ROY BARTH

POINT OF IMPACT

WITH CAROLYN ZALESNE

FOREWORD BY
BILLIE JEAN KING

www.roybarth.com

DEDICATION

To my loving parents and avid tennis players, **Bob and Pat Barth**, who introduced my sister, Patty, and me to the game as soon as we could hold a racquet. As I grew, they saw my love and talent for tennis and encouraged and supported my dream to be a professional. I thank them for giving me the gift of tennis.

To my wife, **Colleen Barth**, who has traveled with me on tour, stayed home to care for our sons, helped me recover from life-threatening surgeries, and cheered me on at every challenge. She has been my ultimate doubles partner.

ACKNOWLEDGMENTS

I have one life story, but it took a team to put it in print.

Thanks to **Jeffrey Denny, Jim Loehr, Judy Fogarty, Chuck Taylor, Lydia Angle, Lisa Liberman, Katie Fisher, Judy Zalesne,** and **Bryan Hunter** for their willingness to read a draft and offer seasoned insights and worthy suggestions.

Special thanks to **Carolyn Zalesne**, my writing partner, from whom I learned so much. Her creativity and attention to detail, all while fact-checking my memory, kept me on point. She also taught me a few new computer skills along the way. It was a fascinating process.

And thanks to all the players, partners, opponents, coaches, students, colleagues, bosses, doctors, family, and friends for the memorable roles they played in my life. I am most grateful.

FOREWORD

When I wrote, "Perspective is about the words you use to define yourself and your experiences," and, "It's not about winning or losing but creating the opportunity," I may not have been thinking specifically about Roy Barth, but I could have been.

We have known each other since I was 17 and Roy was 13. His parents were staples of the San Diego tennis community in 1960 and invited me to stay at their house when I played in a tournament at nearby Morley Field. I first saw Roy play at the Los Angeles Tennis Club in the Junior Pacific Southwest Championship. He played with such tenacity and focus. As a junior, he did what I wish more juniors would do today: watch the ball hit the strings.

Our paths have crossed many times since 1960. Whether Roy was playing at Wimbledon, promoting doubles play among juniors in the USTA, hosting Fed Cup team matches at Kiawah, or supporting higher standards for teaching accreditation within the Professional Tennis Registry, I've seen him display that same disciplined focus on the "point of impact" at every opportunity.

Roy's perspective is right on target and we can all learn from his love, passion, and dedication to a sport we love.

Billie Jean King
February 2020

(photo courtesy of the PTR, credit Dayle Thomas)

PREFACE

Focusing on the "Point of Impact"

In this book I share the many life lessons I learned as a junior, collegiate, and professional tennis player and director of a world-renowned tennis teaching center.

I grew up in the tennis world of the 1950s and 1960s during which there was no professional tour; playing collegiate tennis and entering amateur tournaments were all junior tournament players like me could aspire to. But my generation saw big changes, and before my playing career was over, I was a founding member of the men's Association of Tennis Professionals (ATP) and I made a living playing in the world's biggest tournaments against the game's best players.

The excitement of the newly formed ATP increased the popularity of tennis worldwide for recreational, amateur, and professional players alike. In more than 65 years of playing and helping hundreds of players of all levels improve, I learned that the foundation points of the game — and the life lessons they inspired — are timeless.

I call my story *Point of Impact* after my most cherished tennis lesson, which became my greatest life lesson. One of my first coaches explained that the only time I had control of the ball was when I was hitting it. To make that control last, he taught me to watch the ball hit my racquet strings — the point of impact — and stay focused on that instant through each stroke. That disciplined concentration was central to my on-court success and then became the standard for my instructional philosophy and my approach to managing a world-class tennis operation. Every budget, administrative challenge, instance of adversity, and relationship demanded that same attention to detail and confidence to take chances on the people and passions that mattered most.

The "point of impact" was only the beginning. On my journey from No. 3 in the tough Southern California juniors circuit in 1958 at age 11, to playing No. 1 singles and doubles at UCLA, to competing for seven years on the pro tour, I learned other valuable life lessons — among them to "take one point at a time," "hang on like a crab," and "develop character on the court." In my many years at Kiawah, I relied on these playing principles to shape my management style and earn Kiawah Tennis the distinction of being named the No. 1 Tennis Resort in the World.

Along the way, these lessons also helped me overcome life-threatening illnesses so I could share many more years with my beloved wife, Colleen, our family, and our friends — and, of course, enjoy more court time.

I tell my story in two parts. Part One: Life Lessons from the Game of Tennis, and Part Two: Life Lessons for the Business of Tennis. The venues and decades are different but the lessons are the same. And they are still relevant. What I learned from seasoned coaches, elite players, and successful managers about demeanor, preparedness, focus, sportsmanship, goals, and character should inspire and motivate new generations of players, parents of players, instructors, coaches, commentators, directors, managers, writers, and observers of the game I love.

Tennis has been an extraordinary teacher. From my career-long view of the game on and off the court, I am excited to share how it became a metaphor for my whole life.

Roy Barth
February 2020

TABLE OF CONTENTS

Part Two
Life Lessons for the Business of Tennis

Appendix
Quick References, Bonus Resources, and More Photos!

INTRODUCTION

Monday, October 25, 2004

I woke up at 4:00 a.m. to be sure not to be late. Open heart surgery. I felt fine, which made the plan for the day seem so strange. No pain. No signs of slowing down. I looked in the mirror at my chest. It didn't look like it did when I was a college and professional tennis player in my 20s, but it had been years since I worked out as I had back then. Still, though, I was in pretty good shape for 57. I'd never even been hampered in a match by anything more serious than blisters or muscle cramps. I took one last look. I will never be the same. I'll be sidelined for a while. I'll have a scar. I'll look old. I'll probably feel old. But I am fortunate my doctors can fix this. *Former President Bill Clinton just had this same procedure two months ago and he's a year older than me. I can get through this.* I put on my shirt and turned off the light.

The roads were empty at that early hour and parking was easy. I checked into the Medical University of South Carolina (MUSC) at exactly 5:30 a.m. In the time the waiting room clock advanced an hour, I felt I had aged a year.

I couldn't believe I was even there. I had only gone to see my doctor a week earlier because two of my longtime tennis friends developed serious heart conditions. Ron Bohrnstedt had double-bypass heart surgery and Brian Cheney needed a stent. Both Ron and Brian were thin, in great shape, and had no history of heart disease. They could be me.

Even though I took cholesterol medicine every morning and felt no symptoms, my internist ordered a non-invasive cardiac calcium scoring test to determine the level of plaque buildup in my arteries. A score of "zero" would mean no plaque and low risk of heart attack. A score over 200 could mean a 90 percent chance an artery was blocked, and I'd be at a high risk for heart attack. My score was 800. My internist immediately referred me to Dr. Bruce Usher, the Head of the Cardiology Department at MUSC. After administering a stress test, Dr. Usher delivered the bad news: I had life-threatening arterial blockage that would require catheterization. There was a 95 percent chance I would need a stent.

As it turned out, needing a stent would have been the good news. The forty-minute catheterization procedure revealed that my main artery — the left anterior descending artery (LAD), also known as the "Widow Maker" — was 100 percent blocked. A stent was not an option.

According to Dr. Usher, I had probably lived this long because my body developed its own circulatory bypass around my heart blockage, known as "collateral circulation." He attributed that to my being a fit athlete. I felt great about that; all those years of training, conditioning, and eating well had paid off.

My fit body might have gotten me that far, but it wasn't going to get me much further. Almost no one survives an LAD heart attack, and that's where I was headed. It could happen when I'm sitting still or teaching out on the court. There may be no warning.

Dr. Usher put me in touch with Dr. John Kratz, MUSC's top heart surgeon, who explained that if I ever wanted to be active again I would need bypass surgery — actually *double* bypass surgery, because apparently I also had a smaller artery that was 70 percent blocked. I did not expect any of this.

Just two months earlier, my blocked arteries and I played the USTA National Father-Son Clay-Court Championship in Cincinnati, Ohio, in 100-degree heat. I was exhausted in the second match of the day. Players were joking that we "could die out here." I really could have.

The upside of the bypass procedure was the 25 years it could add to my life. The downside was the 1 percent chance I could die on the table. I liked the odds, and I really had no choice. I scheduled the surgery.

At 9:00 a.m. an anesthesiologist came to administer my IV drip. He asked me what kind of "cocktail" I'd like. I guess that's anesthesiology humor.

I laughed, but not at that.

"What is so funny?" my wife, Colleen, asked.

"I was just thinking about my report to the Executive Committee I asked Theresa Silo to read for me at today's meeting. She should be reading it out loud to everybody right about now."

The anesthesiologist didn't look amused, but he would have if he had known what was in the report. *At least if I don't make it through the surgery, my colleagues will know I knew the good news before I died.*

"Cocktail time!" the anesthesiologist declared. I felt cold, then tingly, and then numb.

Five hours later I woke up in more pain than I have ever experienced. Breathing was excruciating. *Why did I agree to this? I felt fine before.* Colleen begged the nurse to give me more morphine or oxycontin or whatever would help. The pain killers were not killing the pain. The doctors finally got the dosage correct, or my body just gave up. I eventually fell sleep.

My seven years on the pro tennis tour kept me away for months at a time, but I was never so happy to be home as I was after four days in the hospital. My shower! My bed! An excellent start to my recovery.

After sleeping only a few hours, I woke up feeling restless. Maybe a hot shower would help. Colleen placed a small bench in the shower in case standing made me dizzy or weak. *Ahhh ... hot water. This feels great. Just what I needed.* But after a few seconds, I felt faint and then I felt nothing. I called for Colleen and reached for the bench. When she arrived, I collapsed in her arms. Minutes later we were in an ambulance on our way back to the hospital.

A resident cardiologist from Dr. Kratz's team asked me some basic questions. I understood what she was asking, but she and Colleen seemed not to understand my answers. *I am pretty sure I'm making sense. Why do you all look so worried?*

The CAT scan revealed a large, ugly tumor.

"You have a lesion on the front left lobe of your brain. We need to remove it but you will be fine, and I can save your hairline," reported Dr. Sunil Patel, one of the top neurosurgeons in the country. His four accompanying residents nodded their heads in agreement. Dr. Patel was very comforting.

I stayed in the hospital for five days before the procedure so they could monitor my vital signs. I don't remember much of that time; perhaps the pain medication from the heart surgery kept me from focusing. The television was on but I'm not sure what I watched. Maybe a Robin Williams movie. The kids had been in and out. I think my boss and his wife stopped by, or maybe they didn't. I'm not sure.

I do remember the nurses telling me I'd become quite the celebrity in the hospital. Very few people are deemed fit enough at 57 years old to undergo two life-threatening surgeries within ten days. *I hope I survive so I can feel famous.*

The night before surgery Colleen stayed with me instead of going home. She slept in my room on a chair that didn't look comfortable enough to sit in, let alone sleep in. She'd been great these few weeks. *Everyone was taking care of me but who was taking care of her? She looked tired.*

The night nurse came to check on me.

"How are you feeling?" he asked.

"A little confused. What does my brain surgery have to do with my heart surgery?"

"That's what they are going to find out," he said. "Don't worry. You are in good hands." He gave me another blanket and dimmed the lights. "Try to get some sleep. I'll be right outside your room if you need me."

My surgery was scheduled for early in the morning — it was dark when they came to get me — but at 10:00 a.m. I was still lying on a gurney in a pre-surgery room looking up at the ceiling and feeling a little cold and very hungry. Dr. Patel had been delayed. There was a steady hum of hospital equipment, or maybe it was the air conditioning. *I'm not that scared. I probably should be but I've learned to stay positive in the face of worthy opponents my whole competitive life. This seems no different.*

An attendant came to wheel me into the operating room. I started to count the ceiling tiles as we moved. A big grid. Very clean. Very orderly.

I'm still not sure what this has to do with my heart surgery. The perfect grid hovered above me. Life isn't nearly so predictable.

The hallway seemed endless. There were too many tiles to count. *It's in God's hands now.*

We finally reached the surgical suite. The attendant positioned me in the center of the room and someone locked my gurney into place. Lights. Machines. Lots of beeping. I counted about eight people in there, all wearing scrubs, cloth caps, and quiet shoes. Someone wrapped my upper arm in a blood pressure cuff. *This is their office. They seem so organized, barely speaking as they go about their tasks. This is a once-in-a-lifetime day for me, but they are here every day. Do they notice me? Yes! A nurse smiled when our eyes met.*

I heard myself saying, "I hope you guys didn't drink too much last night."

They laughed. Another nurse cupped my head in her hands and shifted me into position. Her hands were gentle, her smile calming.

I'm glad my father isn't alive to know about this; I'd hate for him to worry that I'll die this way.

Colleen told my mother there was no need for her to fly east and promised to call after the surgery to tell her how everything went. I was lucky to have such great parents. *Have I been a good parent?*

As the medical team administered the anesthesia, I didn't know three things:

1. A representative from the neurology department had already told my family I probably had a glioblastoma — an aggressive cancerous brain tumor requiring three to six months of chemotherapy and radiation — and they should prepare for some rough times ahead. Colleen asked whether there was a chance the tumor might not be cancerous. "There is a chance, but it's not likely," the neurology representative explained. My older son, Jonathan, pulled his baseball cap down over his eyes to hide the tears streaming down his face. My younger son, Sandon, who had come to Charleston for my heart surgery, was already on his way back to Clemson. Jonathan's wife, Meredith, called him. "Come back to Charleston," she whispered, "your father has a brain tumor."

2. If I hadn't had the double bypass heart surgery, my body would have been too weak to undergo brain surgery and the tumor would have had to remain.

3. Colleen had been going home from the hospital at night to find the light on our answering machine blinking wildly. She was too mentally and physically exhausted to listen to any of the messages, but she saved each one as she flipped through the names of the callers, noting how incredibly supportive the tennis world is. Among the names was Billie Jean King.

PART ONE

LIFE LESSONS FROM
THE GAME OF TENNIS

CHAPTER ONE

Honor the Role Your Parents Played in Your Success

Learning to Play

My father, Robert (Bob) Bruno Barth, was a quiet, hardworking electrical engineer who taught himself to play tennis at the age of 14, studied the game, and became quite good. In the late 1930s he played for UCLA, one of the country's top collegiate tennis programs. As an adult, he played every weekend in the tennis-perfect San Diego climate and even used his vacation days from work to play on our neighborhood courts at Morley Field and Balboa Park Tennis Club. He encouraged my mother, my older sister, Patty, and me to play and hoped we'd love the game as much as he did.

When I was five, I watched my father and his partner Bob Galloway win some 35-and-over doubles titles in San Diego. My dad was very competitive. He said if I wanted to become good enough to play in tournaments, I had to learn his three most important approaches to the game: 1) practice enough to prepare for competition or it would be a waste of time and money, 2) be disciplined enough to control my temper (he said showing frustration on the court just encourages your opponent; I certainly didn't want to do that), and 3) do my talking with my racquet. Heavy stuff to tell a young kid, but it stuck.

My father had the most character of anyone I've ever known. He was hardworking, strict, tough but fair, and vigorously devoted to his family. He sacrificed his own vacations and luxuries to pay for travel expenses, practice courts, and tournament entry fees so Patty and I could compete in the Southern California Junior Circuit, in tournaments in the Pacific Northwest, and in national tournaments in the South and Midwest.

My parents holding me in 1948. They were already dressing me in tennis whites!

My father's parents, my grandparents, were Bruno and Elizabeth Barth. Bruno emigrated from Germany to San Diego and pursued a career in electrical engineering. Elizabeth was born in Kansas. Bruno was a quiet, industrious, and disciplined man. When I was seven, my grandparents' house was featured in a magazine article about "Push Button Houses" because they had the first electric garage door opener in San Diego. Maybe my grandfather designed it or built it — I'm not sure — but I do remember standing on the street watching the door go up and down a million times while people took pictures.

Bruno was very serious and seemed ill-at-ease around kids, at least around grandkids. He thought my father's profound love for the game of tennis was a waste of time and discouraged my father's interest in playing. The contrast between how my father grew up and how I grew up, specifically regarding tennis, made me appreciate my father's sacrifices even more.

My grandfather owned his own electrical engineering firm, encouraged my father to become an electrical engineer, and employed him as an apprentice, but had no intention of turning the business over to him. Nothing had ever been given to Bruno and he didn't want to show favoritism towards his son. My father left his father's engineering firm to work for a competitor. He never talked about that experience but I know it crushed him. Later in my life I found myself in a similar position and handled it much differently.

My mother, Patricia (Pat) Barth, loved tennis as much as my father did. She played in a local women's league at Balboa Tennis Club and most of her friends were tennis players. She used to bring me with her when I was a baby, set me on a blanket with some toys, and tether me to the net on the empty court next to her game. To say that my being "comfortable at the net" started at an early age is not an exaggeration.

According to my mother, the first word I spoke wasn't "mama" or "dada"; it was "Wilbur." The tennis pro at Morley Field was Wilbur Folsom. Whenever he got a phone call in the pro shop, the shop attendant would yell out to the court: "Wilbur, Wilbur, telephone!" I heard this name so many times I felt compelled to repeat it.

My mother was the nicest person; she could find goodness in anyone. Her father, Perry Powers, taught her to "be kind to people because you don't know what cross they bear." She lived by that notion, teaching me by example the art of respecting others. Someone once told me he thought if he could be half as nice as Pat Barth, his life would be much more rewarding.

My mother also taught me the importance of volunteering time and talent to worthy organizations. She served as president of the parent-teacher organization in my elementary school, was a long-standing president of Balboa Tennis Club at Morley Field, and volunteered for the "Meals on Wheels" program in our area. I never forgot how involved she got and how fulfilled she seemed by these opportunities.

I can trace my mother's family back to the Civil War. My great-great-grandfather, Pierce Powers, was married to Sarah Powers and lived in Jackson, Ohio. Pierce worked in the ironmaking business until, at age 30, he responded to Lincoln's last call for volunteers to fight for the Union. The injuries he sustained in battle caused his untimely death just two days after he returned home. Sarah was left to raise their four young children alone. Her son, Perry, 7, was my great-grandfather.

Perry was what I would call a "mover/shaker." He worked in the coal mines as a child but, at age 20, moved to Davenport, Iowa, to become a typesetting apprentice. Enamored by the power of publishing and the profound influence of the printed word, Perry chased an on-the-job education in the printing and publishing business from Iowa to Illinois to Michigan. When Perry answered an ad to run a newspaper in Cadillac, Michigan, in 1887, he became the editor and publisher of *The News and Express*. Perry was a staunch Republican and voiced his opinions through his newspaper's articles and editorials. He served on the state and local boards of education, as auditor general, and as state labor commissioner. Cadillac even named a street after him.

Perry was also — *and I still can't believe my mother had this newspaper clipping* — a tennis player! Apparently he was a member of the Cadillac Tennis Club in 1888. I'd love to know more about this "recreation and entertainment" club. Did they actually play in those clothes!?

Cadillac Tennis Club, 1888

One of the many forms of recreation and entertainment in Cadillac's early days was that of tennis. Shown are members of the Cadillac Tennis Club in June, 1888. It included many prominent Cadillac people. Seated left to right are Augusta Burlingame, Miss Cummer (later Mrs. Fred Diggins), John Dixon, Elizabeth Yost, Maude Valentine, (later the wife of Rev. Lee Mitchell), and an unidentified lady. Standing left to right, John Fletcher, Mrs. Ida Cummer, an unidentified schoolteacher, Perry F. Powers, newspaper publisher George Lamb and another unidentified lady.

My great-grandfather, Perry F. Powers, was a tennis player!
He is in the back row, third from right.

Perry and his wife, Jessie Warren Powers, had three sons. Their second son, also named Perry, was my grandfather. He was a devout Republican like my great-grandfather but was not interested in the publishing business. He worked as a stockbroker instead. Perry married my grandmother, Rebecca, who studied music in college in the 1920s when few women pursued higher education. She was a talented pianist and worked with young protégés.

Perry and Rebecca had a son, Richard (Dick); a daughter, Patricia (Pat, my mother); and a daughter, Mary. My mother was nine in 1929 when the stock market crashed and her father lost everything. Perry moved the family to San Diego to start over and got a job in the insurance business. Rebecca continued to give piano lessons until she suffered from disabling rheumatoid arthritis. She was bed-ridden as long as I can remember. Her son, my uncle Dick, shared her lifelong love of music. He played the French horn in the San Diego symphony.

Perry was the grandparent I knew best. He was outgoing and politically opinionated like his father. Whenever my family got together with him, he and my father — a disciplined and thoughtful Democrat — would take somewhat playful jabs at each other. My mother refused to get between her father and her husband, so she just ignored them.

When my mother was 64, her bridge partner, Jeanne Doyle Garrett, who was also the women's tennis coach at San Diego Junior College, talked my mother into enrolling in a few courses just so she could play on the school's tennis team. Wielding her well-disguised drop shot and strategic lob, my mother won at least half of her matches against opponents a *third* her age. My mother was extremely competitive but also very maternal. First she would win, and then she would comfort and console her much younger opponents.

My parents met while studying at San Diego State University. My father went to UCLA for two years and then transferred to San Diego State to complete his engineering degree. My mother was at San Diego studying education; she wanted to be a teacher. After graduating from college, my father went into a six-month officer training program at the Naval Academy in Annapolis, Maryland. He and my mother were married in the chapel at Annapolis in 1943.

My parents started their married life in Annapolis but when my father was sent to Guam to repair warships, my mother moved back to San Diego to live with her in-laws. My father never talked much about his wartime experience. I wish I had asked him about it.

Among my parents' many accomplishments — which included producing Patty and me — they won the Husband-and-Wife Doubles

Championships at the La Jolla Beach and Tennis Club in 1953, and then again at the Hotel del Coronado on Coronado Island in San Diego in 1960.

Before I picked up a tennis racquet, I picked up tennis balls for Wilbur Folsom, the pro at Morley Field, which was only three miles from my house. Wilbur paid me 25¢ to collect the balls for him during his lessons. My mother told me to pick up the balls without calling attention to myself and to listen during the lesson because I might learn something. I loved being on the court.

Unfortunately, one of my first playing experiences was not so happy. My mother was running a clinic at a nearby elementary school and I got hit hard in face with another kid's racquet. I sat out for a while thinking maybe the game wasn't for me. My parents gave me time to shake off the incident, didn't enroll me in any more clinics, and never said a word about my not playing. But they took me to watch Patty. They knew I shared their competitive spirit and bet if I saw Patty improving, I would want to play again. They were right. After all, I was their kid who, as a Cub Scout, rang every single doorbell in the neighborhood trying to sell more wrapping paper than any other Cub Scout. It worked.

When Patty brought home two tennis trophies, I was really jealous and I got back on the court. Deep down I knew tennis was more fun than that one bad day. I'm glad I didn't end my tennis career at age six.

I won my first trophy when I was nine. It was four inches tall but, to me, it was the biggest and best trophy ever. I was hooked. I still love winning trophies.

My father was quick to point out that the earlier rounds of tournaments don't have trophies and it's in those early rounds where I'd need some of my most crucial concentration. He said winning the early rounds only gets you to the next round so I'd have to focus on more than trophies.

*In front of Grandma and
Grandpa Barth's house,
holding two trophies.
Age nine.*

My parents were regulars in the San Diego tennis community for more than 60 years and enjoyed an admirable reputation as both fierce competitors and nice people. They encouraged Patty and me to play but never pressured us. They helped us develop skills to win matches but never got mad if we lost. And they taught by example how to take tennis seriously but never lose sight that it was a game. Character came first with them. I'd like to think it does with me too.

CHAPTER TWO

Treat Your Partner
and Opponent with Equal Respect

My First Friends, Partners, and Opponents

Fred Kinne, the editor of the *San Diego Evening Tribune* and a World War II Air Force pilot, was a very good local player who ran free tennis clinics for boys every Saturday morning at nine o'clock on the public courts at Morley Field. I loved those Saturday mornings. That's where I first met Carlos Carriedo. Carlos lived near me, just on the other side of Balboa Park. We were the same age but he was the better player when we were young. I met the other two best junior players in the area — Rocky Jarvis and Johnny Sanderlin — through junior tournaments. Rocky lived in La Jolla and Johnny lived in Granite Hills. The four of us became friends and rivals.

Rocky was my first regular doubles partner. We were only ten years old, but we were ranked No. 2 in doubles in the 11-and-under age group in Southern California, behind Johnny and Carlos. The most fun about playing doubles with Rocky was staying at each other's houses and going fishing together. He lived in La Jolla, California, a beautiful seaside community eight miles north of San Diego. We fished off the

La Jolla rocks, went deep-sea fishing off Mission Bay, and even drove to Nevada with his father to go fly fishing. Years later, Rocky attended Harvard University where he played varsity men's tennis. After graduating, he stayed in the Boston area and became a teaching professional.

Many of my doubles partners — from Rocky through college pairings — ended up being great friends. If I was going to be on the same side of the court, share strategies, and celebrate wins, I preferred it be with someone I liked. Through doubles, I made some lifelong friends; played with a lot less stress than in singles; and improved my angled volleys, overheads, chip service returns, and lobs, all of which also helped my singles game.

Some singles opponents, like Carlos Carriedo, however, were just always a challenge. When I first started playing Carlos, he lobbed every ball a mile high over my head on *every* point. It was maddening. Over the next four years, he kept improving and became one of the top players in Southern California. Losing to him and his frustrating strategy just motivated me to want to win the next time. As we got older, my matches with him got closer. I got stronger and more confident attacking the net. This put pressure on Carlos' game.

Carlos was an interesting guy. His father, Lente, worked nights driving a truck. When he got off work, Lente would take Carlos and his brothers to the courts at Morley Field and sleep in his car while the boys learned to play tennis. Until I saw that, I never considered how fortunate I was that my father worked during the day and my whole family played together on the weekends. Despite Carlos' unorthodox playing style, I had tremendous respect for his talent.

I was sixteen when I finally beat Carlos — and then I beat him the next two times we played — but he got his revenge when he beat me 6-4 in the third set in the final of the National Boys' 16-and-Under Hard-Court Championship in Burlingame, California. In the semifinals, I had upset No. 1-seed Bob Lutz in a tight three-set match, and Carlos had defeated Ron Bohrnstedt. I took that loss in the final pretty hard; it was the closest I came to a national junior singles title.

Carlos' father thought tennis would pave the way for his son's higher education, and it seems he was right. After high school, Carlos was awarded a full tennis scholarship to Notre Dame and then went on to earn a law degree from Berkeley.

Johnny Sanderlin was probably the best doubles player of the four of us. His father, George, was a professor who moved the family from Maine to Southern California when he joined the faculty at San Diego State University. George was an avid tennis player who swept snow off the courts in Maine so his kids could play. Johnny, the youngest of four kids, was smart and funny and a natural athlete. We were the same age, but I felt as though I learned everything from him. Just by being himself, he taught me friendship, good sportsmanship, dedication, courage, and strength — all the things that give a person character. He was a very important part of my life.

*The four of us in 1957: Rocky Jarvis and me on the left
and Carlos Carreido and Johnny Sanderlin on the right.*

When I was 11, my father challenged me to see how many times we could hit a tennis ball back and forth without missing. We were at University Heights, a recreational facility with three lighted courts for evening play. My father felt that playing at night made me watch the ball more closely, which improved my focus. And "watching the ball" to him meant literally seeing the ball hit the racquet strings. It took tremendous concentration and patience to do what he asked but it became a standard of my game. I learned to maneuver my opponent from side to side until I had an opening to win the point by attacking the net and finishing with a winning volley or overhead. All while watching the ball hit my strings.

Our record that night under the lights was a 310-stroke rally lasting 20 minutes.

In 1958, I was ranked No. 3 in singles in Southern California in the 11-and-under age group, despite my feeling incredibly nervous before each match. All the skill-based lessons and all the hours of practice didn't teach me how to overcome my pre-match nerves. I figured out though, that once I started to move and sweat, the nerves left me. Even the legendary tennis great Rod Laver said that you don't play well unless you are nervous at the beginning.

Me at Morley Field.
11 years old.

I loved playing with my father and his friends at the Balboa Tennis Club. Balboa was a small six-court club located across the street from the world-famous San Diego Zoo and adjacent to an old-fashioned merry-go-round, which is still there. The club had a small clubhouse, showers, and snack shop that served great hamburgers. My parents played mixed doubles together on Saturday and Sunday mornings, and in the afternoons, my father would arrange men's doubles games and invite me to play, even though I was only 11. He always made me play the net. Desperately wanting to show my father and his friends that I could compete, I went for every volley. I missed a lot but tried not to get discouraged. My father applauded my initiative rather than become angry over any lost point. He encouraged me to keep at it. Not surprisingly, volleying became one of the strongest elements of my game.

I felt honored to be asked to play with my father and his friends on those weekend afternoons, but that paled in comparison to the day my father suggested we play together in the Father-Son tournament at San Diego's historic Hotel del Coronado. In our first round, we played the father-son team of Captain Reynolds, who was 64, and his son, Nick, who was 35. My dad was 41 and I was 11.

My father and me at the Father-Son Tournament
at the Hotel del Coronado in San Diego, 1958

Despite it being a tournament — with a check-in desk, posted draws, refreshments, T-shirt favors, and umpires — our first round felt like the sets I played with my dad and his friends at Balboa: I was at least 20 years younger than everyone else on the court. As the "kid," I could have behaved childishly when I missed a shot or double faulted. I could have thrown a tantrum or even cried when things didn't go my way — I'd seen plenty of other kids behave this way on the court — but it was never my inclination. I never saw my father act out in such situations and he would never have understood my doing it. He taught me that I needed to live with myself no matter the score. Most important, he might never have wanted to play another father-son event with me, which would have been a big loss in my life. We got beaten badly that day, but we were gracious in defeat. It was great to play with my father.

(Later I learned that we got beaten not only by good tennis players, but pretty good musicians, as well. Nick Reynolds, who learned to play guitar from his father, was a founding member of The Kingston Trio.)

The next year, my father and I played in the first annual National Father-Son Hard-Court Championship at the legendary La Jolla Beach and Tennis Club in La Jolla, California. We played in this event for the next eight years, even when I was in college. We reached the quarterfinals in our last year. I always looked forward to playing with my father, and I was so happy he wanted to play together as much as I did.

I enjoyed playing doubles with my mother and sister too, especially at the annual La Jolla Tennis Championships. Nicknamed the "Jewel City Net Classic," this nine-day tennis tournament featured the traditional singles, doubles, and mixed events, but also offered family doubles events including husband-wife, mother-son, mother-daughter, father-son, father-daughter, and sibling partnerships. My family entered all the age-appropriate divisions.

In 1959, Bob Ortman, a local sportswriter for the *San Diego Evening Tribune*, wrote an article entitled "Family Fun 'Racquet' With Barth Clan," in which he highlighted our family's tennis life. "Busy people, these Barths," he said. Accompanying the article was a picture of the four of us on the court together. It's a nice memory.

Family Fun 'Racquet' With Barth Clan

"Family Fun," San Diego Evening Tribune. July 2, 1959

The San Diego area, which includes La Jolla, has always been a prominent tennis haven, so much so that talented players from other areas sought out its challenging competition and year-round tennis-perfect weather. One of those players was Tom Gorman from the Seattle, Washington, area — which does not have year-round tennis-perfect weather. His early tennis skills surpassed the challenges available to him there, and he came to San Diego in the summer when he was 14, a year older than me.

Even though Tom wasn't part of the Southern California Junior Circuit, we played together as partners and opponents. Tom had a very dry sense of humor and we quickly became good friends. Although he came to San Diego frequently, he remained loyal to his hometown and was the Washington State High School Champion three years in a row.

Like Rocky, Carlos, and Johnny, Tom was a fierce competitor but also an honorable person: no unsportsmanlike conduct, no bad line calls, no gamesmanship, and always a friendly handshake at the net. Tom went on to be a two-time All-American at Seattle University and, in 1995, he was inducted into the Intercollegiate Tennis Hall of Fame. I am fortunate that he and I would stay friends and become formidable doubles partners way beyond our early years in Southern California.

I've seen all kinds of behavior on the tennis court through the years, and I still conduct myself in my parents' image. Partners and opponents alike have been my friends; I can't imagine behaving any other way.

CHAPTER THREE

Listen to What Others Teach You

Lessons from Legendary Coaches

As Patty and I grew, my father found it increasingly difficult to teach his own children. I expect his decision to relinquish control of our progress was a defining moment for him. He was proud of the solid start he and my mother had given us but knew his teaching skills were limited. For Patty and me to get to the next level, we would need the guidance of seasoned professionals. My father arranged for us to take lessons from three of the most prominent pros of the day.

Wilbur Folsom

My first lessons were with Wilbur Folsom, the same pro at Morley Field whose name was the first word I spoke and who had paid me 25¢ to pick up the balls on his lesson courts. Wilbur was about 50 years old when he taught me in 1958, but he had been a tennis legend in San Diego for years. He was an avid high school player who might have gone on to a collegiate career if not for being hit by a car at age 18, two days after he graduated from high school. The accident took his left leg but not his love of tennis.

Wilbur was confined to a wheelchair after the accident but found he could still enjoy hitting tennis balls against a wall from his seated position. When he got his prosthetic leg, he got back on the court and learned to play again, but he also discovered he could earn money teaching tennis. He worked his way through college at San Diego State teaching tennis and then went up to Los Angeles and got a job working with the tennis team at UCLA. While he was there, he earned a law degree. Wilbur's son Bill told me his father always said he enjoyed being out on the court teaching tennis more than the prospect of being a lawyer. Wilbur returned to San Diego and taught tennis at the University Heights Recreational Center before spending his many years teaching at Morley Field. He was a formidable opponent and improved the games of hundreds of tennis enthusiasts over the years — many of whom went on to play college and professional tennis.

My father played against Wilbur and used to say that Wilbur would "take one big step on his good leg and a short hop on his wooden leg, place the ball anywhere, and give us fits."

Wilbur Folsom in the pro shop at Morley Field. (photo courtesy of David and Bill Folsom)

Wilbur is probably best known for discovering Maureen (Little Mo) Connolly. In 1943, eight-year-old Maureen Connolly walked by her neighborhood tennis courts and stopped to watch two pretty good 12-year-old players hitting. She asked if they would hit with her for a few minutes when they were finished. They declined. In tears, Maureen moved on to the next court and watched Wilbur Folsom giving a lesson. Wilbur noticed Maureen, handed her a racquet, and asked her if she wanted to try to hit balls back to his student and then help pick up the balls after the lesson. In return, he agreed to pay her five cents and teach her some basics of the game.

Eight years later, at age 16, Maureen won her first of three U.S. Championships (now US Open) singles titles. In all, Little Mo won nine major singles titles (including Wimbledon three years in a row), two major doubles titles, and one major mixed doubles title. In 1953, Maureen became the first and (still) only American woman to win a "Grand Slam": all four major tournaments in the same calendar year. She credited Wilbur with having taught her the fundamentals of the game.

For me, Wilbur was a strict, detailed-oriented teacher with a soft-spoken manner. He would put his right hand up next to his head and ask me to hit the ball at his hand. At first, I hit the ball and just *prayed* it wouldn't strike Wilbur in the head. Then I learned to control my swing and direct the ball within two feet to the outside of Wilbur's hand. With each shot, I got more confident about my target. The other boys he taught swung their racquets like baseball bats. Not only didn't the balls come close to Wilbur's hand, they literally flew over the fence.

Maureen (Little Mo) Connolly

Patty and I were fortunate to take lessons from Maureen, although I was sorry for the reason she was available to teach us. Maureen loved two sports — tennis and horseback riding— and when she wasn't taking tennis lessons from Wilbur or practicing on our local courts against men in their 30s (including my father), she was riding at the local stables. A few weeks after winning her third consecutive Wimbledon singles title, Maureen was thrown from her horse when it was spooked by an oncoming cement truck. Maureen's broken leg and torn tendons ended her professional tennis career at 19 years old. She remained in the San Diego area and, as a favor to my father, agreed to work with Patty and me.

For three years, Maureen built on the foundation that Wilbur instilled. She taught me to direct the ball with my hand because "*where the hand ends up is where the racquet ends up, and thus where the ball ends up.*" This worked for ground strokes, serves, overheads, and volleys alike. She taught me how to hit under pressure: "*Speed up your swing rather than slow it down when you get tense.*" She taught the importance of a dedicated work ethic, stressing that I should never let up in a match no matter what the score. "*If you ease the pressure on your opponent, no matter how far ahead you are, they can always come back and beat you.*" And she advocated taking breaks from the court during the year. She was right. I played on my high school basketball team which gave me a healthy mental break from tennis and was great for my physical conditioning.

One of Maureen's signature talents was "moving after hitting." All the film clips of Maureen playing show her feet in constant motion. She taught me not only to move my feet when the ball is in the air coming toward me, but also after I hit the ball. A common response to pressure situations in a match is to stop moving the feet. She said if I felt nervous — which I always did — concentrate on keeping my feet moving.

Maureen emphasized that it's not how long we practiced, it's how efficiently we practiced. She would rather me practice two hours with purpose and intensity than four hours with neither.

The most enduring lesson I took from Maureen was her insistence that I remain a "nice person," even if I beat an opponent badly. Playing to win and being a respectful opponent were not mutually exclusive.

Maureen married fellow horseback riding enthusiast Norman Brinker, a Navy man attending college in San Diego. Norman was a member of the US Olympic Equestrian Team and went on to revolutionize the restaurant industry, first in the Southwest and later nationally and internationally. Maureen and Norman had two daughters.

When I was 13, Maureen and her family moved to Scottsdale, Arizona. She went back to school and got a degree, and then she traveled the world giving clinics for the Wilson Sporting Goods Company. She also did television commentary at Wimbledon.

The year after she moved to Scottsdale, Maureen invited my father and me to spend a weekend with her to work on my game. She never hit the ball right to me and ran me so hard I threw up. She made me learn how to hit on the run so I would be prepared for tournament competition. That was the last lesson I took from Maureen.

In 1966, Maureen was diagnosed with ovarian cancer. In October 1968, eight months before she died, Maureen came to my sister Patty's wedding looking radiant as always and lighting up the room. Maureen died on June 21st, the first day of the 1969 Wimbledon tournament. She was 34. I was in London that day playing at Wimbledon. The next day, the newspaper headline read "Little Mo Dies." A televised movie of Maureen's life, entitled *Little Mo*, aired on NBC in 1978.

In 2019, the U.S. Postal Service issued a commemorative "forever" stamp picturing Little Mo hitting a backhand. The image is a painting of her copied from a photograph. When I saw it, I was reminded not only of her athleticism, but of her grace, determination, and focus — qualities I've always admired.

My father and Maureen Connolly.
Maureen's U.S. commemorative stamp.

Les Stoefen

After Maureen moved to Scottsdale, I started taking lessons from 1934 Wimbledon doubles champion and singles quarterfinalist, Les Stoefen. He was also a member of the United States Davis Cup team. Les was 6'4" and taught tennis at the La Jolla Beach and Tennis Club wearing an open shirt and sandals and holding a beer in one hand. His image was highly unorthodox, but he could teach. And he could play. And he looked good doing it — so good, in fact, that his service motion was the model for the guy atop the tennis trophies in the 50s and 60s. Really!

When I started taking lessons from Les, I already had some success as a junior: No. 1 in doubles and No. 5 in singles in the national 13-and-under age group.

One of the first things Les taught me was how to hit angle volleys. He stressed the importance of using my hands, not my arms, and hitting in a short, relaxed motion. Thanks to this gift from Les, my volley became my best shot. I could out-volley anyone at the net.

Les Stoefen the La Jolla Beach and Tennis Club
(photo courtesy La Jolla Beach and Tennis Club)

My father had taught me to watch the ball hit the strings on my ground strokes, but Les taught me to watch the ball even longer, and on every shot. He insisted I watch the "point of impact" on my ground strokes, serves, volleys, and overheads until I finished my follow-through because it would help me hit the ball in the center of the strings, follow toward my intended target, and not telegraph where the ball was going. Les believed the most common mistake in tennis is looking up from the stroke too soon.

"The only time a player has control of the ball is when he or she is hitting it," Les would explain. "When a player looks up at the point of impact, he or she is worrying about where the ball is going rather than concentrating on the stroke itself. By looking up too soon you look into the future at the expense of the present."

The "point of impact" fundamental has been a cornerstone of my success as a player and as an instructor.

I was blessed to take lessons from the best teachers of the time, and I loved learning. I listened intensely and did what they told me. Wilbur was out there on a wooden leg insisting I hit toward his hand. Maureen was a record-setting Wimbledon phenom who would never hit the ball right to me. Les Stoefen kept emphasizing the angled volley and the "point of impact." Respecting their talents and passions for their craft served me well as a young tennis player and throughout my life.

Les Stoefen and Maureen Connolly at the La Jolla Beach and Tennis Club (photo courtesy La Jolla Beach and Tennis Club)

CHAPTER FOUR

Maintain a
Positive Attitude During Illness

Losing My Doubles Partner and Best Friend

The first sound I heard as I awoke from that 2004 brain surgery was Colleen's voice. "You're OK, you're OK, you're OK," she kept repeating. "Why wouldn't I be OK?" I thought. I squinted. It was bright.

I must be outside. Am I at Morley Field? Balboa Park? La Jolla? Wait. No. I didn't know Colleen then. She wouldn't have been there. Who was holding my hand? It felt warm and comforting.

The tumor turned out to be a benign meningioma, not the aggressive cancerous glioblastoma the doctors and my family feared. Even though it was not life-threatening, the tumor had started to wrap around my optic nerve and could have eventually cost me my sight.

And I think I finally understand what my brain surgery had to do with my heart surgery. Apparently, the meningioma no one knew about was growing slowly on its own but, at the time of my heart surgery, it was not large enough to cause headaches or vision changes. However, I learned that bypass surgery can trigger swelling around a tumor. The heart procedure itself causes fluid shifts in the body — both from the increased blood flow through the heart and from the "pump" that keeps the body alive during surgery. In the absence of a tumor, these fluid shifts are normally tolerated. But, in the presence of a tumor, they can, in the immediate post-operative days, cause an existing tumor to swell, put pressure on the brain, and cause a loss of coordination and balance, or even a stroke. This swelling is likely what caused me to collapse in the shower that night. Had I not had heart surgery, I probably would not have known about my brain tumor until it grew enough on its own to impact my eyesight, or worse. By that time, it might have been too late to remove it. Fascinating.

On the way home from the hospital, Colleen mentioned all the unheard voice mail messages she saved for me, including the one from Billie Jean King. Wow.

I am so glad I lived to thank everyone.

The euphoria I felt over the not-cancer diagnosis caused me to temporarily lose control of my fiscally conservative self. I bought a new car for Colleen, some new furniture for the house, and some new landscaping for the yard. I even tried, unsuccessfully, to turn down a bonus at work. Money didn't seem to matter; I felt great just to be alive.

I returned to work in 2005 in a limited capacity and started to get my life back in order. Three months after my brain surgery, I was cleared by both my neurologist and my cardiologist to hit tennis balls. The interesting thing about brain surgery is there are no nerves in your brain and so there is no pain with recovery. All I had was a black left eye and I was tired and weak. As my strength and stamina increased, I grew anxious to get back on the court. The teaching symposium I attended in Hilton Head proved to be the perfect opportunity. I asked my colleague Jeff Gray if he would hit with me. I was a little shaky, worried that any abrupt movement would pull the "wiring" loose that was holding my chest together. I hit a few balls. Nothing hurt! I hit a few more. I was elated to get this part of my life back. Colleen joked that I'd surely be disappointed if I thought I'd be getting back to the shape I was in at 22. I was happy to settle for the shape I was in at 57.

During my recovery, I had missed some other doctor's appointments, including my annual dermatology checkup with Dr. Marianne Rosen. I finally saw her in May 2005.

Dr. Rosen found two melanomas, one behind my left knee and one on my back below my neck. She referred me to Dr. Paul Baron, a highly respected oncologic surgeon in Charleston. Dr. Baron was concerned about the thickness of the melanomas and whether they might have spread internally to the nearest lymph nodes. He needed to remove three lymph nodes to see if the cancer was spreading.

I was optimistic. I survived double bypass heart surgery and brain surgery six months earlier and now I was facing another long procedure with life-threatening implications. I had already recovered from worse. At least I hoped that was the worst.

What I didn't expect was a ten-day wait for the results. After my heart surgery, my arteries were no longer blocked. After my brain surgery, the meningioma was gone. Waiting to learn whether cancer had metastasized was excruciating. I had a hard time concentrating at home and at work. I found myself thinking about my life, my family, and my career.

And about my best childhood friend, Johnny Sanderlin.

I knew Johnny from junior tournaments when we were ten years old. He played doubles with Carlos Carriedo when I partnered with Rocky Jarvis. I don't remember exactly how Johnny and I became doubles partners, but I do remember how much we enjoyed playing together and how we became best friends. Together he and I won the 13-and-Under Southern California Championships, which qualified us for the National tournament.

I probably would never have met Johnny if not for tennis. He lived in Granite Hills, which is only about 20 minutes from my house in San Diego, but we were in different school districts. I went to McKinley Middle School and Wilson Junior High and then Hoover High. I don't recall where Johnny went to middle school or junior high but I know he went to Granite Hills High.

Johnny was a shy kid who liked to play chess and miniature golf, so much so that he built himself a miniature golf course in his back yard. He also had an asphalt tennis court next to his house. When we weren't taking lessons, playing, or traveling to tournaments in Southern California, we were at Johnny's house practicing tennis or playing miniature golf, or in my garage playing ping-pong.

Johnny Sanderlin,
age 12, in 1959

Our practice paid off — in tennis, not miniature golf or ping-pong — as Johnny and I continued to play well together. In 1959, when we were 12, we played a match in a county doubles tournament against a local sportswriter named Dave Gallup and his partner. It was not the first time we'd played Dave. Two years prior, Johnny and I faced him and a different partner in the same tournament. At ten years old, Johnny and I won 6-4 in the third set. In 1959, Johnny and I won again, this time in straight sets, and Dave chose to write about us in his column:

John Sanderlin and Roy Barth are a pair of shy,
quiet-as-a-mouse sprouts who look perfectly harmless

– until they start punching the ball past you on a tennis court ... It was two years ago that this agent took his first lesson from John and Roy ... when these cherubs showed up as our opposition ... it was 6-4 in the third for the little guys. I never saw two kids grow up so fast.

And they are much tougher now ... Both boys have uncanny steadiness and control. Sanderlin's subtleness is perhaps his greatest asset. His play is effortless, almost casual. He appears to be merely tapping the ball, yet it goes past you like an arrow. He rarely makes a mistake ... Pretty soon they are going to get really tough.

He was right, but not in the way he thought.

In 1960, Johnny's mother, Owenita, heard about the first annual USTA National Boys' 13-and-Under Championship Tournament scheduled in Chattanooga, Tennessee. She called my parents to see if they would let her take me to play in the tournament with Johnny. The idea of traveling outside California to play in a tournament was exciting enough, but when she proposed we travel by train, the train part sounded more fun than the tennis part. Two thirteen-year-old boys on the Sky King train from San Diego to Chattanooga for three days and nights. What a great adventure.

Johnny Sanderlin and me (left) before boarding the Sky King train to Chattanooga, Tennessee, in 1960

Johnny later wrote about this trip in his journal:

> *It was the first time we had ever been anywhere in a train and [Roy] was grinning all over the place — that special three-cornered grin of his. Roy wasn't a very different-looking person — he had brown hair cut short in a flat-top crew-cut like all the other guys that year, and he was medium weight and medium height — but when he'd get to horsing around and teasing, he didn't look like anybody else but himself, his eyes twinkled so mischievously. Everybody liked Roy because he was so full of fun, and nice to people. I was lucky to have him for a friend.*

The two biggest challenges of the trip for us were the 100-degree temperatures with high humidity and the clay courts. I had never played on a clay court before and, although Johnny had played on clay in Maine when he was seven years old, he admitted he'd forgotten what it was like. We lived in San Diego with year-round temperatures in the 70s, low humidity, and hard courts. The first night in our hotel room — which had no air conditioning — I slept on the floor because it felt much cooler than the bed. And the next day, Johnny and I stepped onto a clay court for the first time together.

Playing on clay demands more focus and patience than does playing on hard courts. The soft clay absorbs some of the ball's bounce, causing it to "sit up" a little longer, giving players more time to prepare and hit the ball more consistently. Rallies tend to be longer and the matches are more physical. Proper hydration is crucial.

Johnny and I entered both the singles and doubles tournaments. In singles, Johnny lost in two sets in the second round to a good player from Florida named Hugh Currey. I didn't see Johnny's match, but he told me later he never really found his rhythm. He lost his energy in the extreme heat and humidity, and he struggled to keep his feet moving. I reached the quarterfinal round where I faced Dickie Dell from Bethesda, Maryland. I was leading 4-1 in the third set and all I could think of was how hot it was and how good a cold Coca-Cola would taste. I lost the next four games and lost the match. Seems I never forgot that loss.

Johnny and I made up for our singles losses by reaching the final of the doubles draw. We played a close match in the semifinals against a good team from Florida — Bill Harris, the top seed in singles, and his partner Ed Cunningham — beating them 6-3 in the third set. Afterwards, we went to scout out the other semifinal match. We saw Richard Howell and Bill Shippey win the other semis by lobbing every ball. Before our final match the next morning, Johnny and I got up early and practiced hitting overheads. Our scouting and preparation paid off. They tried their lobbing strategy on us, but we didn't miss a single overhead in the match and beat them 6-1, 6-2.

My best friend and I won a national doubles title at age 13! It was thrilling. Doubles is great that way: we practiced and played and got to share the win together. It was wonderful to have a best friend.

Johnny and I knew we could compete with the best in Southern California, but playing well in Tennessee showed us we could compete nationally. We were ranked No. 1 in the country in 13-and-under boys' doubles.

The same week, my mother traveled with Patty, who was 15, to the USTA National Girls' 15-and-Under Championship in Louisville, Kentucky. Just as I did, Patty reached the quarterfinals of the singles and won the doubles.

Life was good, until it wasn't. At 14, Johnny learned he had leukemia.

Johnny overheard his parents talking with his doctor outside the exam room door and went home to look up some words in the dictionary; he figured it out himself. Apparently, he had been diagnosed when he was eleven — the doctors told his parents Johnny could not possibly live for more than 15 months — and his parents never told him. This explained why his mother was always the parent who took the players when Johnny went; she needed to be sure he took his medicine. It also perhaps explained why such a talented a singles player had more success in doubles. He just did not have the energy singles demanded.

Once he knew, Johnny never complained about being sick; he

preferred to talk about his future. Johnny was an "A" student who skipped third grade when his family moved from Maine to San Diego, and then skipped traditional eighth grade — moving right into ninth-grade work — when his illness caused him to be home-schooled. Johnny continued to dream about playing tennis for UCLA as his brother, David, had and then maybe playing at Wimbledon. We both did.

When I went to Los Angeles to see the Pacific Southwest Professional Championship — one of the biggest pro tournaments in Southern California — and saw legends Rod Laver, Roy Emerson, Lew Hoad, Billie Jean King, and Darlene Hard play, I came back and described to Johnny each match in as much detail as I could. We wanted to be as good as they were.

In May of 1962, Johnny's doctors told him the medication that had kept him alive long past his original prognosis had stopped working and they suggested an experimental treatment of "internal radiation." They would have to go to a hospital in Berkeley and stay for at least a month because after the treatment Johnny's immune system would be so weak he'd have to be in isolation. He told me to think about maybe getting another partner for the Southern Cal junior tournament. I didn't really want to.

Johnny loved to write. He kept a journal of his life and wrote lengthy letters, especially during his illness when he was sidelined from sports.

Dear Roy,

I just thought I'd write and fill you in on all the gory details of my operation. For two weeks before the operation they were drawing blood and did two bone marrow [treatments] (they aren't as bad as they sound, as they only take three or four minutes). Then on Monday the 14th I had a "trial run" which was supposed to help them to figure out how much radiation to give me on Thursday. First they stuck a needle in my right arm and then one in my left. Then they took me into this room where there was some sort of horrible animal looking me in the face. It was the box. This box was about 8 feet long, a little over three feet wide, and about 5 feet tall. It had glass sides and a narrow bed inside for me. Underneath were two air conditioners. The box itself was pressurized and there were all sorts of filter and radiation equipment on the end where my feet were. Plus an intercom. In each window there were two big black gloves. You probably have never heard of this before, mainly because it is the only one in the world. The box, not quite made on the assembly line, cost as much as a good house! It has been used only twice before, so it is still an experimental thing. Dr. Winchell, a doctor from New York who came to Berkeley just for my operation, invented the box. Anyway, I got in the box and they proceeded to "connect" me. Tubes coming from one end of the box were connected to the needles in my arms, while a blood pressure band was put on my arm. On both ankles and both wrists were elastic things like tight wristwatches and wires from them leading out of the box to an electrocardiograph. They also had to keep constant track of my temperature, and there were two ways of taking temperatures, they chose the worst way, and it proved to be very uncomfortable.

During the "trial run" I was in the box for 6 hours, and for the "real thing" the radiation was given for 6 hours but I had to stay in the box still connected for another 15 hours. During the first 6 hours my temperature rose to 104° yet this was expected. The operation destroyed most of my blood cells although it cannot destroy all of them without destroying me. Therefore, some of the "bad cells" are left. However, by way of a 30 minute transfusion, some of my mother's bone marrow was given to me. It is hoped that her bone marrow will fight against the remaining bad cells. That was something that my bone marrow was unable to do. Then they did a skin graft, *putting some of my mother's skin on my stomach to see if it would "take." If it does take, there's a better chance that this operation will fix me up for good.*

For the last two weeks they have been taking blood samples every day. I had to stay in the same room because, until my blood count built up again, I could very easily have got an infection. I was in "isolation." Everything in my room had to be sterilized and no one could come in unless they scrubbed themselves clean and wore special gowns and a mask over their mouth and noses. I had a private nurse 24 hours a day while I was in isolation so the nurse and the room alone cost $1,500. My usual day went like this. I had breakfast at 9:00 and a sponge bath about 10:00. Somewhere in between they would come and draw some blood. The lunch cart came at 12:00 and dinner at 5:00. I had a TV and a radio so I listened to the Giants games on the radio and also watched a lot of TV. Yesterday I got some good news. They took me out of "isolation" since I had been doing so well and my doctor told me that if my blood count was good on Thursday, I would be able to go home by the weekend. If not, I will probably be able to go a few days after that.

Have you got a doubles partner for the Southern Cal yet? They told us that we would be here until June 17th, so our plans changed in a hurry when we found out I could go so soon. If you still don't have a partner, you could put my name in and it's possible that I could play. However, if you can get a partner, please do as it is doubtful that I could play, and I wouldn't want to leave you with no one. It is doubtful for two reasons — whether I'm really ready for it , and whether my dad will let me, and you know my dad!

Neither of us played Southern Cal that year. Johnny came home and tried to get back into tournament shape. We played one local match together but he was not strong enough to compete.

Over the next weeks and months, I spent a lot of time with Johnny at Scripps Memorial Hospital in La Jolla when he went in for blood transfusions. I thought he was getting stronger. He was able to go to school, play chess, and even hit some tennis balls. In the hospital, we would pass the time playing each hole of his miniature golf course in our heads, trying to figure out which of us had won more ping-pong games, and reliving every detail of our train trip to Chattanooga and our national doubles victory.

In early 1963, Johnny and I were again talking about playing together in the Southern Cal Junior Championship and going on to the Boys' 16 Nationals in August, but again Johnny said his father probably wasn't going to let him play.

The call came on February 8, 1963, from Johnny's older sister, Frea. The look on my mother's face was unmistakable. Johnny died early that morning, three days before his sixteenth birthday, four months from his high school graduation, and ranked third academically in his graduating class.

Johnny won a national tennis championship while he had leukemia. I was a pall bearer at the funeral. I didn't understand why such a good person had to die so young. I still don't.

In 1968, Johnny's mother wrote the book *Johnny* to ensure her son would not be forgotten. She wrote it in Johnny's voice, taking his words directly from Johnny's diary. Whenever I read the book, I feel Johnny is still alive and we are still a team. Although Johnny's mother altered the chronology of a few events, the dialogue is exactly as I remember. A few times a year (still!) people ask me if I am the "Roy" in the "Johnny book." I am proud to say I am.

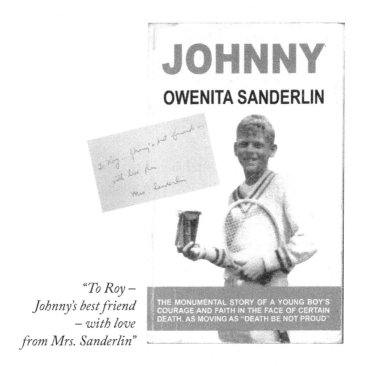

JOHNNY

OWENITA SANDERLIN

THE MONUMENTAL STORY OF A YOUNG BOY'S COURAGE AND FAITH IN THE FACE OF CERTAIN DEATH. AS MOVING AS "DEATH BE NOT PROUD"

"To Roy –
Johnny's best friend
– with love
from Mrs. Sanderlin"

W.F.L. Smith, one of Johnny's classmates from Granite Hills High School, purchased the *Johnny* book in 2012, almost 50 years after graduating from Granite Hills. He posted the following comment on Amazon:

> *Johnny was in my high school class at Granite Hills High*
> *School class of 1963 in El Cajon, California. Everyone has*
> *a high school buddy but Johnny was the entire classes buddy.*
> *Even the bullies had a smile for him because he had a smile*
> *for everyone. He knew as did we that he wasn't going to*
> *make it out of high school alive. It never stopped him from*
> *being the best tennis player in the district. Even when he*
> *was all puffed up with his illness he would go out onto the*
> *tennis court and play. We all admired him for his courage*
> *and I don't believe there was a single person in that class*
> *that wouldn't have given his or her life to see him saved.*
> *He was the finest young man I ever met. I'm sure that for*
> *some reason God wanted to start a tennis team and that is*

why he called Johnny. He stepped off this world and right straight into heaven. I will never forget him and his courage. Every time I start to feel sorry for myself and need to perk my self-esteem up I think of him and realize just how humble we should be. He was an inspiration to say the least.

Johnny's father, George, established the "John Sanderlin Tennis Tournament" in his son's memory. It's an annual junior boy's tournament in San Diego.

Ten long days after my melanoma surgery in 2005, I arrived at Dr. Baron's office to find out if the cancer had spread to my lymph nodes. I hoped he'd greet me in the waiting room and pronounce me cancer-free right there. But he didn't. I sat down near a few other patients. Within ten minutes I was shown into the office. Dr. Baron shook my hand and asked me how I was.

"I was hoping you'd tell me," I joked uneasily, thinking maybe these were the last moments of my life before I'd learn I had cancer. I had a stomachache. *So, this is it. I survived open heart surgery and brain surgery, and now skin cancer was going to kill me.*

Dr. Baron began by making small talk. He was very serious. He picked up my chart and pointed to some images of lymph nodes. I presumed they were mine, but I was struggling to keep up.

"....so, it seems that your lymph nodes are clear and there are no signs the cancer has spread."

I must not have reacted because Dr. Baron continued, "And that's a good thing, Roy."

My fog lifted. I had dodged another bullet. My heart was pumping soundly, my brain tumor was gone, and I was cancer free. I wished Johnny had had the same good fortune.

CHAPTER FIVE

Develop Character:
It's More Important than Winning

National Juniors and UCLA

When Johnny told me his father wouldn't let him play in the 1963 USTA National Boys' 16s doubles because of his illness, I asked Bob Lutz to play. Bob was a great doubles player with an excellent serve-volley combination and return-of-serve. He was powerful and moved well. He preferred the ad side of the court, so I played the deuce side. Together we won the Boys' 16s doubles in Southern California; the USTA National Boys' 16s in Kalamazoo, Michigan; and the USTA National Boys' 16s hard-court tournament in Burlingame, California. While I never liked playing singles against my doubles partner, I did manage to beat Bob in singles as well. It felt like a good win for me at the time — all wins are good — but I had no idea it would be the first of a career-long rivalry between Bob and me. The next year as partners we got to the semifinals of the USTA National Boys' 18-and-Under tournament.

Bob and I were successful on the court, but we weren't close friends the way Johnny and I were. I missed that relationship. Bob went to

Stanford for a semester before transferring to the University of Southern California. He didn't lose any varsity eligibility and he helped USC win three NCAA team championships. He also won an NCAA singles title his sophomore year and the NCAA doubles titles with Stan Smith in his sophomore and junior years. He and Stan Smith went on to win four US Open doubles titles together.

Bob Lutz was a formidable adversary for 16 years. I played with him in the juniors and against him in college and in the pros. I must have faced Bob over thirty times in my career. He was always favored but I managed to win some of those contests, and they were some of my most rewarding victories.

Someone once asked me which player, of all my opponents, motivated me to raise my level of play the most. Without hesitation, I replied, "Bob Lutz!"

Bob Lutz (right) and me in 1963

I learned a lot about character playing Bob so often. Win or lose, Bob always competed hard and fair. Not once did he give me a bad line-call. He also never argued a call. On close calls, he would give away the point. He exemplified what my parents taught: the way a player behaves on the court reflects his or her personality and character. Like Bob, I needed to be able to live with myself. In the end, character is what defines you, not winning or losing.

Tennis has always offered me a way to make good friends. In addition to Rocky, Carlos, and Johnny, I became friends with Don Parker, a junior player I met in local tournaments when we were 14. He also took lessons from Wilbur Folsom. Unlike my other tennis friends, Don and I were in the same school district and could play together on the Hoover High School tennis team. We traveled to tournaments and double-dated on the weekends and to our prom.

My best non-tennis friend in school was Pete Kofoed. Pete's family moved to San Diego in 1962 when his father was hired as the minister of our church, the Trinity Methodist Church. Pete and I became friends in church and then Pete, Don, and I hung out together in high school. I've heard Pete say that he was "not an athlete like Roy and Don," but that's one of the things Don and I loved about him. Pete's first love was music. He was in the Hoover High band and orchestra and directed the pep band at basketball games. We graduated high school together in 1965.

Pete would have loved a career in music — and proudly played the trombone in the Marching Band — but he earned a degree from UCLA in political science, graduated from law school, and has enjoyed a successful career in the insurance industry. Don played tennis for two years at San Diego City College under coach Odus Morgan, won All-American honors for doubles in 1967, married his high school sweetheart, and then transferred to UCLA. Upon graduating, he thought he might want to be a lawyer but instead found success in the field of human resources, specifically executive recruiting in the banking industry. Pete, Don, and I have been friends for 60 years.

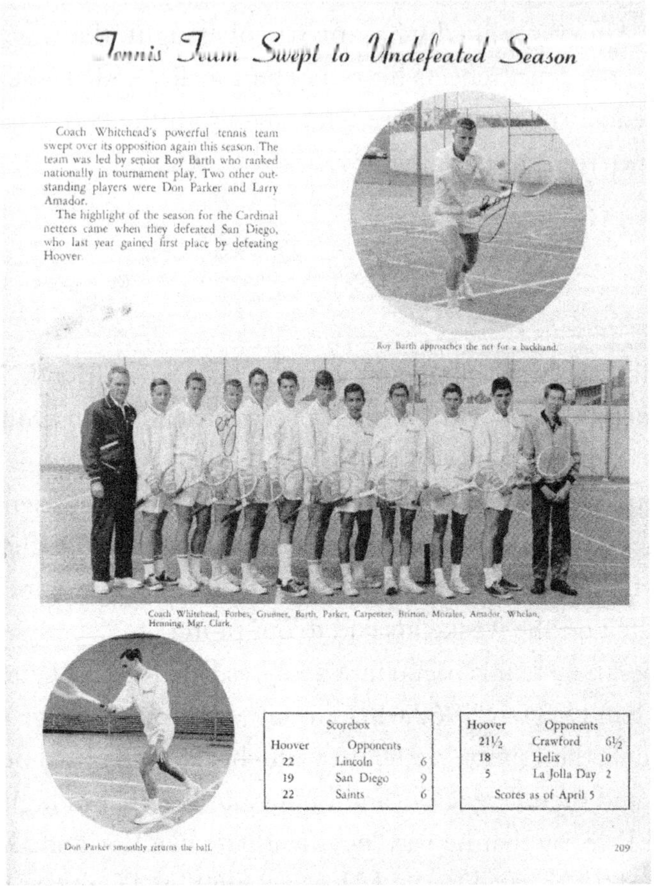

Tennis Team Swept to Undefeated Season

Coach Whitehead's powerful tennis team swept over its opposition again this season. The team was led by senior Roy Barth who ranked nationally in tournament play. Two other outstanding players were Don Parker and Larry Amador.

The highlight of the season for the Cardinal netters came when they defeated San Diego, who last year gained first place by defeating Hoover.

Roy Barth approaches the net for a backhand.

Coach Whitehead, Forbes, Grunner, Barth, Parker, Carpenter, Brinton, Morales, Amador, Whelan, Henning, Mgr. Clark.

Scorebox

Hoover	Opponents	
22	Lincoln	6
19	San Diego	9
22	Saints	6

Hoover	Opponents	
21½	Crawford	6½
18	Helix	10
5	La Jolla Day	2

Scores as of April 5

Don Parker smoothly returns the ball.

209

Hoover High School Yearbook 1965.
Tennis team page featuring Don Parker and me.
(photo courtesy Rita Cantos Cartwright)

My whole life I dreamt of playing tennis for UCLA. My father played there. Arthur Ashe played there. Johnny's older brother, David, played there. Johnny and I planned to go there together. I couldn't imagine playing anywhere else.

I had some work to do to prove myself to UCLA though, and fracturing my ankle in a basketball game in my junior year didn't help. I was sidelined in the spring when I should have been preparing for the

1964 National 18-and-Under tournament in Kalamazoo, Michigan.

I recovered enough to play but I lost in the third round of the singles draw, which didn't increase my chances of getting a scholarship to UCLA. But Bob Lutz and I got to the semifinals in doubles — losing to Stan Smith and Jim Hobson, which did help my chances.

UCLA was one of the top tennis programs in the country at the time. J.D. Morgan, the men's tennis coach and assistant athletic director, who had also been a teammate of my father's at UCLA, invited my father and me to visit UCLA during the 1965 NCAA Men's Championship. Arthur Ashe was on that team, as was Johnny Sanderlin's brother, David. We visited the day Arthur won the NCAA singles and doubles for UCLA. It was inspiring. UCLA also won the NCAA Team Championship that year.

Other schools expressed interest in me as well. Brigham Young University in Utah offered me a full scholarship and the No. 1 singles slot in my first year of eligibility, which would be my sophomore year. Long Beach State University near Los Angeles offered the same. Their offers were quite tempting, and UCLA hadn't offered anything yet.

I had a few other things going for me to interest UCLA: J.D. Morgan and my father had been teammates; Odus Morgan, the tennis coach at San Diego City College and J.D.'s cousin, knew me from my lifetime of tournaments in San Diego; I was a strong doubles player; and my high school grades were excellent — I was ranked 16th in a senior class of 950 — so I would not have had to work if I got a scholarship. I knew I would have to work my way up UCLA's ladder though. I was OK with that. After all, it was UCLA.

J.D. Morgan himself called to offer me a full tennis scholarship. I felt like I was accepting for two of us. *We made it, Johnny!*

The summer before college, fellow Californian Brian Cheney and I both competed in the junior tournaments leading up to the USTA National Boys' 18-and-Under Championship in Kalamazoo, Michigan. We were not partners, but at the conclusion of the tournament we were named co-recipients of the Allen B. Stowe Sportsmanship Award.

We didn't even know there was such an award, which means we

were recognized for just being ourselves. Brian and I received this honor in the tournament's eighth year; it was the first — and only — time the award was presented to two recipients. Six weeks later, our picture was in the program for the Pacific Southwest Professional Championship tournament.

I would have liked to have done better in the tournament — I reached the quarterfinal round in singles and the semifinal round in doubles with Ron Bohrnstedt — but I left Michigan with my Sportsmanship Award feeling good about having treated all the players with respect on and off the court, making fair line calls, and acknowledging my opponents' good shots. As I've said, character counts too.

*Brian Cheney and me winning the USTA Boys'
18s Sportsmanship Award in 1965 (photo courtesy
Thelner-Hoover Photographic Artist)*

CHAPTER SIX

Hang On like a Crab

Transitioning to College Tennis and My First Major

I entered UCLA in the fall of 1965 with 3,000 other freshmen, including basketball icon Kareem Abdul-Jabbar, whose name at the time was still Lew Alcindor. I was planning to major in business, but the year I enrolled UCLA dropped its undergraduate business curriculum. I chose economics instead — the closest major to business — and discovered I was going to pursue a degree in something I didn't really like. I was in for a rough ride academically.

My first semester at UCLA was overwhelming. I was one of 150 students in my freshman classes, and no one cared if I showed up or not. Even though I graduated at the top of the Hoover High School senior class in San Diego, I felt like everyone at UCLA was smarter than me. I couldn't wait to get to UCLA and, when I did, it was pretty stressful.

Fortunately, I felt at home on the tennis team. I went to class in the morning, practiced with the team from 2:30 p.m. to 5:00 p.m., had dinner at 6:00 p.m., studied from 7:00 p.m. to 10:00 p.m., and went to bed at 10:15 p.m. I worked hard in the classroom and on the court. I loved having a coach push me mentally and physically against players of similar skill.

I also had a great roommate: Hank Goldsmith from Great Neck, New York. We grew up 2,700 miles apart but immediately bonded over our love of playing tennis and watching basketball. We went to every home UCLA basketball game together in an era when UCLA, coached by John Wooden, won ten national championships in 12 years. Hank and I also played freshman tennis.

It seemed everyone I met at UCLA was from California, or at least the western states, so Hank's being from New York stood out. Apparently Hank and his family visited a friend in the Los Angeles area at the time he was applying to college. When Hank returned to New York, he applied to a handful of East Coast schools — and to UCLA. His parents made him promise that if he went to UCLA, he'd come home for holidays and summers. He did, which worked out nicely for me, too.

As freshmen, we were not eligible to play on the varsity team, but the best practices were the ones with the varsity players. Our freshman team played other freshman teams — including our rival USC — and smaller colleges like the University of Redlands. We also traveled to many of the same tournaments throughout Southern California I played in as a kid.

My father and me my freshman year at UCLA, 1966
(photo courtesy UCLA Atheltic Department)

During my freshman year, Allen Fox was invited to practice with the team. Allen was a former three-time All-American and NCAA singles and doubles champion who, when he graduated from UCLA in 1961, was ranked No. 4 in men's singles in the United States. He played for the U.S. Davis Cup Team three times, was ranked five times in the Top 10 in the U.S. men's singles, and reached the quarterfinal round of Wimbledon in 1965.

Allen was back at UCLA studying to earn a PhD in Psychology. I loved practicing with him. He was about 5'8" — a little shorter than me — and played a similar counter-punching style. He was tenacious on the court and difficult to beat. He worked the point, running me from side to side until he had the opportunity to get to the net and put the ball away. He never gave me any "free" points and rarely made an unforced error. Allen taught me never to give up.

Maureen Connolly also taught me never to give up, but not in the dramatic way Allen did. I'll never forget when Allen grabbed a fistful of my shirt with his outstretched fingers, shook me, and said, "You must hang on like a crab and never give up." The memory of that moment won me many matches.

Allen Fox, back at UCLA to earn a PhD in Psychology, helped me with my mental and physical game (photo courtesy Allen Fox)

In my freshman year, Coach J.D. Morgan paired me in doubles with Los Angeles native Steve Tidball for a Men's Invitational Tournament in Phoenix, Arizona. At first, Coach Morgan paired Steve with big-serving Louis Glass — Arthur Ashe's freshman protégé from New York — but Louis' poor grades prevented him from playing. I took his place. This was a prestigious invitational tournament and some of the biggest names in men's tennis accepted: Brazilian Davis Cup player Thomaz Koch; Mexican Davis Cup and USC player Joaquin Loyo-Mayo; U.S. Davis Cup player, USC player, and my long-time partner and opponent Bob Lutz; as well as USC star and U.S. Davis Cup player, Stan Smith. Steve and I had a great tournament, losing a marathon match in the final to Koch and Loyo-Mayo. Steve and I remained a formidable doubles team for the rest of our freshman year. I couldn't wait for my first year of varsity eligibility.

That summer I played in my first major tournament: the 1966 U.S. Championships on the grass at the West Side Tennis Club in Forest Hills, New York. (Two years later, the tournament's name would be changed to the US Open.) I had never been to New York before and was a little daunted by the prospect of going into Manhattan. Fortunately, I had a personal tour guide: my college roommate Hank Goldsmith, who had made good on his promise to his parents to return home to New York each summer. I got Hank a ticket to come watch me play and he offered to introduce me to New York City. Exciting! But first I had to concentrate on my matches.

In the first round, I defeated American Nicholas Kourides 6-3, 6-1, 6-0 — my first major match win! My reward was to face world No. 2 and defending French Open Champion, Australian Fred Stolle, in the second round. I lost to him in straight sets, as did almost everyone else in the tournament. Stolle didn't drop a set on his way to the final until he faced John Newcombe. "Newk" won the first set but Stolle won the next three and the title. In my first major tournament, I won a match and then lost to the best player in the draw.

What I remember most about the match against Fred Stolle was not that I lost, or what the score was (6-4, 6-1, 6-4), but that I played every point the best I could against the No. 2 player in the world in my first major tournament. After losing the second set 6-1, I could have given up. The crowd was with the favored Stolle and I was an unknown. No one expected anything from me, except me. I had every intention of "hanging on like a crab" on every point. And I did. This tenacity would serve me well in school, on the court, and in business.

That night Hank and his parents took me to my first show in New York. We saw the British comedy *There's a Girl in my Soup* at the Globe Theater in Manhattan's West End. It was a near-perfect day.

My first US Open, 1966, Forest Hills, New York.
Left: Hank Goldsmith watching me play.
Right: Hank's picture of me serving against Fred Stolle.

CHAPTER SEVEN

Concentrate on One Challenge at a Time

Surviving My Sophomore Slump

The study of economics examines how a system works: assessing strengths and weaknesses, resolving problems, and balancing supply and demand. My sophomore year was a perfect case study of a system (me) going from a strong economy into recession as the Gross Domestic Product (my value) declined for two consecutive quarters, literally. Beginning in the fall of 1966, UCLA changed its academic schedule from semesters to quarters. Rather than two 15- or 16-week semesters, classes were offered in four 10- or 11-week quarters. Unfortunately, my professors didn't adjust their coursework, opting instead to cram their same 15-week syllabus — in all four of my classes — into the shorter time frame. For someone already overwhelmed by the subject matter, I struggled even harder to keep up. Any extra time I could have studied was already consumed by varsity tennis practice and matches. Our team was under pressure to win the Pacific-8 (Pac-8) Conference, the NCAA titles, and the national title against our rival USC.

In addition, I joined the Sigma Nu fraternity, which I had rushed in my freshman year, and I signed up for the Army ROTC as my tennis coach, J.D. Morgan, encouraged me to do. Coach Morgan thought this would protect me from being drafted. I no longer enjoyed any manageable schedule and I struggled to prioritize. My economic indicators had turned "unfavorable."

To add extra volatility, I hated ROTC. The authority figures were retired veterans of the Korean War who seemed to have been forever compromised by their experience. They subscribed to the "break you down to build you up" philosophy and thought nothing of screaming at and demeaning us. On our first day of marching exercises out on the practice football field, an upperclassman ROTC instructor approached me in formation and noticed that my last name was the same as his. He proceeded to stand two inches from my face and yell at me to growl like a tiger. He told me he expected twice as much from me as he would not permit me to embarrass his name. Just great.

The ROTC classroom was no better. While there were thousands of Korean War veterans who served the country with honor and distinction — and many who could have thoughtfully inspired college students — the retired Korean War veterans who taught me at UCLA just talked endlessly about how they used specific tactics to "kill as many Gooks as possible." It was horrible and it gave me nightmares. And it certainly put tennis in perspective. Doing battle on the court I worked to be more competitive, strategic, and tactical than my opponent but, win or lose, we still engaged in a friendly handshake at the net. I was suited to go to war on the court, but that was it.

In my sophomore year, I also had a new tennis coach. Glenn Bassett took over as UCLA's men's varsity tennis coach when J.D. Morgan was promoted to athletic director. I would miss Coach Morgan. He had been my dad's teammate at UCLA, and he was the one who called to inform me of my full scholarship. He looked out for me and I liked how he coached. J.D. was a motivator, which was just what I needed my freshman year.

Glenn Bassett was a conditioning coach. Not all the players on my team did well under Coach Bassett's style, but fortunately I flourished. Coach Bassett was bullish about practice, practice, and more practice

— a style he gleaned from UCLA men's varsity basketball coach Johnny Wooden. Wooden was in his 18th year of what would become a legendary 27-year, 10-national-championship-winning basketball coaching career at UCLA. I enjoyed watching him coach when I went to the games.

Like Coach Wooden, Coach Bassett emphasized the process: practice hard and let the competition take care of itself. He would run intensive drills and have us play points for two and a half hours and then make us run two miles. Every day. Coach Bassett also encouraged us to drink water during practice because Coach Wooden encouraged his basketball players to drink water during practice. (Before Wooden, drinking water during practice was considered a sign of weakness and lack of conditioning, even as elite football players on fields around the country were dropping dead from dehydration. Seems obvious now, but it wasn't then.)

Coach Bassett was a master of positive reinforcement. He found something specific in each of our games he could encourage us to improve. For me, it was volleying. Thanks to my father and Les Stoefen, I had always been a good volleyer, but under Coach Bassett's watchful eye, I became a great volleyer. Every time I hit a successful volley, he would acknowledge it. "You never miss a volley," he would say as I came off the court. His scrutiny of that shot made me never want to miss. I went whole matches without missing a volley.

Trying hard never to miss a volley playing for Coach Bassett on the UCLA Tennis Team (photo courtesy Andrew Sinatra and the UCLA Athletic Department)

Coach Bassett kept Steve Tidball and me together as a doubles team. Our sophomore year, we reached the semifinals of the NCAA Championship. Bassett's team was the upturn of my tough year, which was about to get worse.

When the final exam schedule came out toward the end of my sophomore year, I learned that all five of my finals were scheduled for the first two days of finals week — the Monday and Tuesday following the last week of classes. I would have just two days once classes ended to study for five finals. *How on earth am I going to manage this?*

In the weeks leading up to finals, I studied harder, slept less, and started losing concentration, which made it harder to study, which kept me from sleeping, which further impacted my concentration. My schoolwork and tennis were suffering. I was in a downward spiral. I was crashing. I panicked.

The weekend before finals, I went home to San Diego to see my parents. My mother called Dr. Minna, our long-time family doctor, who saw me immediately. He told my parents my eyes looked "lifeless" and suggested I spend a night for observation in the psych ward of the San Diego Country Hospital. It was the lowest point in my life. From national tennis champion at 13, to a full tennis scholarship at UCLA, to the local psych ward. I couldn't believe it.

Dr. John Rombeau, the oldest brother of one of my tennis competitors, Jim Rombeau, took a personal interest in me. He determined that I was not mentally ill but just under extreme stress. (Again, obvious now, but not so then.) He released me to the care of Dr. Minna, who advised me to eliminate as much stress as possible to get me through my exams. Together we devised a plan: I would tell Coach Bassett I would be skipping practice until finals were over, I would try to convince a few professors to reschedule my exams to give me some more time, I would drop out of my pledging duties in the Sigma Nu fraternity, and my father would help me create a study schedule so I would know specifically when to study for each exam. I regrouped and recovered, doing well in all my finals except one. Most importantly, I didn't have to quit school.

The summer of 1967 gave me a much-needed break from classes and there was no tennis team, but my tournament life was in high gear and I had the chance to read for pleasure instead of for school.

One book — *Psycho Cybernetics* by Maxwell Maltz — stayed with me. Maltz, a well-known plastic surgeon, wrote about the importance of positive self-image. Before the stress of my sophomore year, I'm sure I would never have given this book a second look. After that experience, I embraced the idea of thinking only positive thoughts about myself, tennis, and life in general.

Maltz was right: there was no room for unproductive negativity. Playing tennis well demands positive thinking. It was just me out there and I was either my best friend or my worst enemy. When I missed a shot, I had the choice to tell myself it's OK and to watch the ball closer next time or to berate myself for having an inconsistent backhand. The "negative" choice could cost me the next few points. In order to win, I needed to see myself winning and be confident I could close it out. I was a lot happier choosing to think positively, and my tennis game continued to improve. I focused on getting the most out of every day.

That 1967 summer, I played on the USTA's Junior Davis Cup team and on the United States Men's Tour, which included a stop at the U.S. Men's Doubles Championship at the Longwood Cricket Club in Boston the week before the U.S. Championships in Forest Hills, New York. Steve Tidball and I continued our successful college partnership outside of school by upsetting Charlie Pasarell and Cliff Richey. This was a nice lead-up to the U.S. National Championships.

In my second year at Forest Hills, I beat American William Brown in four sets and then I defeated Mexican Joaquin Loyo-Mayo in a tight five-set match, avenging my doubles final match loss to him two years prior. Losing to No. 2-seed Australian Roy Emerson in the third round was not so bad. He had already won the U.S. Championships twice in singles (and four times in doubles) and I felt honored just to play him on such a big stage.

And New York meant a chance to visit with my friend Hank Goldsmith, who came to see me play. Even though we didn't live together after freshman year, we went to basketball games together at school and I looked forward to seeing him in New York. He always found us the best restaurants.

Had my father and my doctors not taught me how to prioritize and focus on one challenge at a time, I would have self-destructed. I don't know whether I would have quit school and been drafted, or whether I would have taken time off from tennis to focus on my degree. I would not have liked either option. While the feeling of helplessness at the time was frightening, it was cathartic. Never again would I want to feel that way, which is incentive enough to keep my commitments in perspective.

CHAPTER EIGHT

Get the Most Out of Your Talent

Great Junior Year at UCLA

Determined not to repeat the devastating pressure of my sophomore year, I made some big changes when I returned to UCLA in the fall. First, I dropped out of ROTC before I had to sign a document officially committing to the service. Quitting ROTC increased my chances of being drafted before I finished school but, if I couldn't keep my grades up, I'd definitely be drafted sooner and without a degree. I planned to just walk into the ROTC office and inform them I needed to drop out of their program. A half hour later, I was involved in a test of wills to see whether their resolve to keep me was greater than my resolve to resign. They were bigger than me and wore uniforms with medals. I was a slender nineteen-year-old kid who was behind in my homework and needed to get to tennis practice. No more ROTC.

Second, I dropped out of my fraternity. The social life seemed fun and a welcome relief from studying, but I just couldn't find the time to appreciate it. The Sigma Nu leadership understood my priorities and said I could always come back.

Third, I reduced the number of classes I took each quarter. I could not balance too much theoretical and academic undergrad economics with so much real and physical varsity men's tennis. I was still only eligible for three years of varsity, and this would delay my graduation date, but no matter how long my classes took to complete, I wanted to get the most out of them.

With no ROTC or fraternity and a lighter class load, I really enjoyed the year. In September 1967, I entered the Pacific Southwest Tennis Championship and beat Charlie Pasarell in three sets. That was a big singles win for me, not only because Charlie ended the year ranked No. 1 in the U.S., but because in conjunction with my third-round appearance in the U.S. Championships, my 1967 year-end national men's singles ranking jumped from No. 32 to No. 14.

At the start of 1968, I was a junior playing No. 1 singles and No. 1 doubles with Steve Tidball. We were one of the top collegiate doubles teams in the nation — ranked as high as No. 4 — thanks to some big wins, including that win over Pasarell and Richey in Boston. *It seems like just yesterday Johnny Sanderlin and I were putting on his miniature golf course and dreaming of playing for UCLA. He would have loved this.*

Steve was a great partner but we didn't quite gel at first. When we were freshman, he was brimming with confidence and I wasn't. Steve was a pretty laid-back guy who just walked on the court expecting to win. I liked that attitude. I had been a little intimidated by my freshman experience and didn't play with the same confidence he did.

Our sophomore year was the opposite: my tennis confidence soared and Steve's waned. Since I felt nothing off the court was going right, I was sustained by tennis wins. Steve wasn't happy with his results from the previous summer, and he had hurt his shoulder. He didn't care as much about winning as he used to. We were just not in sync.

That year, Steve and I independently approached Coach Bassett to discuss our issues.

"Don't tell me," Coach said. "Tell each other."

We did. We worked out our issues and leveraged our strengths and weaknesses to motivate each other. By the time we were juniors, we were proficient partners and good friends.

Steve Tidball
and me as the
No. 1 doubles team
at UCLA.
(photo credit: Bob
Redding of the
San Diego Union
newspaper)

Our doubles success improved my singles game and I started beating favored opponents. Coach Bassett's main objective that season was to beat USC, the country's top men's collegiate tennis team. The UCLA-USC matches were a big deal. I played singles against my old partner and adversary, Bob Lutz, in front of 3,000 UCLA fans and a local TV audience. I won 8-6 in the third set, beating Bob for the first time since the National Boys' Hard-Court Championship when I was 16. It felt great.

The following week I was named the "John Wooden UCLA Athlete of the Week" and received a handwritten note from Coach Wooden.

> *What I liked the most about your match against Bob Lutz*
> *is that you got the most out of your talent.*

This meant a lot coming from such a highly respected coach.

Steve and I reached the final of the NCAA doubles championship that year but lost to Bob Lutz and Stan Smith for the second year in a row. Lutz and Smith were now two-time NCAA doubles champions and, with Stan winning the NCAA singles, they were both NCAA singles champions as well. I didn't think Steve and I would ever beat them.

My "talent" that junior year off the court was paring down my responsibilities to the few I could handle, and then taking my talent on the court to new heights. It was a successful year.

CHAPTER NINE

Understand Your Industry

Amateur to Professional Tennis Tour

Nineteen sixty-eight was a pivotal year in men's professional tennis, and the end of my third and beginning of my fourth year at UCLA. The post-college professional men's tennis options were changing, my game was coming into its own — I was already a top player in the amateur ranks — and I would soon have to make some decisions about my future.

Before 1968, the top male tennis players in the world were either professionals or amateurs. This difference was less about talent and more about income. Tennis began as a game for aristocrats and the wealthy when high-level competition was about prestige, not money. But as the game grew in popularity among the working class, players who excelled could not afford to play without compensation. Many talented players quit the game because they needed to earn a living. Enter the first professional tennis promoters and the first professional tennis tours.

The opportunity to make a living playing tennis was attractive but restricting. The pro tour offered a guaranteed, contract-based income, but its events were series of exhibitions, pre-arranged head-to-head competitions, and annual Champions Tournaments, not the more well-known venues. The most prestigious events — the Australian, French, Wimbledon, and U.S. tournaments, known as the "majors" — were for amateurs only.

Some notable players began as amateurs and then became professionals. Bill Tilden, who won 15 major singles titles as an amateur in the 1920s, turned pro in 1930 and spent the next 15 years as a touring pro. As an amateur, Pancho Gonzales won the U.S. Championships at Forest Hills in 1947 and 1948 before signing with Jack Kramer's pro tour in 1949 and barnstorming around the country playing one-night exhibitions. Rod Laver won all four majors in a calendar year (a "Grand Slam") and played on the Australian Davis Cup team before turning pro and limiting himself to the exhibition-style matches of the pro tour. Roy Emerson won 12 majors as an amateur before turning pro, including a *career* Grand Slam (all four major tournaments but not necessarily in the same year) in both singles and doubles, the only male tennis player (still!) to accomplish that.

Some professional players remained independent, but most were contracted to either the National Tennis League (NTL) or the World Championship of Tennis (WCT), both established in 1967. The NTL was founded by George MacCall, who signed Roy Emerson, Rod Laver, Andres Gimeno, and Ken Rosewall, among others. The WCT was established by David Dixon. The first eight players he signed were known as the "Handsome Eight": John Newcombe, Tony Roche, Niki Pilic, Pierre Barthes, Roger Taylor, Butch Buchholz, Dennis Ralston, and Cliff Drysdale. By 1968, David Dixon had sold his share of the WCT to Lamar Hunt and Al Hill, Jr., but not before signing the first women professional tennis players: Billie Jean King, Rosie Casals, Francoise Durr, and Ann Haydon-Jones.

Amateur players like me could play on college teams (freshman year and then three years of varsity eligibility as long as they maintained academic standards); enter local, regional, and national tournaments; qualify for the four major tournaments; and receive invitations to join their country's Davis Cup team (teams of countrymen playing other countries, named for founder Dwight Davis). These tournament associations all played under the rules of the International Lawn Tennis

Federation (ILTF). Winners received trophies or small mementos but no prize money. Amateurs invited to the major tournaments were given a travel allowance. The top amateurs were given "appearance money" or guarantees, whether they won a match or not. In the United States, private housing was also offered at the non-major events. Playing tennis in the Olympics was not an option; tennis had been dropped as an Olympic sport in 1924 and wasn't reinstated until 1988.

These two avenues of men's top-level tennis did not coexist peacefully: the pro players wanted to play in the most prestigious tournaments, and the once-revered world of amateur tennis was losing top name players to the paying ranks of the pro tours.

In 1967, The All England Club — where Wimbledon is played — invited professionals Rod Laver, Roy Emerson, Pancho Gonzales, and others to play at Wimbledon to see if the fans would come out and support them. They did. The success of that event prompted The All England Club to open the Wimbledon field to both amateur and professional players the next year. When the 1968 Wimbledon became the first major tournament to offer prize money and let pros and amateurs play in the same tournament, the two tennis worlds intersected and the "Open Era" officially began.

The Australian Championships became the Australian Open, the French Championships became the French Open, and the U.S. Championships became the US Open. Despite the new "open" format, Wimbledon still chose to be called The Championships, Wimbledon.

The first few years of the Open Era were far from harmonious. Power struggles between the International Lawn Tennis Federation (the governing body of the amateur players) and the NTL and WCT (the two prominent professional promoters) led to tournament boycotts and tour rivalries, but not the on-court kind.

In 1970, The WCT professional tour absorbed the NTL professional players. This gave the ILTF amateur group just one adversary, but the tension did not ease. Each group banned the other from their events. In 1971, the Australian Open was a WCT competition while the French Open, Wimbledon, and US Open were ILTF events.

This was the chaotic men's professional tennis world of my era, but I could not allow myself to get caught up in the disarray. Once I stepped on the court, I focused on the game, which was the same no matter the name of the tournament or which tour promoted it.

CHAPTER TEN

Take One Point and One Day at a Time

Playing in My First Wimbledon

No matter who was invited to play and how they got there, Wimbledon was, to me, the ultimate tennis stage. In the days before the current point-based ranking system, whoever won Wimbledon was deemed the No. 1 player in the world. As young players, Johnny Sanderlin and I dreamt that someday we would be good enough to play there.

In June 1968, I was playing in the NCAA tournament in San Antonio, Texas, when I received a telegram from Wimbledon inviting me to play in the men's singles draw. Players were accepted into Wimbledon based on their national ranking. In 1967, I was ranked 14th in U.S. men's singles, which made me eligible for the 1968 draw. I stared at the telegram for much longer than it took to read what it said.

> WESTERN UNION
>   ROY BARTH
>   CONFIRM SOONEST ENTRY
>   MAIN DRAW WIMBLEDON STOP CONFIRM
>   AMATEUR STATUS STOP
>   THE COMMITTEE
>   ALL ENGLAND LAWN TENNIS CLUB

An invitation to play in the main draw at Wimbledon which, for the first time, would include the best amateur and professional players in the world. *I must still be dreaming.*

I didn't have time to go home to San Diego. I flew right from San Antonio to New York and from New York to London (my first trip overseas!) to play at Wimbledon the *next day* against Clark Graebner, one of the top American players. *Twenty-one years to prepare for this moment and I'm lucky if I have everything I need.*

I paid five pounds (about $10) to stay in a small bed and breakfast owned by Mrs. Sealy in Earl's Court near an underground "Tube" (British subway) stop. Fortunately for me, it rained on Day One and I had a whole day to acclimate to the atmosphere and the time change. As a player in the main draw, I was given a $300 allowance for Fred Perry clothing — the clothing sponsor of Wimbledon — and a rainy Day One was the perfect time to go shopping. With Mrs. Sealy's help, I made my way to the warehouse and picked out a few shirts, a long-sleeved knit V-neck sweater, and some shorts. I was really enjoying the clothing perk when the shop attendant asked if I would wait a few minutes while she *monogrammed* the clothes for me. I had arrived.

Sporting my new Fred Perry clothes from my first Wimbledon in 1968.

I lay in bed that night planning the morning schedule, trying not to think about my match in the afternoon. I would take the Tube one stop west from Earl's Court to Baron's Court on either the Piccadilly (blue) or District (green) line, walk to the Queen's Club to practice and have lunch, and then take the Players' Limo for the 25-minute drive to Wimbledon. Plenty of time to relax and not be too nervous.

Unfortunately, the tennis gods were not with me that next morning. Over breakfast, Mrs. Sealy told me that the Tube was on strike. Officially, it was a dispute between the National Union of Railwaymen and the British Rail entity over a pay increase. I guess if the Tube employees wanted to make a statement, the opening day of Wimbledon was dramatic timing. I panicked. All of England and I would be trying to hail a taxi at the same time. *Didn't anyone care that I was playing in the most famous tennis tournament in the world?*

I started to walk with all my gear in the direction of Baron's Court. I finally tracked down an available taxi and I got a ride the rest of the way to the Queen's Club, where the players' limousine was already waiting to take me to The All England Club. I didn't have time to practice or eat — I barely had time to change into my Wimbledon whites — and I was an hour late for my match. Fantastic.

I was pretty sure I had just come all this way — geographically, professionally, and personally — to face certain default. *How could this happen? How did the other players, including my opponent, get here on time? How did all the spectators get here?* I still don't know.

My only hope was to explain my morning to the officals as though they didn't know the Tube wasn't running, which of course they did. They let me play. Clark was already on Court 14 impatiently pacing back and forth, not caring at all about me or the Tube strike. The excitement of the morning had taken my mind off playing the match. Now I had to focus. I was nervous and excited at the same time.

I started my first match at Wimbledon on an empty stomach and without having practiced. Before I knew it, I had lost the first two sets and I was serving at 3-5 in the third set of the best-of-five set match. I was down to match point on my serve. Clark needed to win one more point to move on to the second round. As crazy a day as it had been, I was not going to give him the match. But perhaps he thought he'd already won because he seemed to lose some concentration. Between our points, he was watching the match on the next court.

I won my serve and then took advantage of Clark's waning focus. He missed some first serves and stayed in the backcourt after his second serve. I attacked those second serves, went on the offensive, and broke his serve. I came back and won the third set 7-5. I think I surprised both of us.

In the first game of the fourth set Clark was serving and it started to rain, but the officials didn't stop play. We each served one game, slipping on the slick grass. At 1-1 in the fourth set, the officials stopped play for the day.

I had better luck with the taxis the next day and got to The All England Club early enough to appreciate my surroundings. I took a deep breath and looked around for the first time. *I was playing at Wimbledon.* The place was magnificent, even on a cloudy day. The grass was beautifully manicured and showed no wear marks along the baseline or at the service "T," as it would in the coming days. The ball boys manually changed the scores on the scoreboard in the corner. All the outer courts (Courts 2-15) were grouped together with only a narrow alleyway between them for spectators, whom I hadn't noticed until just then. The umpires were wearing suits and ties. The players looked quite regal wearing white.

We started the fourth set where we left off the day before — at 1-1 — and I quickly fell behind 3-5. Somehow, I managed to hold my serve, break his serve, and win the fourth set 8-6. I really "hung on like a crab" in this match. Allen Fox would have been proud.

Going into the fifth set, I forgot all about being in my first Wimbledon tournament. I loved playing on grass and felt very comfortable on Court 14. I found some rhythm in my serve-and-volley combination and, for the first time in the match, I was holding my serve easily.

My God, I can win this match!

Word got out around the tournament grounds that Graebner, a

top ranked U.S. player, was in a "dog fight" on Court 14. Suddenly the walkways around this small outer court were packed with spectators. Things were heating up. Clark was asking advice from well-known agent and lawyer Donald Dell from the sidelines (which was against the rules) and calling me names as we changed ends of the court. I started walking around the other way to avoid him.

At 5-5 in the fifth set, Clark was serving and lost the first two points, giving me my first opportunity to break his serve and then serve for the match. I hit a great return to his feet, and he miss-hit a half-volley over the net for a winner. What a lucky shot! I would have been up triple breakpoint with a great chance to break his serve if he had missed that. Instead, it was 15-30, the momentum shifted, and he held his serve. We stayed even until I served at 9-10. We split the first four points: "30-all." I needed two points to stay in the match and Clark needed them to win it. He played them by hitting the two best returns he'd hit the entire two-day, five-set contest. He won. I was out.

I shook hands with Clark and with the umpire and left the court. Amid the crowd of spectators, I felt alone. The pro tennis tour can do that. I was still in college, which at the time was considered young for the tour, even among amateurs. And I really was alone, on and off the court. No family, no coach, no partner — no one to share my tough loss with.

My parents used to love to watch me play — and applauded my efforts, win or lose — but they were only able to attend matches close to home. My father worked long hours and took little time off, and traveling was expensive. I did call long distance from my hotel room every night to tell them about my matches. Even from far away, they were the closest thing I had to a "team." I would have loved them to be waiting for me when I came off Court 14.

As I walked by myself from the court to the locker room, someone touched my shoulder. I turned around.

"Roy, you know you have what it takes when you play well at Wimbledon," she said.

It was Billie Jean King, sharing with me one of the most memorable moments in my life.

Had I won that match, I would have moved into the Top 10 ranking of U.S. male players. I was feeling sorry for myself when Billie Jean applauded my effort and changed my outlook on the experience. She turned a court loss into a life win. Years later I was fortunate to tell her how much that meant to me.

CHAPTER ELEVEN

Don't Burn Out

European Clay, U.S. Grass, Hard-Court College Tennis,
and Two 5-Set Matches in One Day

Despite the epic first-round loss at Wimbledon, my game was at a new level. Clawing back on that stage after being down two sets was not easy. Thank you, Wilbur Folsom, Maureen Connolly, Les Stoefen, Glenn Bassett, Allen Fox, and *Psycho Cybernetics*. I "hung on like a crab," thought positive thoughts, and gave it my best. And I lost to an excellent American player; Clark Graebner went all the way to the semifinals that year, losing to Australian Davis Cup player Tony Roche.

Clark could be mean on the court but off the court he was much more pleasant. I had come to Europe unexpectedly and had no plans to remain there, but Clark introduced me to some tournament directors and I was able to stay in Europe for a month, playing tournaments on the European red clay in Germany (Ingolstadt, Munich, and Hamburg) and Switzerland (Montana-Vermala). Afterwards, I came back to the States to play the grass-court season before the US Open.

In the pre-Internet days, tournament registration was a mail-in protocol with strict deadlines. I had played the US Open in the two previous years and I knew the entry deadline. In 1968, when my entry form needed to get in the mail, I didn't send it. I was exhausted, feeling a little as I had at the end of my sophomore year when over-committing myself landed me in the hospital, and I certainly didn't want to relive that experience. I had gone non-stop from the varsity tennis season in the spring, to the NCAA championships in San Antonio, Texas, to Wimbledon in London, through the European clay circuit, and then back to the U.S. for the grass circuit. I was tired. I still had the Pacific Southwest and the Pacific Coast Professional tournaments coming up in September and a whole final year of varsity eligibility ahead of me starting in October. I was in New England and could have easily gone to New York, but I decided to head back to the West Coast for a much-needed break. It seemed like a good decision at the time.

In the fall of 1968, I was back at UCLA for my fourth (but not final) year of classes, and my last year of varsity eligibility. I took a few classes — most of them in my ever-challenging economics major — and practiced with the team.

After a couple of weeks off from competition, I played in the Pacific Southwest Professional Championships in mid-September. I reached the second round in singles but then lost to 1957 U.S. men's singles champion, Mal Anderson, in three sets.

The doubles draw was considerably more exciting for me. Steve Tidball and I played No. 3-seed Smith and Lutz in the first round on center court of the famed Los Angeles Tennis Club. Two weeks prior, Smith and Lutz had won their first US Open doubles title and I knew they would be confident. I also knew they would attract a big crowd. I was right. Every one of the 4,000 seats in the stadium was filled by spectators wanting to see the defending US Open champions. Steve and I played one of the best doubles matches of our career together, upsetting our longtime rivals 9-7, 10-12, 6-4. It was a huge win. Even though we lost the next round to Arthur Ashe and Ron Holmberg, we got a big write-up from Jeff Prugh in the *LA Times* about our first-round upset. Prugh called us "a couple of quick, aggressive seniors from UCLA." I was good with that.

BRUIN DOUBLES TEAM STUNS USC'S SMITH, LUTZ

Times Staff Writer

All summer, on clay and grass courts from Milwaukee to Forest Hills, the doubles team of Stan Smith and Bob Lutz looked invincible.

As national collegiate champs from USC, they had not lost a match since the first round at Wimbleton and it appeared as if they might never lose again.

It finally happened Sunday as darkness fell over the green carpet on the Los Angeles Tennis Club's center court.

And it took a couple of quick, aggressive seniors from UCLA, Roy Barth and Steve Tidball, to do it.

On a day when a record crowd of 4,110 filled the tennis club grounds to overflowing, Barth and Tidball rang up a thrilling 9-7, 10-12, 6-4 victory to reach the third round of the $30,000 Pacific Southwest Open tournament.

It was the highlight of a day in which Tom Okker and Lt. Arthur Ashe advanced, as expected, and in which Billie Jean King and Dennis Ralston were forced out of the tournament by recurring injuries.

Mrs. King, who was top-seeded in the women's singles, had to default her opening match to 17-year-old Pam Teeguarden of Los Angeles because of tendinitis in her left knee.

The three-time Wimbledon queen was advised by three doctors to forego playing in the tournament after she was unable to shake off the same injury that bothered her at Forest Hills.

Ralston, on the other hand, decided to play his second-round match with Australian amateur Colin Stubs, but his pulled stomach muscle prevented his service from being very effective. As a result, he dropped a 2-6, 6-1, 6-4 decision.

"It bothered me in the first set," said Ralston, the No. 8 seeded pro who was hampered by the same injury at Forest Hills. "But in the second set I really aggravated it. It even hurts me to laugh."

Meanwhile, Okker was highly impressive in his Southern California debut and needed only 60

Please Turn to Page 5, Col. 2

My match fortunes continued. Steve Tidball and I beat Smith and Bob Lutz for the *second time in six months* in one of my most memorable days of tennis competition, and not just because we beat Smith and Lutz. We were at the Pacific Coast Men's Doubles Championship at the La Jolla Beach and Tennis Club in March of 1969 facing defending champions and No. 1-seeds Smith and Lutz in the semifinals. Due to rain delays earlier in the week, both the semis and final had to be played on the same day. We played our semifinal match on Court No. 1, an intimate court with room for only 400 spectators. We split the first four sets 2-6, 13-11, 2-6, 6-3. In the fifth set, we served first and stayed on serve until we broke Lutz at 9-10. We held on to win 11-9 and take the three-and-a-half-hour match.

After a 90-minute break to eat lunch and rest, we were back on the same court to contest the final against USC's number No. 2 team of Joaquin Loyo-Mayo and Marcello Lara. Steve and I came out firing and took the first two sets 6-4 and 6-3. We should have been exhausted but

POINT OF IMPACT | 77

we played just as strong as we had earlier in the day. The next two sets were tougher. Our opponents knew we had played a marathon match earlier that morning and they started to lob us high and deep, really trying to wear us out. It worked. We battled hard but lost those next two sets 4-6 and 8-10. In the fifth set, our opponents were serving at 8-7 and I was sure the match was all but over. We were exhausted. What a shame it would have been to beat the No. 1 team in the semifinals and lose to the No. 2 team in the final, especially when I had been returning serve and volleying better than ever. Somehow, Steve and I won that game and the next two to take the set 10-8 and win the match.

We won two five-set matches in one day. Seven hours of competition. I was so tired that night I couldn't appreciate what we had done until the next day. Our prize was a $35 Sony clock radio, which is long gone, but the memories of that day are still with me.

Union SPORTS

MARCH 3, 1969   PAGE C-1

San Diego's Roy Barth, left, strikes one of many overheads he and partner Steve Tidball were called upon to execute yesterday against a pair of lobbying Mexicans, Joaquin Loyo-Mayo and Marcello Lara. Barth and Tidball prevailed in five sets to capture the 80th Pacific Coast Doubles championships at the La Jolla Beach and Tennis Club.

In May 1969 — my final season of college tennis — I once again faced my long-time USC rival Bob Lutz in the No. 1 singles match in the Pac-8 Championship at Stanford University. It was a really hot day and we started by splitting sets. Bob was running away with the third set. Serving at 1-4, I noticed he was slowing down. That day I was in better shape than he was, and I won the set 6-4 and won the match. And UCLA won the coveted Pac-8 title.

1969 UCLA Tennis Team.
Kneeling: from left, Jun Kuki, Steve Cornell, Tito Vasquez, co-captain
Roy Barth. Standing, from left, Jim Allen, Ron Bohrnstedt, Jeff Borowiak,
co-captain Steve Tidball, Elio Alvarez, Joel Ostroff, and the Coach
(photo courtesy UCLA Athletic Department)

That win was a nice way for Steve and me to complete our successful college doubles partnership. We were co-captains. We played No. 1 doubles. We won two All-American honors. We were runners-up for the NCAA doubles title. We appreciated our coach and what he taught us. And we had fun. My best doubles partners had been my close friends: Rocky Jarvis, Johnny Sanderlin, Don Parker, and Steve Tidball. A few years later, Steve was the best man at my wedding.

I completed my freshman season and three years of varsity eligibility, but my college experience was not over. Easing my course load the last two years kept me from burning out again, but if I wanted to graduate, I'd need to remain a student the next fall without tennis — at least without college tennis. I was fine with this.

And so was UCLA. Even though I had completed my varsity eligibility, UCLA graciously extended my scholarship for the next two quarters.

There was no reason I couldn't continue to play professional tennis, though. I was 22; if I was going to be a professional tennis player, this was the time to be playing. And if I was going to be a college graduate, this was the time to stay in school. I would make it work.

CHAPTER TWELVE

Focus on What You Can Control

Transition to Professional Tennis:
The Year of My Best Results

At first, life on the tour didn't seem much different from playing tournaments over summer vacation between years at UCLA, except I could now earn prize money in the major tournaments and play on the pro-only circuit. I still registered, showed up, and played. But there were differences I hadn't anticipated. As in any transition from college to the "real world," tennis on the tour demanded I make it completely on my own. Gone were the many good players eager to practice with me, the support system of my family and teammates, and the coach in my corner pushing me to improve. Now it was just me all the time, needing to be self-disciplined and self-motivated, just like at that first Wimbledon.

I played my second Wimbledon in the summer of 1969, losing in singles in four sets to American Tom Edelfsen, but making it to the second round in doubles. My doubles partner, Alex Olmedo, was a former NCAA singles title winner from USC and a former Wimbledon and Australian Open singles champion. He taught tennis at the Beverly Hills Hotel in Los Angeles. When he asked me to play doubles with him, I agreed immediately. Together we beat Frenchmen Jean-Pierre Courcol and Bernard Paul 8-10, 6-1, 6-3, 6-3 in the first round but then lost to the seasoned team of Ken Rosewall and Fred Stolle in the next round.

After the 1969 Wimbledon, I stayed in Europe, as I had the previous year, to play red clay events in Belgium, Switzerland, and Germany. The slow red-clay-court surface demands players be so patient and so fit; it really toughened up my game for the upcoming U.S. grass season.

In August, I came back to the States to play grass-court tournaments in Southampton, New York; Merion, Pennsylvania; South Orange, New Jersey; and Brookline, Massachusetts, before playing in the US Open at Forest Hills. The transition from slow red clay in Europe to fast grass in the States was productive; I had my best results in those grass tournaments, including reaching the round of 16 in Southampton and defeating Roscoe Tanner, Barry McKay, Jim Osborne, and No. 3-seed Australian Bill Bowery to reach the quarterfinals in the U.S. Professional Championships in Brookline, Massachusetts. It was the best tournament of my life thus far.

NO. 2 FOREIGNER FALLS AT LONGWOOD

Barth Bounces Bowrey

THE BIGGER THEY ARE—

CALIFORNIAN ROY BARTH SEEMS TO BE MAKING UPSETS HIS THING. HE KNOCKED OFF SEEDED JIM OSBORNE IN THE 3RD ROUND AND DUMPED AUSTRALIAN SEED BILL BOWREY, YESTERDAY.

HERALD TRAVELER SPORTS
THURSDAY AUG. 21, 1969 C PAGE 37

My win against Roscoe Tanner in Boston was an important one. I have always heeded Maureen Connolly's advice to do something totally within my control: be a "nice person" in victory as well as in defeat. I must have been a gracious winner that day because years later Roscoe Tanner recommended me for a job that changed my life.

The 1969 US Open that fall in Forest Hills on the grass was my best showing in a Major tournament. In the first round I defeated Miguel Olvera, a Davis Cup player from Ecuador, after losing the first two sets 3-6, 1-6 and coming back to win the next three 6-4, 8-6, 6-0. I started to serve harder, creating more "free" points for myself. I also attacked the net at every opportunity. I "hung on like a crab" and wore him down. In the second round, I defeated American Ron Holmberg, the 1956 Wimbledon junior champion, three-time All-American from Tulane, former Top 10 U.S. player, and major semi– and quarterfinalist in the early and mid-sixties. At almost ten years my senior — he was 31 when I played him in 1969 — he was on the downside of his pro career. I beat him in straight sets. In the third round, I faced the big-serving Swede Ove Bengston and won in three sets.

Going into the fourth round, my first serve percentage was 80 percent, the third highest in the draw. My first serve-and-volley combination had always been a strength and that year my opponents had difficulty managing it, until I faced former Wimbledon champion Roy Emerson. He beat me in three straight sets, marking the second time in three years he stopped my progression at Forest Hills. It was my best result at the US Open though — I played in *eight* of them — and it was thrilling to still be in the main draw over Labor Day weekend. I especially appreciated my good friend Hank Goldsmith coming to watch me play.

That deep run into a major tournament really underscored my early tour experience. I'd won three matches in front of thousands of fans at Forest Hills over six days, yet every night I would go back to New York City on the subway to a lonely hotel room. I prepared to play legend Roy Emerson in the fourth round with no one to coach or encourage me, except for my parents by phone from San Diego. Those early days really challenged my mental toughness and independence.

The first fall tournament of 1969 was the Pacific Southwest Professional Championship on hard courts at the historic Los Angeles Tennis Club. I made the news by upsetting No. 1-seed Tom Okker (the "Flying Dutchman") 6-4, 6-1 in the second round. The following week in Berkeley, California at the Pacific Coast Championships, I upset American Charlie Pasarell 17-19, 6-3, 6-2 in my second-round match that lasted almost four hours, the longest match of my tennis career.

We played a lot of points that day, but the one I remember most was a set point in the first set. Charlie served and came into the net to volley so I lobbed the ball over his head. As he ran back to get it, he slipped and fell on the court but somehow still got the ball back to me. I had the whole court to put away the short lob. *Don't miss it!*

I missed it. My head came down too soon and I hit the ball right into the net. As hard as I try, I just can't forget shots like that in my career. I had complete control over it and lost my focus. What was important though was not letting it cost me the match. I did lose that first set but came back to win the next two. Our match started at 1:00 p.m. and finished after five. This club was in the business district in San Francisco and some passers-by watched for a few minutes during their lunch break, and then came back later after work and we were still playing. This was the match that got me into the Top 10 in the U.S. men's singles for the first time.

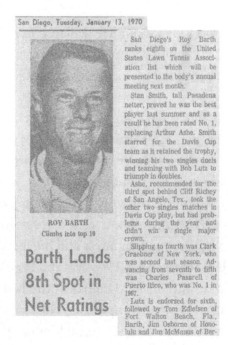

San Diego, Tuesday, January 13, 1970

ROY BARTH
Climbs into top 10

Barth Lands 8th Spot in Net Ratings

San Diego's Roy Barth ranks eighth on the United States Lawn Tennis Association list which will be presented to the body's annual meeting next month.

Stan Smith, tall Pasadena netter, proved he was the best player last summer and as a result he has been rated No. 1, replacing Arthur Ashe. Smith starred for the Davis Cup team as it retained the trophy, winning his two singles duels and teaming with Bob Lutz to triumph in doubles.

Ashe, recommended for the third spot behind Cliff Richey of San Angelo, Tex., took the other two singles matches in Davis Cup play, but had problems during the year and didn't win a single major crown.

Slipping to fourth was Clark Graebner of New York, who was second last season. Advancing from seventh to fifth was Charles Pasarell of Puerto Rico, who was No. 1 in 1967.

Lutz is endorsed for sixth, followed by Tom Edlefsen of Fort Walton Beach, Fla., Barth, Jim Osborne of Honolulu and Jim McManus of Ber-

As a professional tennis player, I enjoyed earning money when I won, but that first summer on the pro tour was not about money. It was about my national ranking. I was nearing the end of my college coursework and the military loomed large after graduation. I felt the better my ranking, the more likely tennis was to keep me off the front lines. I just had to keep playing well.

I returned to UCLA in October for the fall quarter of 1969 as a student with no scheduled tennis practices and no spring tennis team season to look forward to. After playing the most successful five weeks of my competitive tennis career in prestigious venues across the country, I really would have liked to keep my match momentum going. But to finish my degree, I moved into a small apartment near UCLA with Steve Tidball and tried hard to focus on early morning lectures in complex international economic theory. This was not an easy transition.

I also missed my friends. My high school pals, Don Parker and Pete Kofoed, had both started college elsewhere but transferred to UCLA and graduated on time in June of 1969. My first roommate, Hank Goldsmith, completed his degree in history that same June and returned to New York to work for his family's printing business. Thank goodness Coach Bassett allowed me to practice with the UCLA team.

I finished my classes in mid-March 1970 and celebrated by play-ing a professional tournament in Jacksonville, Florida. In doubles, I partnered with Chauncey (Chum) Steele III from New York. He and I upset Arthur Ashe and Zeljko Franulovic from Yugoslavia. It was the first of my three career wins against Arthur Ashe, all of them doubles. Chum had a big serve which really helped our cause. The money I won in Jacksonville was just enough to pay my travel expenses for the next tournament: the Caribbean circuit in San Juan, Puerto Rico and Kingston, Jamaica.

In the Caribbean, I renewed my doubles partnership and friendship with Tom Gorman. I had run into him earlier that year and we reminisced about the days he came down from Seattle to San Diego when we were teenagers. Since neither of us had a permanent doubles partner in 1970, we decided to team up for the rest of the year. Our styles were complementary. I was a steady counterpuncher with precision volleys able to set Tom up to hit winners. Tom was all arms and legs and had an effective "kick" serve and punishing overhead, both huge advantages in doubles. We were a good team.

Waiting for me in the mail when I returned home from Jamaica was my college diploma. I had completed my course requirements and was graduated from UCLA with a bachelor's degree in economics, a discipline I struggled to like but a degree I am proud to have earned. I sat alone at my kitchen table and took the diploma out of the envelope. Not as exciting as wearing a cap and gown and filing into the arena with Don, Pete, and Hank for sure, but that was one of the trade-offs I chose when I joined the tour. I was about to turn 23 and I had both a college degree and a career. For now, I was either going to continue to play tennis professionally or be drafted into the military.

Every male of my generation knew he might have to serve in the military once he finished school. When I was in high school, Vietnam was in full swing and I knew if I didn't go to college, I would have gone straight into the service. Since I went to college, I was exempt until graduation.

As a graduate, however, I was fair game. The U.S. Davis Cup team of Ashe, Pasarell, Smith, and Lutz toured Vietnam in 1969 playing exhibition matches to entertain the troops. Arthur Ashe was stationed at West Point when he won the US Open in 1968. But I was no Arthur Ashe. As well as I had been playing and as favorable as my ranking was, I still couldn't depend on my tennis success to keep me playing if I had been drafted. I would have to take my chances.

As it happened, I missed being drafted by one month. My birth date was the 213th number but they only drew up to the 185th birthday that year. Instead of going to Vietnam, I stayed on the professional tennis tour.

That spring, Tom Gorman and I traveled to Europe. In Paris, I played in my first and only French Open at the Roland Garros tennis complex. I lost in the first round to No. 5-seed Yugoslavian Zeljko Franulovic, whom I had beaten in doubles earlier that year. In doubles at the French, Tom and I got a walkover in the first round and then lost in the second round to Franulovic and Joaquin Loyo-Mayo, 9-7 in the fourth set. Franulovic played really well that tournament. He got to the final — losing to Jan Kodes — but along the way he defeated his doubles partner Loyo-Mayo, Lew Hoad, Arthur Ashe, and Cliff Richey. As his victims, Tom and I were in good company.

Tom Gorman and me in 1970.
Ranked No. 2 in the United States men's doubles.

Playing the French was unique. In 1970, the French Open was the only major tournament — and probably also the only pro tournament, except maybe the Swedish Open — to use the Tretorn pressure-less tennis balls. Tretorn, the Swedish rubber shoe company, made rubberized tennis balls they called the "permanent pressurized ball or pressure-less ball, designed for the bounce to come from the rubber material, not from the pressurized air inside." The goal was to make a ball last *years* rather than games. The Americans didn't care how long the balls lasted; they hated playing with them because it was difficult to hit them for an outright winning shot. Rarely would I think that the best way to prepare for a tournament would be to take a hopper of dead balls out to the practice court, but maybe that's what I should have done.

After the French, I went to England to play the grass-court tournaments leading up to Wimbledon. At Wimbledon, I drew Australian great and No. 2-seed John Newcombe in the first round and lost in three straight sets. John had a great service motion for the serve-volley combination. He was able to serve and then come in so close to the net for his first volley that he took away my strategy of returning the serve to his feet. That strategy worked for me against most other top players but not against Newk.

The 1970 Wimbledon Championships offered players who lost in the first or second round the opportunity to play in a consolation tournament — called the "Plate Event." These extra matches provided an excellent opportunity for me to work on my game. I defeated Australian Davis Cup player John Alexander 6-4, 6-4, Russian Davis Cup player and Russian No. 1 Alex Metreveli 6-3, 6-3, and Australian Dick Crealy 6-4, 10-8. I lost in the final to South African Davis Cup player Robert Maud 6-4, 6-4.

The finals of the Wimbledon Plate Event. Court No.1, All England Club, 1970. One of the largest crowds I ever played in front of.

Reaching the Plate final brought me two exciting perks: 1) playing on the No. 1 Court, which was next to Centre Court, where Billie Jean King and Margaret Court were playing the women's singles final. I could hear that crowd cheering during my match. And 2) using the "upper" locker room with all the top players during the second week of Wimbledon.

After Wimbledon, I came back to the States and played singles and doubles on the summer clay tour in Washington, D.C., Cincinnati, and Indianapolis, where Tom Gorman and I continued to enjoy our success as a doubles team.

That summer I got my first of two tour nicknames. Local newspapers in different cities reporting our matches listed me as "Ray" instead of "Roy." It happened so many times that Tom and other pros didn't just call me "Ray," they called me "Raaaay." I still hear that every so often.

After Indianapolis, I planned to play in another clay-court tournament in Louisville, Kentucky, before playing three grass-court tournaments as preparation for the US Open, but I never got to Kentucky. Instead, I was invited to represent the United States in the Russian National Tournament in Moscow because I had defeated their top Russian, Alex Metreveli, at Wimbledon in July. This trip was a swap: a small group of Americans — Butch Seewagen, Mike Estep, Val Ziegenfuss, Peggy Michael, and I — went to Russia to play in their national tournament and then Russia would send its top players, Metreveli and Olga Morozova, to play in our US Open. I was excited to go.

I was taught in school that communism and Russia were evil. In high school history class — around 1964 — we were shown a film portraying communism on a map as a fire burning out of control. In 1970, I looked out the windows of the plane as we approached the Moscow airport and I laughed thinking I'd see flames. There were none. But it did make me think. The Bay of Pigs Invasion was in 1961 and it strengthened Cuba's ties to Russia and communism. The Cold War was ongoing; the Space Race and the arms race pitted Russia against Western countries. I was about to land in "enemy" territory.

August in Moscow was overcast and dreary. The drive from the airport to Moscow was lined with high-density, low-cost Khrushchev-era condominiums that seemed to be occupied, although I learned they were once considered only temporary housing. I also saw the bus stops jammed with foreigners coming to Moscow every day hoping to find work.

During our stay we didn't see any young people in downtown Moscow, which seemed quite odd. And the food was awful. Breakfast at the hotel was chipped beef and yogurt; I lost six pounds in ten days. I'm sure the top Russian players had nicer accommodations. Our hotel, which was built in the 1920s, was called The Hotel California. (Yes, really. The famous Eagles song of the same name didn't come out until 1971 and I doubt it was about this place!). The rooms were furnished with only a bed and a side table. We had heard so much about the KGB and its spy reputation that we talked loudly into the toilet pretending we were being bugged. Maybe we were. In the hotel elevator we cracked jokes just to watch the Russians' reaction when we all started laughing. They never smiled. It was so depressing.

When we weren't playing tennis, Sergio, our interpreter, took us out to sightsee and shop. He took us to Gums Department Store in a huge mall in the middle of Moscow and told us it was the largest department store in the world. He also pointed out the best restaurant in the world, and a building in the center of Moscow, which he said was the tallest building in the world. Everything was the *tallest, largest,* or *best* according to Sergio and we didn't know whether to believe him or not. Only a year earlier — in 1969 — the U.S. landed the first men on the moon and the Russian media called it a hoax.

Butch, Mike, and I tried to get Sergio to comment on communism, but he wouldn't bite. He was 21 years old, very friendly, and only talked about the positives of Russia, which was propaganda at its best. He was trained well. The only newspaper we could read was a communist paper written in English. That day the headline was about Bobby Kennedy's son, Robert, Jr., being busted for drugs.

We managed to get out without Sergio for a few hours one afternoon and took a taxi to look for a store that sold Russian flags. We thought it would be cool to take home Russian flags as souvenirs, but we couldn't find any. Instead, I purchased a Russian fur hat, a hammer-and-sickle communist pin, and two black-enamel jewelry boxes, each decorated with a hand-painted Russian scene.

The playing conditions were as challenging as the accommodations. The clay court was like a hard court with sand on top. It was so slippery I couldn't get any traction. The ball boys and ball girls paid no attention to the match, and the umpire didn't speak English so I had no chance of debating a bad call with him. I lost in the first round in five sets. I was grateful the sport of tennis provided me this opportunity, but I couldn't wait to get back to the States.

The next week I played in the Eastern Grass-Court Championship in Merion, Pennsylvania, and a gentleman at the tournament players' party asked me about the trip to Russia. I joked about thinking the hotel room was bugged and how we talked loudly into the toilet and at the lamp posts. He laughed and seemed genuinely interested. I found out later I had been talking to Richard Helms, the director of the Central Intelligence Agency (CIA). How embarrassing! Helms was a good friend of the tournament director, William Clothier III.

In 2008 — 38 years after that first trip to Moscow — I returned there in my capacity as the vice chairman of the United States Davis Cup Committee to watch the Davis Cup match between the United States and Russia. Downtown Moscow had changed dramatically. There was a newly built mall across the street from our five-star hotel and luxury cars filled the streets. There were night clubs and casinos and Rodeo Drive-type shopping. The young people attending the Davis Cup matches were fashionably dressed. There was a distinct upper class not evident years before.

But on the outskirts of Moscow I saw signs of Russian society still suffering from oppressive communist leadership. The Khrushchev-era apartment buildings, the ones that looked old in 1970, were still home to many. Hundreds of foreign workers still lined up at the bus stations wanting to come to the city to work. The small minority upper class was eclipsed by the majority working class still living in projects built in the 1950s. It was still depressing.

Both Russia trips were quite emotional; after I got home in 1970, I needed a few weeks to focus on winning again, and in 2008, I returned to work with a renewed sense of appreciation for my life in the United States.

I stayed on the East Coast after Merion in 1970 to play in South Orange, New Jersey, and the US Open in New York. The 1970 Open was the first major tournament to allow a fifth-set tie-break to be played if the players reached six games each. In earlier years, a tie-break was played in any of the first four sets if needed, but the fifth set was always played until someone won it by two games. Playing out the fifth set could take hours, delaying the next match and impacting the tournament schedule, not to mention taking a profound toll on the players. I welcomed the fifth-set tie-break rule. I think most other players did as well.

In the first round of that Open, I defeated American G. Turner Howard in four sets. In the second round, I played South African Ray Moore. He won the first set, I won the second and third sets, and he won the fourth set. In the fifth and deciding set, we got to 6-6 and became only the third match at the Open to play a fifth-set tie-break. I won five straight points in the tie-break, which helped me win the set and the match. My reward for winning the second round was playing Arthur Ashe — which was always a privilege — but a rain delay at the start of the tournament pushed the later matches together and we didn't get a day of rest between rounds. Ashe, the No. 7 seed, had beaten Roscoe Tanner in four sets in his second round and seemed to recover better than I did. I lost to Ashe in three straight sets. I felt I could have played better against him if we'd had the rest day.

The Vietnam draft, communism in Russia, UCLA's graduation date falling in the middle of a tournament, the pressure-less balls at the French Open, playing John Newcombe in the first round at Wimbledon, and playing Ashe without a day's rest at the Open were all things in 1969 and 1970 I could not control. Yet I was enjoying my most successful run on the tour because I worked hard not to be distracted by those things. I just focused on hitting the ball and playing strategically. However, getting along with a new doubles partner and finding someone special with whom I could share my life were things I could do something about. So I did.

CHAPTER THIRTEEN

Cultivate Important Relationships

The Pro Tour, My Hippie Partner, and My Wife

The last fall tournament in 1970 was the Pacific Coast Pro Championship in Berkeley, California. I played doubles with Tom Gorman and we made it to the final by beating Dennis Ralston and Arthur Ashe 7-6, 6-4 in the semifinals. It was a great match and my second doubles win against Ashe that year. Gorman and I lost to Smith and Lutz in four sets in the final. By the end of the year, Tom and I were still great friends and we were ranked the No. 2 doubles team in the country.

(A few years later, Tom did something I really admired. He was up two sets to one and leading in the fourth set against Stan Smith in the best-of-five semifinals of the 1972 year-end Masters Tournament in Barcelona, when he hurt his back. Even with increasing discomfort, he managed to get to match point. Rather than try to win that one point, get off the court, rest his back, and prepare to face Ilie Nastase in the final the next day, Tom defaulted the match. He sensed his back injury was bad enough to keep him from playing in the final and didn't want to cost Stan Smith the opportunity. There are some players who would do that and some who wouldn't.)

After the 1970 Pacific Coast Pro Championship, I flew back to Los Angeles to figure out what to do with my time. It was the first fall since I was a little kid I wasn't enrolled in school. I got an apartment in San Bernardino Valley — about an hour east of Los Angeles — and after three weeks there I was bored. I went to a travel agency and purchased a round trip ticket to Europe. I entered the qualifying rounds of indoor tournaments in Paris, London, and Stockholm, and earned a spot in the main draws in London and Stockholm.

When I returned to Los Angeles, I met Mel Davies at a party. He was the brother of Mike Davies, a former British Davis Cup player and the current the executive director of Lamar Hunt's World Championship Tennis (WCT) pro tour. The WCT was one of the major tennis promoters that contracted with top professional tennis players and paid them to appear in tournaments, exhibitions, and head-to-head competitions nationwide. The players were considered "contract pros." It was the steadiest income-producing work a professional player could get at the time.

Mike was looking for an American player to replace Butch Buchholz, whose painful tennis elbow forced him to retire from the tour. Mike offered me a three-year contract with the WCT for 20 tournaments a year with a guarantee of $600 per tournament plus air travel. I was excited to sign. At the time, I was ranked No. 12 in the U.S. in men's singles and No. 2 in the U.S. in men's doubles. The WCT would put me in the big leagues, playing the world's top players on a regular basis: Rod Laver, Arthur Ashe, Roy Emerson, Fred Stolle, Ken Rosewall, and Tony Roche. I was going from playing the top college players in the nation to playing the top professional players in the world. This was a big step.

It was January 1971 and my WCT commitment didn't start until the end of the month, so in the interim I stayed in Los Angeles to practice with the UCLA team. My college doubles partner, Steve Tidball, who was teaching tennis in Los Angeles, introduced me to Paul Cohen, a student of his who lived in Westwood Village near UCLA. Paul was a stockbroker at Bear Stearns and avid tennis player. He and his wife invited me to stay in their guest room. Paul convinced his neighbor, Colleen McAndrews, who worked with Paul as an assistant stockbroker, to go out on a blind date with his "friend Roy who is visiting and doesn't know anyone in Los Angeles." Colleen agreed and we had a fun evening. She and I started dating.

When the WCT season started, I was paired with my new doubles partner: Torben Ulrich from Denmark. He played for the Danish Davis Cup Team, as had his father and brother before him. I would have liked to continue to play doubles with Tom Gorman but he didn't join the WCT that year.

Torben and I were distinct opposites. He sported a beard and long braided hair (he had country singer Willie Nelson's look before Willie Nelson did); I was clean cut. He ran miles a day and did yoga; I was in good shape but just from tennis. He routinely got detained at airports for carrying a bag of tea leaves that looked like marijuana; I don't even like tea. He used to annoy fellow travelers by hitting tennis balls against the wall in the airport during long layovers; I would never do that. He played left-handed; I played right-handed. He was the "young hippie"; I was the "middle-aged conservative" – except he was 42 and I was only 25.

And he would never give a straight answer. If someone asked how he was, he would reply, "Ohhhhh, I don't know. It depends what you mean." He drove me crazy.

*WCT partner
Torben Ulrich and me,
Berkeley Tennis Club, 1971*

As a team on the court, we were no more in sync. Three matches with him stand out.

1. We played together against four-time Wimbledon doubles champions John Newcombe and Tony Roche in Dallas. Our match started at noon. When John and Tony returned my serve near Torben at net, Torben ducked to let the ball go by, losing us the point. It seems Torben was half asleep. I learned later that he stayed up until 4:00 a.m.

2. In our match against South African Cliff Drysdale and British player Roger Taylor, Torben warned me to keep my volleys away from Roger's lethal forehand. I served to Cliff and got back such a great return at my feet that I was lucky just to get my racquet on the ball, let alone direct it away from Roger's forehand. The ball went back to Roger with enough room for him to run around it, line up his killer forehand, and fire it right at Torben. Torben ducked and let the ball fly by him and bounce in the court. *Did my partner just punish me for not doing what he told me to do?* Another opposite: for Torben, the priority was to play "correctly," not necessarily to win. I would do whatever it took to win, except cheat.

3. The most embarrassing match we played together was an evening indoor match in Vancouver, Canada, in 1971. We hadn't won a match together all year on the WCT tour. We had had two three-set matches against Rosewall and Stolle, among others, but just couldn't put together a win.

In Vancouver, we were playing the No. 1-seeded team of Tom Okker and American Marty Riessen. We had all been on the road for about ten months by then and we were weary and anxious to get home for a break. That morning, Torben borrowed Marty's car to go to the travel agent's office to arrange a trip home to Copenhagen the next day. Torben assumed we would lose to Okker and Riessen that evening, giving him a few days off. We won a tight first set 7-5.

At 4-4 in the second set, we broke Marty's serve to go ahead 5-4. All we had to do was win Torben's serve and we would win our first WCT doubles match — and a few hundred dollars. Torben missed his first serve into the net. His second serve went flying up into the cheap seats. I was ready to crawl under the court. *What was he doing?*

Torben served the next point, Tom returned it, and Torben caught the ball on his racquet. He was proving some point, but he was going to cost us the match to do it. Then from Love-30 down he finally played like a professional. After each of his first serves, I gambled and moved across the middle of the net to volley the return-of-serve. We won the next four points and the match.

In the locker room after the match Torben explained that he sensed Marty and Tom were "tanking" so we would win, derailing Torben's vacation plan, and giving Marty and Tom the few extra days off. Torben was even upset with Marty for lending him the car to book an early flight. I guess everyone was just really tired and wanted a few days' rest, but it was all very strange.

When Torben wasn't making me crazy, I enjoyed being around him and I learned a lot from his unorthodox personality. It took some work but I grew to like him as a partner and as a person. I even spent ten days with him and his wife, Lorna, in Copenhagen in 1971. Torben's daily routine was to stay up until 3:00 or 4:00 in the morning and then sleep until noon. Within three days, I was doing the same thing. We couldn't get indoor court time during the day at his club, so we practiced from midnight until 1:30 a.m. It's amazing how quickly you can totally change your internal clock.

Torben loved music, probably more than tennis. He was a jazz disc jockey on a local radio program when he wasn't on tour and encouraged his son, Lars, to pursue his own love of music. Lars founded the European heavy metal band, Metallica, and was its drummer — at only 16 years old.

Whenever I lost a WCT tournament, I flew back to Los Angeles to see Colleen for a few days. We had a comfortable relationship, but we were not engaged, and I didn't realize she was dating other guys when I was out of town. I learned later she assumed I was dating other women in other cities. I laughed at the idea — I barely had time to see her, let alone other women.

In April 1971, I went overseas to play in a WCT event in Tehran, Iran. From there I planned to play in the French Open in Paris and the grass-court circuit leading up to Wimbledon. In Tehran, I was to play John Newcombe, the No. 1 seed, in the first round. The night before the match I had dinner with some players at the Kings Club tournament venue and I got severe food poisoning. I was rooming with Frew McMillan, a doubles specialist from South Africa, and I got so sick that night I took a blanket and pillow and slept on the bathroom floor so I wouldn't wake Frew. I lost eight pounds overnight and defaulted my match in the morning. I decided to fly back to Los Angeles to recover. Apparently one player gets sick in Tehran every year and that year it was me.

Feeling sick to my stomach, I flew four hours from Tehran to London and then fourteen hours from London to Los Angeles. On the long flight I sat next to an evangelist who held my hand and started chanting out loud that he was going to "save" me. It was really embarrassing but I felt too lousy to care. When I landed, I called Colleen at her parents' house to tell her I was back in town. She seemed glad to hear from me and got her parents' permission for me to stay over. The evangelist gave me a ride to the house. I guess he "saved" me from having to take a taxi.

I arrived at the house in my weakened state hoping to spend time with Colleen while I recovered, but she had plans to go out that night. She and a fellow stockbroker she was dating (when I was out of town) were hosting an office party at his house. Colleen's father felt so bad for me, he gave me the keys to his car in case I wanted to leave, but insisted that I was welcome to come back if I needed a place to stay. I drove around for a while and then returned to Colleen's house. It had been a really long day, considering it started about 23 hours earlier in Tehran, and I just needed to sleep.

I woke up around 12:30 a.m. when Colleen got home. She told me that the guy she was out with had proposed to her, but she turned him down. *She knew someone well enough for him to propose?*

I went back to Europe to play in the Italian Championship in Rome and in the grass-court tournaments leading up to Wimbledon, all the while thinking that I really didn't want to lose Colleen.

In London, South African Davis Cup player Robert Maud introduced me to a tennis fanatic from Yugoslavia who was in the diamond business. I took a taxi to the Hurlingham Tennis Club to meet him. I couldn't believe I was on my way to buy an engagement ring. Colleen and I hadn't even discussed marriage yet. The gentleman showed me a tray of diamonds — all of them round or pear-shaped, except one gorgeous triangular-shaped stone. Since I didn't know what kind of diamond Colleen might prefer, I called to ask her.

"If things work out between us," I said, "what kind of diamond would you like?"

Silence.

"I don't know," Colleen said, leaving me to wonder whether she was answering the question about the diamond or about getting engaged. But that was basically my marriage proposal — from 5,000 miles away.

I bought the triangular-shaped diamond and flew back to Los Angeles after losing to Brian Fairlie from New Zealand in the first round of the 1971 Wimbledon, and then turning down an invitation to practice in Switzerland with French Champion Spaniard Andres Gimeno. I gave Colleen the diamond and we were officially engaged, although I did ask her father for his blessing the next day.

Colleen and I were married at the Bel-Air Country Club in Los Angeles by Father Thomas Dove on December 4, 1971, eleven months after we met.

Mr. and Mrs. Roy Barth.
December 4, 1971, Los Angeles, California.
(photo credit: Eugene Hanson)

I often think about meeting Torben and Colleen around the same time in my life: two very different people in two very different roles, but both important relationships. I worked hard to cultivate my professional partnership with someone as different from me as Torben, and I fought hard for the privilege of having a lifetime partner as wonderful as Colleen.

CHAPTER FOURTEEN

Celebrate the Milestones in Your Life

Forming the ATP, Boycotting Wimbledon,
and My First Tour Title

The infighting on the business side of men's professional tennis continued well into the Open Era. Even though the contract professionals could play in the once-amateur-only majors, the power struggle to control events, rules, and player issues remained between the International Tennis Federation (ITF) and the World Championship Tennis (WCT).

The idea of the Association of Tennis Professionals (ATP) was born in a small meeting room at the Hilton Hotel in Dallas, Texas, in the spring of 1971 by players wanting to get out from under the prevailing associations and govern their own interests. The "who's who" of men's tennis at the time attended this meeting, including WCT players Rod Laver, Roy Emerson, Arthur Ashe, Ken Rosewall, Fred Stolle, John Newcombe, Tony Roche, and Cliff Drysdale. In all, 32 top players — including me — gathered to listen to Donald Dell and Bob Briner discuss the merits of a players' association. Donald Dell was a three-time All-American tennis player from Yale, with a law degree from Virginia, who became one of the first sports marketers and athlete agents. Bob Briner was a pioneer in sports promotion and sports management and later president of ProServe Television. Together they outlined a player-run council designed to give players new benefits and protections, including a retirement fund, increased prize money, and complimentary accommodations for tour events. The international point-based ranking system would be introduced a year later.

My official ATP Publicity Poster
(photo credit: ATP)

A tennis players' association was compelling, especially because the tensions between the ITF and tours like the WCT were costing good players career-defining opportunities. Which explains why, in the prime of my career, I couldn't play at Wimbledon in either 1972 or 1973.

At the beginning of July 1972, when all the best players in the world should have been in London, outside on the grass at Wimbledon, many of us were playing in St. Louis, indoors on the carpet at the Holton Tennis Classic. Although it was the "Open Era," the International Tennis Federation decided to ban all contract players from playing at

Wimbledon that year. If we wanted to play Wimbledon, we would have had to resign from the WCT, breaking our contracts. Unfortunately, in those days the prize money at the major tournaments was still so low that, despite the prestige of playing in them, they weren't worth giving up the guaranteed income of the WCT Tour — if we were forced to make such a choice. It was a sad reality; we all went to St. Louis.

I was especially disappointed not to play at Wimbledon that year because after four years of having gone there by myself, I looked forward to Colleen coming to watch me play. I am sure that John Newcombe — who won the St. Louis tournament — Tony Roche, Marty Riessen, Tom Okker, Cliff Richey, and Cliff Drysdale agreed with me and the others that we'd all rather have been at Wimbledon.

Even though the top players met at the US Open in the fall of 1972 and agreed to accept a self-governing union, the infighting within the business of the game continued to cost players major opportunities.

In 1973, Nikola "Niki" Pilic, a Davis Cup player for Yugoslavia, chose not to play a Davis Cup match (an ITF event), opting instead to play in the Alan King Tennis Championships in Las Vegas (a WCT event), infuriating the Yugoslavian Tennis Federation who went to the ITF and asked them to penalize Niki for not playing.

The ITF, who still controlled the four major tournaments, responded by banning Pilic from playing Wimbledon. The ATP members — now numbering 81 players including me — threatened to boycott Wimbledon unless Niki was reinstated. The ITF and Wimbledon tournament officials would not budge on Niki's ban, so the 1973 Wimbledon tournament was played by qualifiers (those ranked beneath the top players). A few top players, however, chose not to boycott. American Jimmy Connors and Brit Roger Taylor never joined the ATP, and players from communist countries — Ilie Nastase (Romania), Jan Kodes (Czechoslovakia), and Alex Metreveli (Russia) — opted to play. Kodes defeated Metreveli for the title.

Almost as unfortunate as the ATP players not playing in the tournament was the fact that this boycott happened at the last minute — *we were all already in London!* I still wince at the memory of 81 of the world's best tennis players roaming around the streets of London with nothing to do on June 25, 1973, while the first round of Wimbledon was being contested a few miles away by qualifiers and "Lucky Losers."

It was a sad situation all around, but I felt the most compassion for Stan Smith, the defending Wimbledon singles champion, as he lost an opportunity to win back-to-back titles. I also felt a little bad for Colleen and me. I finally got Colleen to Wimbledon, but she still never got to see me play. I really would have liked us to share that together.

Despite the initial challenges, the birth of the ATP was a defining milestone for men's professional tennis and for all of us on the tour. It would eventually change the ranking system, point-driven tiered tournaments, the tournament schedule, television coverage, and even tournament affiliation itself. At first the ATP was just a players' association, but eventually the top-tier tournaments, the lower-level Challenger tournaments, satellite tournaments, and the seniors' Champions Tour all joined the ATP and became known as the ATP Tour. In 1976, Marshall Happer, then-president of the North Carolina Tennis Foundation, negotiated with the ATP to allow players in the Challenger and satellite tournaments to earn ranking points, opening a pathway to the top-tier tournaments for younger players. Men who turned pro after 1972 automatically became members of the ATP and reaped the benefits, including a retirement package based on their number of years on the tour. This was a big win for professional men's tennis. I fully celebrated this new era.

Of all the places I've played, I remember Merion Cricket Club in Haverford, Pennsylvania, most fondly. Not only is it a stunning setting, it is where I won my only pro tour title.

Merion Cricket Club was founded in suburban Philadelphia in 1865 by cricket players looking for a "home" field. Lawn tennis was introduced in 1882, and in 1894, the club held the first Pennsylvania

Lawn Tennis Championship. Merion hosted this event every August, a few weeks before the US Open Championships on the grass at Forest Hills, for 80 years. Nineteen seventy-four, the tournament's last year at Merion, was the year my partner and I won the doubles draw.

Merion was the first place I ever played tennis on grass. At the time, I had no idea that it would become my favorite playing surface. It was in 1966 — three weeks before my first U.S. Championships and two years before I took Graebner to five sets at my first Wimbledon. The grass took some getting used to. Grass-court tennis is a different game from hard-court tennis or clay-court tennis because the ball bounces much lower than on the other surfaces. My return-of-serve was always one of my most reliable shots but returning on grass, where the ball stayed so low, caused me to miss-hit the ball off-center until I got used to the timing. Fortunately for me, the best way to play on grass is to keep the ball from bouncing at all, which means serving and volleying. I was good at that. I eventually improved my return-of-serve on grass by preparing lower in the ready position and taking my racquet back lower to meet the ball.

The first time I walked onto the grass courts at Merion, I knew it was no ordinary tennis experience. Merion's clubhouse, designed by famed Philadelphia architect Frank Furness and built in the late 1800s, is a beautiful, rich, terra-cotta-colored brick and stone building with arched openings that frame expansive wraparound porches and green awnings with white trim. Stretched out along the entire length of the clubhouse, beyond the lush landscaping, is a meticulously mowed lawn of more than 20 grass tennis courts — also green with white "trim." As per club rules, all players must wear white clothing. If not for the style of cars in the parking lot, the new(er) racquets, and the men wearing shorts rather than long pants, my 1960s and 70s surroundings against this dramatic backdrop could have been in the early 1900s.

In 1974, I entered both singles and doubles. In singles, I beat American John Holladay in straight sets before losing to American John Whitlinger in the second round. Whitlinger got to the final, losing in four sets to Brit John Lloyd.

Humphrey Hose, a seasoned Davis Cup player from Venezuela, was my doubles partner. Our playing styles complimented each other nicely. He was bigger and had more powerful strokes, but I was quicker and more agile at the net. We won the first round in three sets against Americans (and fellow San Diegans) Chico Hagey and Brian Teacher, and the second round in three sets against South Africans Bill Freer and John Yuill. In the third round — the quarterfinals — we beat South African Pat Cramer and American Thomas Kreiss, who had done us the favor of upsetting the No. 1-seeded team of Jim Delaney and John Whitlinger. In the semifinals, we were supposed to play Americans Pat DuPre and Rick Fisher but they defaulted, giving us a "walkover" into the final. In the final match, Humphrey and I defeated Americans Mike Machette and Fred McNair in straight sets to win the doubles title.

It was a great feeling. I had won titles as a junior and big matches in college, but it took me six years of playing on the pro tour against the masters of the game to lift my first ATP trophy. These may not have been my toughest matches, but in succession they represented my biggest win.

Grass courts and clubhouse at the Merion Cricket Club, Haverford, Pennsylvania. (photo courtesy Merion Cricket Club)

Eight years earlier I had come to Merion to play my first-ever tennis match on a grass court. I am sure I wasn't thinking then that I would someday win a tour title there. Yet there I was, at the trophy presentation on the meticulously manicured lawn. I had come a long way and I was happy to celebrate the moment.

CHAPTER FIFTEEN

Learn from Those Around You

Inspiration from the "Greats" of My Era

Professional athletes have good days and bad days at the "office" just like everyone else, and while a win was usually a good day for me, a loss wasn't necessarily a bad day. Thank goodness, because I would have had more bad days in my playing career than good ones, and that was not the case. My job allowed me to compete against the greatest players of my time; my experiences playing them and the lessons I learned from them — both on and off the court — made for a lot of excellent days at work.

Arthur Ashe

I am a better person for knowing Arthur Ashe and a better player for having competed against him. I first saw Arthur play during the 1960 USTA National 18-and-Under Championship in Kalamazoo, Michigan. I was 13 and Arthur was 17. I was impressed with his quickness around the court and the accuracy of his serve. I first played against

Arthur — and his partner UCLA star Charlie Pasarell — a few years later at a tournament in Palm Springs. Arthur and Charlie were just sophomores at UCLA but to me they seemed so much older. Bob Lutz and I had won the USTA National 16s doubles title and were invited to play in this event. I was a little intimidated stepping on the court with Arthur, but he was welcoming and gracious, and after he and Charlie beat us in a close three-set match, he even complimented my game. I saw Arthur win his first major men's tournament in the 1964 Pacific Southwest Professional Championship when he was 21; he defeated former No. 1 U.S. player Whitney Reed.

I played singles against Arthur five times in my career and never won a set. He was one of the smartest and most difficult singles players to beat because he could quickly assess his opponent's strengths and avoid them the entire match. It was maddening — and fascinating.

In the second round of the 1970 US Open at Forest Hills, I played Arthur on very little rest. I had won a five-set match the day before against South African Ray Moore and my muscles were fatigued. Ordinarily, I would have had a day to recover between the second and third rounds, but the tournament was behind a day due to rain.

We were assigned an outer court where spectators could only watch from behind a 4-foot high fence. We took our sides and started our warm-up. Arthur was studying my game. I liked when my opponents hit hard because I could use their pace to send the ball back quickly without expending too much of my own energy. Arthur took away my advantage by slowing down the speed of his shot. I had to use a lot more energy — which I didn't have that day — to hit the ball back with pace.

The secret to my disarming return-of-serve was to anticipate where in the box my opponents tended to serve. I would return solidly at the feet of my opponent as he rushed the net. Not only did Arthur toss the ball in the same spot all the time — never telegraphing his target — he mixed up the placement of his serves and then stayed in the backcourt, rather than serve and volley. This took away my "at-your-feet" aggressive return. He always had a plan.

I had more success against Arthur — and other world-class

opponents — in doubles than in singles. In those years, the server in doubles was expected to serve and volley, joining his partner at the net to control the point. My at-your-feet return-of-serve was much more effective here, forcing the incoming server to get low to hit the ball and cough up an easy "put away" for my partner at the net. This combination won my doubles team a lot of points, including against Arthur Ashe.

I beat Arthur with three different partners: Tom Gorman and I defeated Arthur and Dennis Ralston at the Pacific Coast Championship at the Berkeley Tennis Club in 1970; Chauncey (Chum) Steele and I defeated Arthur and Zeljko Franulovic in Jacksonville, Florida, that same year; and Torben Ulrich and I defeated Arthur and Bob Lutz in a WCT event in Vancouver in 1971. Win or lose, Arthur was always gracious. He valued etiquette and sportsmanship; I never saw him argue a line call.

In his career, Arthur won five major titles, three in singles and two in doubles. In 1985, he was inducted into the International Tennis Hall of Fame.

Arthur Ashe serving at the 1972 US Open in Forest Hills, New York (photo courtesy: Tom Fuller)

Arthur was a scholar on and off the court. He was always reading or studying the language of the countries in which we were playing. I regret that I didn't spend more time talking with him about tennis and about life in general. I was a white kid from San Diego who was welcome in any tournament on any court. Arthur was a black kid from Virginia who could practice in the black-only parks and was prohibited from competing in tournaments with white kids. We both worked hard at tennis but he had to work so much harder at life. That he and I ended up in the same places at the same times — and sometimes even on the same court — still fascinates me.

When Arthur went public in 1992 about having contracted AIDS from a blood transfusion during heart bypass surgery, he dedicated himself to raising awareness about the disease and fighting for a cure. The last time I saw Arthur, he was the guest speaker at the Professional Tennis Registry (PTR) Symposium in Hilton Head, South Carolina. I was shocked by how frail he looked. He had never been a large or overpowering man physically, but that day his slight frame was eclipsed by the lectern. I was devastated to think what this humble, proud champion was going through.

After he spoke, he found me in the crowd and greeted me warmly. "How is Colleen?" he asked as though we had just run into each other in the locker room at the start of a tournament. He always asked about others and rarely spoke about himself, which explains why I didn't know as much about his life as I would have liked.

Arthur spent his last years with the same discipline I recall from the tennis court: quietly but effectively achieving his goals. When he wasn't traveling to speak about AIDS awareness and prevention, he was with his wife and young daughter or writing his book, *Days of Grace*. Arthur died in 1993 at the age of 49.

I recently learned from Arthur's good friend and agent Donald Dell that UCLA is offering a course entitled "Arthur Ashe and the Second Half of the 20th Century." What a great way to honor Arthur's legacy. I'd like to take that class — or even be a guest lecturer and share some of these stories.

Billie Jean King

I first met Billie Jean when she stayed at my house in San Diego for a junior tournament in 1960. I was 13, my sister was 15, and Billie Jean was 17. She was a rising star from Long Beach, California. I saw her play at the Los Angeles Tennis Club against top-ranked Darlene Hard in the Pacific Southwest Championships. I loved the intensity of her serve-and-volley style.

My sister Patty and Billie Jean at our house in San Diego in 1960

In my first Wimbledon, in 1968, I played against Billie Jean in mixed doubles. My partner was Vicki Rogers and Billie Jean played with one of her favorite mixed doubles partners, Australian Owen Davidson. They beat us in a close 7-5, 6-4 match and then went all the way to the semifinals, losing to eventual champions Ken Fletcher and Margaret Court. Unfortunately, what I remember most about our first-round match was one shot: one of the most embarrassing moments of my tennis career. I had an easy volley, which I could have hit hard to Billie Jean who was only a few feet from me at the net. Instead, I eased up on it, thinking that was proper sportsmanship when playing with women. It backfired, literally. She took my soft ball and ripped it by me for a clean winner. I never again let up on an easy shot, no matter who was on the court.

That 1968 Wimbledon was the same tournament where only a few days earlier Billie Jean approached me right after my epic no-practice, no-lunch, two-day, five-set loss in the first round and offered me some much-appreciated comfort: "You know you have what it takes when you play well at Wimbledon." Still one of the best moments of my career.

Even a *summary* of Billie Jean's career isn't short. Some highlights include winning 39 major titles: 20 Wimbledon, 13 US, four French, and two Australian; winning three of the four majors in 1972; and achieving the No. 1 women's ranking in five different years. When former professional player Bobby Riggs bragged that the women's game was inferior to the men's game, Billie Jean "accepted the challenge to prove him wrong" and defeated him 6-4, 6-3, 6-3 in the famed 1972 "Battle of the Sexes" match.

Billie Jean was elected to the International Tennis Hall of Fame in 1987.

I feel privileged to know her.

Rod Laver

Rod Laver, a lefty from Australia, was already considered one of the best tennis players of all time when I walked on the court to practice with him in 1971. It was my first year on the WCT tour and we were on an indoor court with no one watching, but I was so intimidated that I may as well have been in a packed stadium. I lost the first two matches I played against him by the same 6-3, 6-2 score: one on the slow outdoor clay in Washington, D.C., and one on a fast-indoor court in Richmond, Virginia. Playing Rod taught me that if I try to play better than I am, I will end up playing worse. It was a good lesson.

That first year on the WCT tour playing the world's top players every week taught me to focus on the ball and not on my opponents' many accomplishments. I am proud to say that over the next couple of years, I took Rod to three sets — twice! In a WCT event in Denver, Colorado, in 1972, I played him on a fast, indoor court at a high altitude, which really suited my game. I won the first set 7-5. Everything I touched found the court. In the second set, we played a very long first game — numerous "ad" points on my serve — which he eventually won. After breaking my serve, he raised his level another notch for the next two sets — hitting winner after winner — as the "greatest player in the world" can do. His agility on the court, coupled with his lefty serve and powerful ground strokes, made him unbeatable. There was nothing I could do but be gracious in defeat.

In the 1973 WCT event at the La Costa Resort and Spa in Southern California, I lost the first set to Rod 6-4 but rallied to win the second set in a tie-break. Even though he won the third set 6-1, I really enjoyed this match. I played well against the best-of-the-best and it was one of the few pro tour events my parents — and even my grandfather, Perry Powers — were able to come watch.

Rod Laver and me
at a reception
in his honor in 2016

In his career, Rod Laver won 20 major titles, which included twice winning the four major tournaments in the same calendar year. He is still the only player in history to do that. In singles, he won two Australian, two French, four Wimbledon, and two US Open titles. In doubles, he won four Australian, one French, one Wimbledon, and three US Open titles. Rod was inducted into the International Tennis Hall of Fame in 1981. In 2000, the center court at the National Tennis Center in Melbourne — home of the Australian Open — was named the Rod Laver Arena.

Björn Borg

I only played Björn Borg once: on grass in the first round of the 1973 US Open at Forest Hills. He was a seventeen-year-old rising Swedish tennis star. I was 26. The year before, he had lost in the first round to former Wimbledon champion Roy Emerson. Borg took Emerson to five competitive sets. The tennis world was watching him closely.

I woke up in the Roosevelt Hotel in downtown New York the morning of our match, physically and mentally prepared to take Borg on. He was a tough competitor and I knew it would be a long day. Three days earlier I learned I would face Borg in the first round and I practiced in Washington, D.C., playing three sets of singles at the hottest part of each day against a good local player. When I arrived in New York, I went right to the West Side Tennis Club, the site of the US Open, and walked around center court. I wanted to soak in the atmosphere, the stands, and the air. I do the same thing in an auditorium before I give a speech in front of a large crowd.

On match day, Colleen and I took the subway from downtown New York City to Forest Hills at about 10:30 a.m. At 11:00 a.m., I started my preferred pre-match routine: hit with a practice partner for 35 minutes or so to work up a sweat, shower, eat, relax, and prepare mentally for my match. *Grass is my favorite surface because it favors the serve-and-volley style and the volley is the best part of my game. I know he is tough, but I can be tough too. I can do this.*

At 3:00 p.m., the temperature on the court was 105 degrees. I started to sweat the minute I left the locker room. I studied Björn as we warmed up. I saw him as the next generation in men's professional tennis: the loopy topspin forehand, a two-handed backhand, and maybe even the long hair and headband.

I expected to be nervous at the beginning of the match, and I was. Playing in front of about 7,000 fans at the US Open in the heat and humidity against a rising star, I tried to concentrate on my game and not on my opponent, but I was having a hard time focusing and my racquet was slipping out of my hand. I don't know how I even held my serve in the first game. I was so tight I couldn't toss the ball anywhere hittable and I double faulted the first two points. *Focus on seeing the ball hit the strings. Don't look up at the crowd. This guy is just another opponent.* I won the first set 6-3 and the second set in a tie-break.

To this day I think I missed winning the third set — and the match — by one inch. *One inch.*

US Open 1973 1st round match. An epic 5-setter.
(*photo credit:* Tennis View Magazine)

We were tied at 4-4 in games, Björn was serving, but I had game point. Björn missed his first serve and his second serve was a safe serve without much pace. I went for a winning backhand return down the line. The ball landed one inch outside the singles sideline. *One inch!*

Björn won that game, won the set, and gained the momentum. I lost some focus. *I was one inch away from serving for the match.* He won the fourth set 6-2.

At 2-2 in the fifth set, my left calf muscle started to cramp. After the next point, my right calf muscle started to cramp. I had never had leg cramps during a match — never, until this very moment. I couldn't push off; I could barely move. The New York crowd was ruthless; they booed me loudly for not running after the ball. *Do they think I'm not trying?* I ended up losing the match 6-2 in the fifth set.

The real shame of that match was that when my legs started cramping, the match was only about 30 minutes from being called for darkness. If I could have just extended the points for a few more minutes, I could have returned the next day with fresh legs. Unfortunately, I lost the last four games in about 15 minutes.

Today, I could call for a trainer mid-match and get my legs massaged for three minutes. In 1973, if a trainer had touched me, I would have been disqualified.

Björn's style was never to show emotion during a match. He just quietly went about his business, much like Ashe, Laver, Emerson, and Rosewall. And he had the best running forehand of anyone I ever played, including Laver and Emerson. Björn moved in that fifth set as effortlessly as he moved in the first set, seemingly unaffected by the extreme heat. *He's not supposed to be so comfortable in this heat; he's from Sweden for God's sake!* That year, Björn went on to the fourth round, defeating Arthur Ashe 6-7, 6-4, 6-4, 6-4 along the way.

Björn won his first major singles title the following May at the 1974 French Open, and he won 12 major singles titles in all: five Wimbledon, six French, and one Australian. Björn was inducted into the International Tennis Hall of Fame in 1987.

Twenty years later I went to see Björn and John McEnroe play an exhibition match in Columbia, South Carolina. After the match I had a chance to say hello to Björn. He was friendly, humble, respectful — all qualities of a great champion — and he remembered me.

Roy Emerson (Emmo)

I was 14 years old the first time I saw Australian player Roy Emerson compete. It was at the final of the 1961 Pacific Southwest Championship in Los Angeles. He was already a Wimbledon singles champion and was seeded No. 1. Emerson was a serve-and-volley "machine." What a treat to watch him play.

Sitting in that stadium I'm sure I wasn't thinking that I'd ever play him, but six years later, in the third round of the 1967 U.S. Championships, Roy Emerson was my opponent. He was the No. 2 seed and he beat me in three sets. Two years after that, I faced him in the fourth round of the US Open and he ended my best run at a major tournament.

What I remember most about that fourth-round loss was that I let my brain get ahead of my body. In the first set I broke Roy's serve to go up 3-1. At that moment, I allowed myself to think about beating him and moving on to play Rod Laver in the quarterfinals. That was a huge mistake. My focus on the match I was playing waned and Roy started steamrolling me, winning the next five games and winning the set 6-3. He took the next two sets and the match easily. After the match, he admitted it was the best he had served in the tournament. Emmo lost to Rod Laver in the quarterfinals 4-6, 8-6, 13-11, 6-4 and Laver went on to win the title and his second Grand Slam.

Roy Emerson was not only a great player, but a natural coach as well. I'll never forget a practice session in 1971 at the Spectrum, an indoor arena in Philadelphia. We shared the court with two other players at 6:30 a.m., which was the only court time we could get because matches were scheduled at 9:00 a.m. I was 24 and had been playing tennis since birth, and I never worked so hard on half a court as I did that morning. Roy just kept us moving. He also offered me advice to improve my one-handed backhand return-of-serve: get very low in the ready-position, turn my shoulders sideways first with an emphasis on an exaggerated shoulder turn, push off from my back foot to my front foot, and keep my shoulders sideways throughout the follow through.

Roy worked himself as hard as he worked us. After playing two matches in one day at the U.S. Pro Championships at the Longwood Cricket Club in Brookline, Massachusetts, Roy went out on a side court and practiced his serve. I saw him serve from the baseline, run as fast as he could to the net, touch it with his racquet, run back to the baseline, grab another ball, and serve again. He did this for *40 minutes without a break.* I saw firsthand that great players like Roy Emerson, Ken Rosewall, and Rod Laver didn't just rely on their considerable talent for success; they also worked harder than most on their conditioning to continue to improve.

I was blessed to practice and compete with Roy Emerson. In his career, he won 28 major titles: six Australian singles and three Australian doubles titles, two French singles and six French doubles titles, two Wimbledon singles and three Wimbledon doubles titles, and two U.S. singles and four U.S. doubles titles. He was inducted into the International Tennis Hall of Fame in 1982.

Ken Rosewall (Muscles)

Another Australian great, Ken Rosewall, was my idol because he was me, only better. We had a similar body style — he was 5' 8" and 150 pounds and I was 5' 9"and 150 pounds — and similar playing styles: quick footwork, precision ground strokes and volleys, and a race to the net at every opportunity. He was called "Muscles" by his fellow Australian players because they thought he didn't have any. That could have been me as well.

Ken was a great practice partner. During the 1969 Pacific Southwest Professional Tennis Championship in Los Angeles, I practiced with him the day before I played top-seeded Tom Okker from Holland. It was the most beneficial practice session I'd ever had. His footwork was graceful and seemingly effortless, and he never missed a shot. I had to work as hard as I'd ever worked just to win a few points. The next day I beat Okker 6-4, 6-1. After having practiced with Ken Rosewall, Okker seemed like an erratic junior player.

I played Ken twice in singles on the WCT tour and lost both times 6-4, 6-4. I knew I was in trouble in my first match against him after he won a 40-shot rally in the first game. He was a steady counterpuncher, a much better version of me. In doubles, Torben Ulrich and I played Ken and Australian Fred Stolle twice and lost both times 7-6 in the third set.

Ken's success and longevity far surpassed mine, and almost everyone's. He won all the major doubles titles and all the major singles titles, except Wimbledon, as well as one major mixed-doubles title. His 18 major titles are accomplishment enough, but it's *when* he won them that further distinguishes his career. He won his four Australian singles titles in 1953 (18 years old), 1954, 1971, and 1972 (37 years old). That's *nineteen years* between his first and last wins in his home tournament. And, at 37 years old, he was — and still is — the oldest man to win a major singles title. (Roger Federer is second with his win at the Australian Open in 2018 at 36 years old). At 39 years old, Ken reached the singles finals of both Wimbledon and the US Open.

Ken Rosewall and me at Kiawah Island in 1987

I flatter myself to compare my game to Ken's, but I do so recognizing that he was my role model. I envied how smooth and efficient his game was, and for how many years it allowed him to compete at the highest professional level.

Ken was inducted into the International Tennis Hall of Fame in 1980.

John Newcombe (Newk)

The first time I played against Australian John Newcombe I was 21 years old and ranked No. 14 in U.S. men's singles. Newk was 24 years old and one of the top singles players in the world. He had also already won ten major titles: two in singles, six in doubles, and two in mixed doubles. We played in the 1968 Pacific Southwest Professional Tennis Championship on center court at the historic Los Angeles Tennis Club. It was all very intimidating.

Newk was a seasoned hard-court player with an effective serve-and-volley combination and a penetrating flat forehand. My strengths were my quickness and my volley. That day my first serve-and-volley combination was efficient, and my return-of-serve was forcing John to miss his first volley. I held my serve and broke his to win the first set. Unfortunately, John raised his game to another level, and I didn't have anything that could overpower him. He won the next two sets and won the match.

The next time I played him in singles was in the first round at Wimbledon in 1970. Two days prior, I was practicing at the Queens Club in Barons Court and the draw came out. *Newk in the first round.* Suddenly, I heard the thick Sydney accent behind me. "Can't wait to play you on Centre Court, mate," Newk said. If he was trying to get in my head, he did.

We played on an outside court — not Centre Court — in the first round. What I found unique about Newk was that while I could usually win points returning to the feet of the incoming serve-and-volley player, Newk got to the net so quickly that my return wasn't a weapon but a liability. I never saw anyone time the rhythm of his serve and volley so efficiently to allow him to close the net so quickly. The grass courts at Wimbledon were extremely fast that day and so was he. I lost in three straight sets.

Newk was clearly the better player that day, but I might have made it a more competitive match if I had been wearing the right shoes. It was a mistake I would never make again. I was wearing smooth-soled shoes, which were for hard-court play. I needed to be wearing shoes with a ribbed sole that would grip the grass. I slipped more in that match than any other. So embarrassing. But I did lose to the best player; Newk went on to win his second singles title at Wimbledon that year.

Newk had an outstanding playing career, winning 26 major titles, 17 of them in doubles, which was a record until it was surpassed by Bob and Mike Bryan. Newk was also the first male player to achieve the world No. 1 ranking in both singles and doubles in his career. Only John McEnroe and Stefan Edberg have done it since. Newk was inducted into the International Tennis Hall of Fame in 1986.

Tony Roche (Rochie)

No one taught me more about playing on the clay-court surface than Australian Tony Roche, and he taught it all in one match. In 1967, I played Tony in the U.S. Men's Clay-Court Championship in Milwaukee. He had won the Italian Singles Championship on clay earlier in the year. On every point, he moved me around the court with his heavy topspin forehand and slice backhand as many times as he needed to until he could move in for the kill off any short balls. I didn't have anything in my game to hurt him. I lost the match but won a lesson in top-level clay-court tennis.

I played Tony three times in singles and three times in doubles. In one singles match I learned a valuable lesson about being on the pro tour: pack your bag carefully. Tony and I split sets in the 1971 WCT professional tournament in Aventura, Florida, on an extremely windy day. I lost the first set and decided to attack his second serve more aggressively in the second set. Due to the wind, he had trouble passing me and lobbing over my head and I was able to win the second set. I tried to keep that strategy going but I couldn't; I had an increasingly painful blister bleeding on my foot. I asked someone to get me a Band-Aid, but I never got one. I had a lot of difficulty moving in the third set and there was nothing I could do about it.

This experience reminded me how isolated pros are on the court and specifically how completely I needed to pack my bag in future matches. I might still have lost that match without the blister, but I would have liked to find out. I was playing well. I never again walked on the court without a fully stocked dispensary: three strung racquets, each at slightly different tensions; three tennis shirts; sweatbands; Band-Aids; energy bars; three over-wrap grips; sunglasses; an extra pair of shoes and socks; a sports drink; and two towels. And, of course, today I could get a medical timeout and call for a trainer to attend to my blister. Nice!

Tony won a total of 16 major titles: 13 in doubles — 12 of them with John Newcombe — two in mixed doubles, and one in singles. He was inducted into the International Tennis Hall of Fame in 1986.

Jimmy Connors (Jimbo)

Jimmy Connors was famous for being able to take an on-court situation, escalate its importance, and use it to pump up his adrenaline to raise his level of play. I saw this firsthand in a fun doubles match on a private court in Beverly Hills. In an exchange at net, I hit a volley down the middle of the court that accidently hit Jimmy in the leg. He made a huge deal about it and spent the rest of the friendly match trying to hit me.

I first met Jimmy when he was 17. He moved to Los Angeles from St. Louis for better coaching and competition. UCLA's men's coach Glenn Bassett invited him to a practice. I had already graduated from

UCLA and joined the pro tour, but Colleen and I were living in Los Angeles and when I was home between tournaments, I practiced with the team. Jimmy was considered a recruit and, according to NCAA rules, recruits could not practice with the team so Coach Bassett asked me to play him. I beat him 6-3 in the third set. My strategy was to crowd the net and gamble that he wouldn't lob over my head. He didn't. After the match I mentioned that he might consider lobbing more if his opponent comes to net. I could see how talented he was, but I had no idea how good he would become.

On the pro tour, I only played Jimmy once. Tom Leonard and I played against Jimmy and Pancho Gonzales in the 1970 Pacific Southwest Professional Tennis Championship. They were an unusual doubles team: Jimmy was an eighteen-year-old rising star and Pancho was a forty-three-year-old two-time major winner. Pancho's big serve and touch volleys nicely complimented Jimmy's powerful ground strokes. And Jimmy's on-court theatrics were as distracting as Pancho picking out a beautiful woman in the crowd and continually talking to her. That match took all our concentration to make it competitive, which we did. We lost 6-3 in the third set.

As Jimmy's career developed, I noticed that he did use the lob quite often to complement his great passing shots. Maybe he remembered my advice. Jimmy went on to win ten major titles: eight singles titles and two doubles titles. He was inducted into the International Tennis Hall of Fame in 1998.

Ilie Nastase (Nasty)

Ilie Nastase, the talented "bad boy" from Romania, thought nothing of drinking a beer during a match to throw off an opponent's concentration. He did it to me and it was humiliating. Like Connors after him, Nastase was well known for acting up in matches in order to undermine his opponent's momentum and concentration.

I played him in the first round of an indoor tournament in Wembley,

England, as part of the 1970 fall indoor circuit in Europe. I got off to a fast 4-1 start in the first set, but he fought back to 4-4 and went on to win the first set 8-6. At the changeover after the first game of the second set, Ilie took a sip of beer and raised the can to salute the fans, implying he could be inebriated and still beat me. He only took that one sip to be dramatic but, unfortunately, he also took the second set 6-4.

The next time I played him was in the second round of the US Open at Forest Hills in 1974, which was the last year the US Open was played on grass. (From 1975 to 1977 the Open was played on clay, and then on hard courts from 1978 to the present). Ilie had won the French Open singles title the previous year and was ranked world No. 1. I had set point in the first set, and Ilie missed his return on my deep first serve. He then proceeded to complain to the umpire that the serve was long. The umpire made me play the point over. Fortunately, I won the point again to win the set, but I shouldn't have had to. I lost the second set, won the third set, and then lost the next two sets to lose the match. He wore me down by making me work for every point.

Every generation of men's tennis has its Nastase: someone who calls attention to himself for gamesmanship as much as (or more than) skill. Some have verbally abused umpires, while others have smashed racquets, smeared out ball marks, and trash-talked their opponents. I would think that instant-replay technology, point penalties, and size-able fines would reduce the number of game-disrespecting theatrical players, but maybe not. I find it hard to watch.

Ilie won six major titles, including the US and French Open singles, French and US Open doubles, as well as Wimbledon and US Open mixed doubles titles. He was inducted into the International Tennis Hall of Fame in 1991.

Stan Smith

I came out of my hotel room in Springfield, Ohio, in 1964 to the sound of someone jumping rope in the hallway. A tall, slender, kid about my age was sweating profusely as he spun a jump rope over his head. He was good at it. He was Stan Smith from Pasadena, California, the winner — at only 17 years old — of the Southern California 18-and-Under singles title earlier in the summer. He and I were on the same junior circuit, the summer national tour that culminated in the Boys' 16s and 18s National Championships in Kalamazoo, Michigan. It's a tournament that comes with considerable bragging rights.

"My goal is to be No. 1 in the world someday," he declared as he started jumping again. I went back into my room.

Stan went on to win the National Boys' 18s singles that summer after being down match point in the third set. His opponent, Chuck Darley from Minnesota, was up 5-2 and match-point and missed an easy forehand volley on top of the net to give Stan the opportunity to come back to win the title.

Stan was a few months older than me and a great athlete. While attending USC — my UCLA crosstown rival — Stan would drive 125 miles south from Los Angeles to La Jolla to take serving lessons from my old coach Les Stoefen. Like Stoefen, Stan was 6'4". With his weapon of a serve, Stan won NCAA Division I titles in singles and doubles.

Stan's height and long-arm reach made him a challenging opponent. My UCLA doubles partner, Steve Tidball, and I had a couple of memorable matches against the formidable Smith-Lutz team, including two wins I count among my best doubles matches. After losing to them in the 1967 semis and in the 1968 final of the NCAA National Championships, we beat them twice in the next year and a half. At the 1968 Pacific Southwest Professional Championship — a week after they won the US Open doubles title — we defeated them 10-8 in the third set. And in the 1969 Pacific Coast Doubles Championship, we won 8-6 in the fifth set.

I never beat Stan in singles but I had two good chances. In the fall of 1969, I played him on an outdoor court at Caesar's Palace in Las Vegas. I was serving and returning really well and went up 5-2 in the first set. I felt as though this could be my match, but then I noticed tennis legend Pancho Gonzales leaning on the fence watching us. I started to get nervous and play tight. Unfortunately, Pancho's presence seemed have the opposite effect on Stan. He raised his level and came back to beat me 7-5, 6-2.

It's a funny thing about getting nervous playing in front of spectators. I did get nervous when I was a junior when only my parents and a few others were watching. But as the venues got bigger, so did the crowds and, after a while, I just got used to them and even forgot they were there. In junior tournaments maybe a hundred people watched the matches. In college maybe a thousand people. In the pros it's a few thousand and, at the majors, it's quite a few more than that. So when one person — albeit one of my tennis heroes — made me lose my focus, I was a little surprised.

My closest match against Stan was in the second round of the 1971 Italian Championships in Rome. I won the first set by attacking the net while he was playing in the backcourt. He changed his strategy to play his traditional attacking game and started to serve and volley. His height made it tough for me to lob over him, and his wingspan made it tough for me to pass him. He won the next two sets.

*Stan Smith and me
at my South Carolina
Tennis Hall of Fame
induction, 1998*

Stan and I faced each other at least thirteen times in my tennis career. He was always a gentleman in victory and defeat. Later in our lives, we lived close enough that we saw each other a few times a year at tournaments and meetings. He would always mention our USC-UCLA rivalry, specifically his USC victories.

As a pro, Stan won seven major titles: singles at the US Open and at Wimbledon, and doubles at the US Open (four times) and at the Australian. In 1972, he reached his goal to be ranked No. 1 in the world.

Charlie Pasarell

I loved playing American Charlie Pasarell, not only because he was a class-act as a person, but because each time I played him my ranking jumped up dramatically. I had two big wins against him. In the fall of 1967, the start of my junior year at UCLA, I won my first big center court match. I defeated Charlie at the legendary Los Angeles Tennis Club 6-4 in the third set after serving an ace on match point. This win over Charlie, who was ranked No. 1 in U.S. men's singles in 1966, vaulted me from No. 32 to No. 14 in the national men's singles rankings.

My other big win against Charlie was the longest and one of the most important matches of my career. We battled for almost four hours in the second round at the Pacific Coast Championships in Berkeley, California. I beat him 17-19, 6-3, 6-2. It's hard to play such a long first set, and it's even worse if you lose it. He had the momentum and I'm sure he wanted to win the match in two sets and go home. But I was determined not to let that happen. I was focused and in great shape and I didn't give up. With that win, and my results leading up to that match, my ranking jumped from No. 14 to No. 8.

With my $300 prize for winning that round, I bought myself a portable color Sony TV set as my trophy. In the quarterfinals, I lost a tough match against Thomaz Koch of Brazil 4-6, 7-5, 6-3.

Charlie's playing highlights included winning the NCAA singles and doubles championship in 1966 while playing at UCLA, holding the No. 1 ranking in men's singles in the United States in 1967, and winning the U.S. Indoor Championships in 1966-67. After retiring from the pro tour, Charlie and South African touring pro Ray Moore designed, developed, and ran a major professional tennis tournament in Indian Wells, California, which they grew from a small local tournament into a Tier 1 (mandatory) tournament for both men and women. The stadium they built seats almost as many fans as the US Open. In 2018, Charlie was inducted into the International Tennis Hall of Fame.

I admire Charlie's ability to transition from success as world-class tennis player into success in the business of tennis. It is the path I chose as well.

Richard "Pancho" Gonzales

I was 11 years old when Pancho Gonzales sprayed a return-of-serve wide and the ball hit me in the head. He came over to see if I was OK. I was fine. I was a ball boy at the La Jolla Beach and Tennis Club on the court during a match between Gonzales and Lew Hoad, two of the top touring professionals at the time. Fourteen years later I was on the court with Pancho again, this time as his opponent, in an eight-man invitational tournament in Portland, Oregon.

Pancho was one of my tennis idols growing up. He had a dynamic presence on the court: fast, penetrating serves from the baseline; booming overheads from mid-court; and delicate, soft hands at the net. Not easy to do.

For more than 25 years, Pancho lived at the top of the competitive tennis world. In 1948 — at the age of 20 — he won the U.S. Open Championships singles title, and then defended his title in 1949, the same year he won the doubles titles at the French and Wimbledon. Then he turned pro, making himself ineligible to return to the amateur-only major tournaments. By the start of the "Open" era in 1968, when professionals could play in the Slams, Pancho was already 40 years old. He competed but never won another major title.

Pancho was quite prolific on the pro tour. He played hundreds of matches and exhibitions against the other top rivals of his day, among them Jack Kramer, Lew Hoad, Pancho Segura, Don Budge, and Tony Trabert.

When I played Pancho in Oregon in 1972, I was 25 and he was 44. I walked onto the court knowing I was about to face one of my heroes, and suddenly I felt like that eleven-year-old ball boy again who was lucky enough to watch the master from the sidelines. This time, though, I had to play the guy. In the first few games, all I could think about was my opponent. Even though he was in his mid-forties, I knew he would be tough to beat.

He won the first set and we were at 5-5 in the second set when I hit a backhand passing shot to break his serve. I won the second set 7-5, and the third set 6-1, defeating one of my childhood idols. I still marvel at that.

As an amateur, then as a professional, and then as a middle-aged force in the "Open Era," Pancho Gonzales won over 100 pro titles. He became a member of the International Tennis Hall of Fame in 1968.

Fred Stolle

The summer after my freshman year of college, I played Australian Fred Stolle in singles in the second round of the 1966 U.S. National Championships at Forest Hills. I was 19 and Fred was 30. Fred was already a seasoned champion, having won the French singles title the year before as well as at least ten men's doubles and mixed doubles major titles. He had also played on the winning Australian Davis Cup team in 1965. My tennis friends told me that Fred was over-the-hill at 30. Apparently, he wasn't. Not only did he beat me in straight sets, he won the whole tournament.

In the early 70s, I had some close matches against Fred but never beat him. Torben Ulrich and I stretched Fred and fellow Australian Ken Rosewall to 8-6 in the third set twice during the 1971 World Championship of Tennis Tour. In singles, I played well but lost 6-3 in the third set in a WCT event in Louisville, Kentucky. Fred had a big serve with great volleys to back it up. He also had an excellent return-of-serve.

As if it weren't enough that the American players called me "Raaaay," Fred and his Australian buddies called me "Tubby." The Australian players nicknamed everybody and, since there were so many Australian players, the names usually stuck. After a year of being called "Tubby," I finally asked Fred and his fellow Australian Bob Carmichael why on earth they would call a slender, 150-pound guy "Tubby."

"In Australia, your last name Barth is pronounced 'Bath,' as in bathtub, so we call you Tubby," Fred said.

To this day, whenever I run into Rod Laver or Roy Emerson or any other player from that era, they call me "Tubby." It makes me laugh. I guess it could have been worse!

I learned a lot from playing doubles against Fred. He had an excellent return-of-serve from his backhand side: a little chip to the feet of the incoming server hoping to get back a winnable volley. And if the server anticipated the low shot, Fred would set up for his chip shot but, at the last minute, lob the ball over the net player's head instead, hoping it would land safely in the backcourt. I successfully incorporated his shots into my backhand return-of-serve repertoire.

Fred won a total of nineteen major titles: two singles titles, ten doubles titles (four with Bob Hewitt, four with Roy Emerson, and two with Ken Rosewall), and seven mixed doubles titles. He was inducted into the International Tennis Hall of Fame in 1985. I like Fred as a player and as a person. He is still a great guy.

Jan Kodes

I faced Czech player Jan Kodes on center court in the Pacific Southwest Professional Championship at the Los Angeles Tennis Club in 1971. I lost to him 6-1, 6-3 in a match where he put pressure on me from the first point to the last point. He ran me from corner to corner, waited for the short ball, attacked the net, and closed out the point. I could match ground strokes with him but didn't have anything with which to hurt him. I needed to do to him what he was doing to me. It was a good lesson.

Jan won the French Open singles title in 1970 and 1971 and Wimbledon in 1973. He was inducted into the International Tennis Hall of Fame in 1990. Jan also played Davis Cup for the Czech Republic for fourteen years.

Francisco "Pancho" Segura (Segu and Sneaky)

To watch Ecuadoran player Pancho Segura — a 5'6" skinny, pigeon-toed player — come onto a tennis court, one might not think him a formidable opponent until he started to play. His unorthodox two-handed forehand, strategic shot selection, and precision return-of-serve made him a bona fide champion.

As an amateur from the age of 18, Segura played college tennis for the University of Miami and won the NCAA singles title in 1943, 1944, and 1945. He turned pro in 1947 and remained atop the world pro rankings for the next twenty years. I have heard that legendary player Jack Kramer described Segura's two-handed forehand as "the single greatest shot in the history of tennis," while at the same time lamenting all the energy Segura expended to run around his backhand so often to hit that forehand.

Pancho was known to have a "little black book" to keep a record of the strengths and weaknesses of his opponents. He could be seen reading it during the changeovers of a match and using what he learned at the critical points. He was a genius of shot selection and tennis strategy.

I first saw Segura play in 1966, my sophomore year of college. He and Pancho Gonzales played on center court at the Los Angeles Tennis Club. Segura was 45 years old and still a force on the tour. That day, he dominated with his powerful two-handed forehand and won the match against Gonzales — eight years his junior — 10-8 in third set. He totally surprised me.

I was fortunate enough to play doubles with Segura in the 1972

WCT pro event at the La Costa Resort and Spa in Carlsbad, California, where he was the resident tennis pro. He was 51; I was 25. Neither of us had a partner so we teamed up for the week.

In the first round, we played the No. 1-seeded team of Australians Geoff Masters and Ross Case. Segura liked to "coach" me between points. I couldn't possibly remember — or do — everything he advised, but I do recall his suggesting my first volley go down the alley, rather than back toward the serve returner. Segura noticed during the match that the player not returning serve would try to intercept my first volley crosscourt by moving toward the middle of the net, leaving the alley open. I won all my service games that match doing exactly that. We won the match 6-4 in the third set against the No. 1 seed.

Pancho was thrilled with our victory and so was I. We started the second round brimming with confidence but lost to top-ranked Americans Charlie Pasarell and Clark Graebner, who overpowered us with their big serves and dominating net play.

Winning a match with Pancho Segura — one of the great tennis minds of all time — is one of my fondest memories. Every time I would see Pancho at a tournament or at a Davis Cup or Fed Cup match, he would call me "Partner." While some may use that term as a casual greeting of friendship, I knew he was remembering our victory.

In addition to dominating collegiate tennis in the mid-1940s, Segura distinguished himself on the pro tour, winning three U.S. Professional singles titles in consecutive years (1950, 1951, 1952), and he was ranked No. 1 in the world in 1950. He was inducted into the International Tennis Hall of Fame in 1984.

Rafael Osuna

One of the best doubles matches I ever saw was the American team of Dennis Ralston and Chuck McKinley playing against the Mexican team of Rafael Osuna and Antonio Palafox. They played on center court during the 1963 Pacific Southwest Professional Championship at the

Los Angeles Tennis Club. I was playing in the junior tournament in Los Angeles at the same time as the Pacific Southwest tournament.

Osuna and Palafox were the defending U.S. Championship winners, having beaten this same Ralston-McKinley team 6-3 in the fifth set. Each of these players had great speed, touch, and accuracy with their volleys — especially Osuna — and each player had already won a Wimbledon title. Osuna had the quickest hands and the keenest precision at the net, making him the player I most wanted to emulate.

Three years later, Steve Tidball and I played Osuna and Chuck Rombeau in the 1966 Pacific Coast Doubles Championship during our freshman year at UCLA. I got to experience the Osuna volley firsthand. He was even quicker and more deceptive as an opponent than he appeared from the stands. I loved watching him volley.

Rafael was nearing retirement at the age of 30 in 1969, but he was talked into playing on Mexico's Davis Cup team in Mexico City against the dominant Australian team. His winning matches carried the Mexican team to an upset victory, and it seemed the whole country celebrated his efforts. Just a week later, he was flying to Monterrey for the day when his plane crashed, killing everyone on board. There was an investigation into the cause of the crash because a Mexican politician was on the plane, but terrorism was never proven.

In his all-too-short life, Osuna won one NCAA singles title, three doubles titles, and two team titles, as well as one U.S. Championships singles title, two Wimbledon doubles titles, and one U.S. Championships doubles title. He also won a doubles title in the 1968 Olympics, where tennis was considered a "demonstration" sport.

Osuna was ranked No. 1 in the world in 1963 and he was inducted into the International Tennis Hall of Fame posthumously in 1979 — the only Mexican player (still!) to earn both of those distinctions.

At the Hall of Fame induction ceremony, Joe Cullman, the president of the International Tennis Hall of Fame, described Osuna as "the fastest human being ever to set foot on a tennis court, and the only one capable of reaching a drop shot and hitting it as a volley." I have always loved that image.

Frank Sedgman

My one and only trip "down under" was in 1971 to play the Australian Open. At that time, the tournament was played on grass, it didn't have a permanent home, and it moved around on the calendar. In the years leading up to 1971, the Australian Open was played in Melbourne, Sydney, Adelaide, and Brisbane. I played it in Sydney at the famed White City Tennis Club. The next year the tournament moved to Melbourne and has been there ever since. The Open had traditionally been scheduled for the third week in January (as it is now), but some years it started as early as the end of December. The year I played, there was a scheduling conflict and we played it in March.

The week prior, I had played singles and doubles in the New Zealand Open in Auckland. I played well but lost in the second round in both singles and doubles. After those losses, I should have headed to Sydney to acclimate. Instead, I stayed to watch the rest of the matches and see a little of Auckland. I arrived in Sydney the night before my first match.

My generation of great players was replete with Australian champions who dominated the Davis Cup competitions. In the 25 years prior to 1971, the Australian team won 15 Davis Cup championships and the United States team won 10. Many of the Australian Davis Cup matches were played on the center grass court at the White City Tennis Club. When I walked out there for my Australian Open match, I felt I was on hallowed ground.

I played Australian legend Frank Sedgman in the first round. By 1971, Sedgman had already won 22 major titles: five singles, nine doubles (including all four tournaments in the 1951 calendar year), and eight mixed doubles, before turning pro in 1953. He was 43. I was 23. Even though grass was my best surface, his excellent serve-and-volley combination and aggressive return-of-serve were on full display that day. He beat me in three straight sets. In the next round, he lost to fellow Australian Fred Stolle.

Sedgman was inducted into the International Tennis Hall of Fame in 1979.

Vitas Gerulaitis

As one of the top junior players in the world, Vitas Gerulaitis had a reputation for being cocky and displaying a volatile temper. I played him in the Eastern Grass-Court Championships in Merion, Pennsylvania, in 1973. Vitas was 19 years old, had an overall excellent game, and was very confident. His only real weakness that day was his second serve and I took advantage of it. With a little strategic pressure on that serve, I broke him once in each set. I used a strategy from the "John Newcombe playbook": stand way over in the ad-court alley when preparing to receive Vitas' second serve. It made him think I would certainly be hitting a booming forehand return off his softer second serve and it dared him to gamble to try to hit an ace down the middle, as far away from me as possible. I created enough pressure in Vitas' mind to cause him to double fault on break point and lose the set. I beat him in straight sets. It was one of my best career wins.

The last time I saw Vitas was in 1991 at the Kiawah Island Resort outside Charleston, South Carolina. He was 36, had retired from the tour two years earlier, and was working as a TV commentator. When I ran into him, he was broadcasting the U.S. Men's Professional Clay-Court Championship from Kiawah.

In 1994, Vitas was on Long Island, New York, to play in a senior pro event. He was staying in the pool house of a private residence. While taking a nap, Vitas died in his sleep of carbon monoxide poisoning from a faulty pool heater. He was 40.

In his playing career, Vitas won Wimbledon doubles in 1975 and the Australian Open singles in 1977 among his numerous tour titles. He was ranked No. 3 in the world in 1978.

Don Budge

I first met Don Budge in 1966 at a men's grass-court tournament in Baltimore, Maryland. I was 19 years old, playing in one of the lead-up tournaments to the US Open on grass at Forest Hills. Don was 51, having retired from the tour at age 40 in 1955, and currently running the Don Budge Junior Summer Camp. I knew enough at 19 to know that Bill Tilden had been the best player in the world in the 1920s and Don Budge had been the best player in the world in the 1930s. Don was known for his devastating backhand and powerful serve.

I talked to him for a few minutes about his career. He had amazing self-discipline: he never drank alcohol on the tour and he ran the hills of San Francisco to get in shape in the off-season. The second time I saw Don was in 1980. We were opponents in a pro-am event in Palm Springs, California. He was 65. On a service return, he took one step to his left and blistered his legendary Don Budge flat backhand down my alley for a winner.

The last time I saw Don he was in his 80s and in a wheelchair. It was at the Davis Cup match between the United States and Australia in 1999 at the Longwood Cricket Club in Brookline, Massachusetts. Another man and I carried Don in his wheelchair down the stairs of the clubhouse. It was difficult to see such a legend so frail and vulnerable.

Don was the No. 1 player in the world five times and won 14 major titles. In 1938, he was the first player to win the Grand Slam: four major singles titles in a calendar year. He was inducted into the International Tennis Hall of Fame in 1964. I can only imagine what it would have been like to face him when he was in his prime.

Jack Kramer

I never played with or against Jack Kramer, and I never saw him compete, but I heard him speak in 1962 at the historic Hotel del Coronado in San Diego when I was 15 years old. For me, he was the highlight of the Junior Davis Cup training weekend. He emphasized the importance of developing two or three weapons to rely on under pressure. He had his precision angled volleys, a booming serve, and a powerful forehand. That really stuck with me; my best shots were my forehand and my volley. In big points, I would look for opportunities to hit them. I believe if I could have also gotten my serve to "weapon status," I could have been ranked in the Top 15 in the world. That's how important a big serve is.

1963 Southern California Tennis Association Junior Davis Cup weekend, Hotel del Coronado, San Diego. Featured speaker: Jack Kramer. Standing (left to right): Joe Bixler, Official, Bill Rombeau, Jon Pearce, Tom Karp, Bill Canning, Official, Brian Leck, Official, Ed Grubb, Official, Stan Smith, Jim Buck, Steve Tidball, Bob Lutz, Bill Kellogg, Perry T. Jones. Kneeling (left to right): Carlos Carriedo, Jim Hobson, John Tidball, Richard Berman, Jerry Sung, Mike Howard, Roy Barth, Jamie Carroll . (photo courtesy USTA Southern California)

Jack Kramer was a dynamic, 6'2" athlete with a world-class presence on the court in the 50s and 60s, but his legacy is just as much — or more — about his impact on the business of tennis. He won seven major titles, including one Wimbledon and two US Open singles titles. Off the court, he lobbied passionately for the "open" format, he was one of the first tennis promoters in the 50s to sign the top players to play on his tour, he served as the first executive director of the ATP, and he was a popular television commentator.

Jack was inducted into the International Tennis Hall of Fame in 1968.

Chris Evert (Chrissy, Ice Princess)

In the semifinals of an eight-woman event on the clay courts of Charlotte, North Carolina, in 1969, fifteen-year-old Chris Evert upset No. 1-ranked Margaret Court. The tennis world took notice. Six years later I was hired to coach the 1975 U.S. Wightman Cup team (United States women vs Great Britain women) in Cleveland, Ohio, for the week leading up to their competition. Our match prep included on-court drills and intra-squad competition. Chris Evert was our No. 1 player. Her teammates were Janet Newberry, Julie Anthony, and Mona Schallau. Julie Heldman was the non-playing captain.

As the team's coach, I learned a lot about "Chris the Competitor." She was extremely focused from the minute she walked on the court and her intensity never waned, no matter the point in the match or the score. She was a "backboard" from the backcourt, never missing a ground stroke. I was only able to take control of a point against her by attacking the net on my first opportunity and hoping to drop a volley short enough to be out of her reach. It was not easy. Chris never showed her temper in competition, although I have seen her throw a racquet or two in frustration during practice sessions. Chris lived by the saying, "You play like you practice," and she practiced with match-tough intensity.

Chris won eighteen singles major titles, including three Wimbledon, six US Open, seven French, and two Australian titles. She was inducted into the International Tennis Hall of Fame in 1995.

Harold Solomon

If it's possible to play the perfect match and still lose, I did that against Harold Solomon in Toronto on February 11, 1973. I had never played him before but I had studied his game and I had a plan. He was a fierce defender; I knew I couldn't beat him in a ground stroke war. My strategy was to engage in a baseline rally only until I could hit a low angled shot to his backhand side. This would force him to come in, reach for the ball on the run, and then I could pass him. Since I couldn't just do that every shot, I snuck into net when he least expected it and caught him by surprise taking high lobs out of the air. My plan was working. Just when I needed a big point, I would find the angle I needed and get my put-away volley.

I won the first set 6-4 and was ahead 5-4 in the second set. I needed just one break of serve to win the match. I got ahead in Harold's service game 15-40. Match point. On the next point, I missed my forehand return and tightened up. 30-40. Match point No. 2. This time I hit my low slice backhand shot perfectly, and Harold reached for the ball and popped it up to my waiting racquet at the net. All I had to do was hit into the open court — as I had been doing all day — and the match was mine.

But in a split second I figured he knew what I was going to do and he'd take off for the open court so I decided to hit it behind him instead, right back to his backhand side. Unfortunately, as even Harold will admit, he gave up on that point — willing to concede the point and the match — and didn't move to the open court. By not moving, he was right where I hit the ball! He returned the shot, won the point, the game, and eventually the match. It was a devastating loss because I let that one point negatively affect me for the rest of the match.

The irony here for me is that one of my Life Lessons is to "focus on one point at a time," and it was because Harold *didn't* focus on that one point that he was able to stay in the match. Maybe there's a "don't overthink things" lesson there too!

In his career, Harold played on the pro tour for 14 years, won 22 singles titles, and reached the final of the French Open in 1976. He also played on the U.S. Davis Cup team and served as president of the ATP in the early 80s.

CHAPTER SIXTEEN

Gain Confidence through Mini-Goals

Surviving on the World Championship Tour

During the 1974 season — my sixth year on the pro tour — I had trouble concentrating on my matches. My mind wandered during key points and I was becoming less and less enthusiastic about the next round or the next tournament. The traveling was often stressful but became consistently so when my excitement about the destination waned.

And the tour was taking a toll on Colleen. She traveled with me and enjoyed that tennis allowed her to see the world and meet interesting people, but she took the losses hard and grew weary of being on the road and living out of one suitcase for so many weeks. We had an apartment in the Westwood section of Los Angeles, but we weren't even there often enough to own live plants. Colleen noted that on the tour we had close friends and intense opponents — who were all the same people. It was an unusual existence.

Whenever I thought about starting a family, I thought our schedule would make it hard to establish the kind of home life I'd want for our kids, and I didn't want to travel without them and miss all the "firsts" in their lives. And I'd miss Colleen traveling with me.

Other players had children. John Newcombe, Roy Emerson, and Fred Stolle had kids at home who only saw their dads for a few days between tournaments. I recall seeing wives and kids in the stands, but only at the major tournaments. There was no right or wrong, just what worked for each player.

For Colleen and me, it was also about cost. The pro tour of the 1970s was not a pro tour of lavish prize money, luxury accommodations, traveling with an entourage, international television exposure, and lucrative endorsements. We barely broke even spending our tour earnings on our one hotel room and expenses. We couldn't afford to have two rooms every night, which we would have needed if we had a baby and I wanted to get a good night's sleep before each match.

I thought about retiring from professional tennis. I was 27 and I had already realized my childhood dreams of playing college tennis for UCLA, turning pro, making the Top 10 in the U.S., and competing against the best players of my generation in the majors. I played all four major tournaments in both singles and doubles. I played hundreds of tour events and exhibitions. I made my parents proud. Despite the rivalries and distinctly different personalities, the men's tour was a family of sorts. And it was familiar. *Am I going to miss this life? What will I do instead?*

Physically, I could have continued. I was in good shape and, but for a few blisters and muscle cramps, my career was injury-free. Some of my colleagues were not so fortunate; their bodies were telling them to slow down or quit. I concluded that it was my *mind* that was tired. And I knew why.

Before I turned pro, I enjoyed success playing as an amateur in local, regional, and national tournaments. Those tournaments, like the major tournaments, organize the players by ability (seeds) and pit stronger players against weaker players in the first few rounds. My national ranking allowed me to be seeded among the top players and I enjoyed a few easier early rounds. These wins in smaller tournaments boosted my confidence.

When I joined the WCT tour, however, I was still playing professional tennis, but the business model was different. I was a "contract pro." The WCT — and similar tours — offered a guaranteed income (plus prize money for winning) to their hand-picked players and booked them into venues around the world to play twenty WCT tournaments, other non-WCT events, and the majors.

On the WCT, we practiced, drilled, and competed almost every week from January through October. I played against the best singles players in the world — Newcombe, Ashe, Laver, and Roche — and the best doubles teams in the world — Rosewall-Stolle, Laver-Emerson, Newcombe-Roche — in the first round *every week*. These guys were tough; there were no more "easier early rounds" for me to win. I lost a lot of matches, and a lot of confidence. I didn't like losing.

I was reminded of my early days at UCLA. I was a top student in high school, but when I got to college, I realized everyone there was a top student in high school, and some students were way smarter than me. I learned to survive by letting my tennis success take some pressure off my academic stress, and eventually I graduated with all the other smart kids.

While playing on the WCT tour, I figured out how to survive by trading winning for "mini-goals." In my first four WCT events in 1971, I lost to John Newcombe, Arthur Ashe, Rod Laver, and Tony Roche. My "easiest" match was against two-time major doubles winner Bob Lutz, who beat me in a tight three-set duel. I always played my hardest and wanted to win, but in the face of my incredibly tough daily competition, my reality was creating my own "wins," despite the score. When I played Rod Laver, one of my mini-goals was to attack the net at every opportunity and not worry about being passed. If I did it, it was a "win." Another mini-goal was to keep my feet in constant motion. If I did that throughout the match, it was a win. I played Rod three times before I was confident enough in my game to forget I was playing the "legendary Rod Laver." I finally took him to three sets, twice. My confidence grew.

I created and managed my own mini-goals for years, keeping my own win-loss record in my head. It was excellent discipline, my goals were good ones, and it took a lot of pressure off me to win each set. But it was mentally exhausting. In 1974, I was ready to consider the next phase of my life.

CHAPTER SEVENTEEN

Benefit from Your
Strengths and Weaknesses

My First Job, World TeamTennis,
and My First Child

If I had had a bigger serve, I could have transformed my close losses into major victories. The serve can make that big of a difference. Despite my efforts, I couldn't make my serve the weapon I needed in those matches. Rather than dwell on it, I focused on recognizing and developing the weapons I did have: my volley, my speed, my first-serve percentage, and my willingness to attack the net. I applied the same thinking to my job search. Since competition revealed my on-court strengths and weaknesses, I decided considering a few tennis-related jobs might help me determine where I'd excel.

In the meantime, I was still on the pro tour. I was in Indianapolis playing the U.S. Men's Clay Court Championship when I met Barbara Wynne, a local tennis enthusiast who dedicated her life to improving junior tennis in Indianapolis. She asked if I would be interested in working with junior tournament players. It would be a good opportunity to see if I liked teaching. She introduced me to Ed Brune, the director of tennis and manager of the Indianapolis Racquet Club. He and I worked out an agreement.

Colleen and I moved to Indianapolis at the end of October 1974. My office was the Indianapolis Racquet Club. I was to give a private lesson and two drill sessions each week to forty advanced juniors for the next four and a half months. It wasn't the work that nearly killed me — it was the daily schedule. I would warm up, teach, cool off, warm up, teach, cool off all day long, six days a week. My back starting hurting for the first time in my career. I couldn't make a living doing this.

I also learned that I'm not the guy to deal with parents, especially angry parents who call me at all hours of the day. One father was so frantic I thought he was telling me his daughter had been injured in a car accident. Instead, he was just upset that his daughter lost to another girl he didn't think she should have lost to. Another upset parent called to complain that her daughter was practicing with a young man she thought was not as good as her daughter. I told the mother that to improve, players must practice with players of all abilities. Within a week, the mother took her daughter out of the program. When I heard the daughter quit tennis when she went to college, I was not surprised.

Dealing with overbearing parents was not fun. My parents were never like that, and I didn't think I could ever be that kind of parent, but I was a bit closer to finding out. That fall, Colleen and I learned we were expecting our first child.

In the spring of 1975, after my commitment to the juniors in Indianapolis, I got a call from Bill Bereman, the manager of the Indiana Loves World TeamTennis team. In the 70s, World TeamTennis was a coed team tennis competition played from May through August. In the inaugural 1974 season, there were 16 teams. Each competition consisted of five sets with a team point for each set won: women's singles, women's doubles, men's singles, men's doubles, and mixed doubles. Each set was played until one team won five games. If a game score got to deuce, the winner of the next point won the game. It's an energetic, fast-paced format and, unlike pro tournaments, cheering from the crowd is encouraged during play. (World TeamTennis is still played today but there are fewer teams and the season is much shorter).

I was invited to play on the Indiana Loves with Ray Ruffels and Allen Stone from Australia, Wendy Overton from Florida, Carrie Meyer from Indianapolis, and Pat Bostrum from Seattle. It was the second year of World TeamTennis and lot of the big names signed on to play in the league, including Virginia Wade, Jimmy Connors, Billie Jean King, Evonne Goolagong, and Fred Stolle. I accepted the invitation to join the team, with the stipulation agreed to by team manager Bill Bereman that I not be made to travel the day my child was born.

I enjoyed playing tennis as part of a large team, but I was a doubles substitute, which meant I was called in to play in the middle of a match, without any warm-up. Every time that happened, I was reminded of the Tube strike in London that caused me to play my first match at Wimbledon without warming up. It was difficult. I also found the spectator participation in World TeamTennis to be quite unsettling. I liked the idea of fan support, but I had a hard time concentrating on each point with all the noise. It was just not something I was used to.

1975 Indiana Loves: Carrie Meyer, Allan Stone, Pat Bostrom, me, Wendy Overton, and Ray Ruffels (photo credit: Indiana Loves)

Jonathan Robert Barth was born on June 10, 1975, and I quickly learned the value of my boss' word. I got a call in the maternity ward at St. Vincent's Hospital in Indianapolis telling me the Loves were playing the Triangles that night and I was expected on a 2:00 p.m. plane to Pittsburgh. I spent *ten minutes* with Colleen and our newborn baby before I had to leave for the airport.

That night in the Pittsburgh hotel was the loneliest night of my life. All I could think about was how baby Jonathan had squeezed my finger when we met. My priorities were changing, and the pro tour no longer fit. I didn't want to be a World TeamTennis sub. I didn't want to coach juniors and field calls from their parents. I wanted to be with my family at the end of the day. I decided to stick with what I know and where I know it; it was time to look for a job back home in Southern California.

CHAPTER EIGHTEEN

Respect the Past
but Focus on the Present and the Future

Taking a Big Chance on Kiawah Island

My father told me that I needed to find my niche, but I wasn't sure how to do that. I had a niche — competitive tennis — but that was coming to an end. I had been competing since I was eight years old. I had never looked for a job before. *How do I know what my new niche is?* I had an economics degree from UCLA, but tennis was what I knew best.

I thought about the options. When I was young, I never looked beyond getting a scholarship to play college tennis, except to think about the possibility I'd be drafted into the military. When I wasn't drafted, I was fortunate enough to join the pro tour. But now what? I thought perhaps my particular combination of skills and experiences would make me a good candidate to work at a resort. I could help tennis players of all levels improve their games. I was patient, outgoing, enthusiastic, and I liked helping others. As a tour player, I knew proper technique and competitive psychology, and I spent years analyzing my own game and studying the strengths and weaknesses of others. Perhaps my extensive playing career would help attract players to the resort.

I learned quickly that former pros already held the best jobs at busy clubs, resorts, and academies in Southern California and they weren't leaving anytime soon. When Pancho Segura retired from the tour in 1962, he got a job as the teaching pro at the Beverly Hills Tennis Club and then the Omni La Costa Resort and Spa in Carlsbad, California. In 1970, he bought a house there. That job probably wouldn't be open for a while.

My roommate and teammate from UCLA, Ron Bohrnstedt, who also grew up in Southern California, played professional tournaments in Europe after college and started looking for a job about the same time I did. I don't know if he was also looking for a position on the West Coast, but he took a job teaching tennis in Virginia before becoming the director of tennis at the Sawgrass Tennis Club in Ponte Vedra Beach, Florida. Stan Smith moved to Hilton Head, South Carolina in 1971 to be the touring tennis professional for the Sea Pines Resort. I hadn't thought about looking on the East Coast.

I interviewed with the Bel-Air Country Club in Los Angeles but during the process I withdrew my application. The club only had two courts. In order to make a decent living, I would have had to teach for 40-60 hours a week for the rest of my life. I could do better.

In other interviews, I had to convince club managers I'd be a good teacher. "Just because you are a good player, doesn't mean you'll be a good teacher," some said.

But it doesn't mean I won't be, either.

As I interviewed for a permanent teaching position, I accepted a short-term position to coach the 1975 U.S. Wightman Cup team (United States women vs British women) for a week in September, in Cleveland, which is where I first met Chris Evert. She was called the "Ice Princess" because she was a tough-as-nails competitor and never showed her temper in competition. Off the court, however, I found her to be the exact opposite. One night that week, she offered to babysit for three-month old Jonathan, allowing Colleen and me to eat out instead of ordering room service again. That's just about the most thoughtful thing anyone can offer young parents.

I kept looking for job opportunities. Tom Gorman, my former doubles partner and good friend, came to Indianapolis to play in a tournament and we met for lunch. I mentioned to him that Colleen and I were looking to get off the tour. The next week, Tom saw Roscoe Tanner, a Top 10 player with a booming lefty serve — the fastest on the pro tour — who was helping the not-yet-open Kiawah Island Golf and Tennis Resort near Charleston, South Carolina, find touring professionals to interview for the resident pro position. Tom suggested Roscoe call me. When Roscoe called, I made arrangements to fly to Charleston for an interview.

The East Coast? I had been concentrating my search in my familiar world of Southern California. My parents still lived in San Diego near Morley Field in the same house on Cooper Street where I grew up. My sister, Patty, whose interest in tennis peaked at age 15 after winning the USTA National 15-and-Under doubles title, was 30, married, and living in Southern California. Colleen's parents and siblings — she is the oldest of eight kids — still lived in Los Angeles. We had a lot of friends there. And I was sure the Pacific Coast beaches, especially La Jolla where I fished with my doubles partner Rocky Jarvis when we were nine, were the best beaches in the country.

On the plane to Charleston, I rehearsed how I would talk about my experiences on the tour and convince them that, despite my limited teaching experience, I could run a tennis program. I would have to show confidence, interest, enthusiasm, and prove myself worthy of being there. And I'd have to do it all by myself, just like when I stepped out on the court.

The next day, I was picked up at my hotel and driven 40 miles through the "Lowcountry" of South Carolina to Kiawah Island. I was shocked by what I saw. Kiawah was a gorgeous, undeveloped, 10,000-acre property with a pristine ten-mile Atlantic Coast beach, rivers, lagoons, saltwater marshlands, and fascinating wildlife. It was stunning.

Kiawah Island had been owned by the Vanderhorst family since the mid-1700s. In 1952, they sold it to C.C. Royal, a real estate developer and lumberman from Aiken, South Carolina, for $125,000. In 1974,

Royal sold it for $17.4 million to the Kuwait Investment Company, who planned to develop a world-class destination resort with three villages, championship golf and tennis, fine dining, private homes, villas, and a 300-slip marina. When I interviewed in March 1976, nothing was open. The first phase, the West Beach Village, was under construction. It included 35 rooms of the 150-room Kiawah Island Inn, one restaurant, the Marsh Point Golf Club, and a nine-court tennis complex called the West Beach Tennis Center.

I approached my interview with Al Forest, Kiawah's managing director, the same way I approached my matches: depending on myself to be focused, serious, cordial, well-rested, and enthusiastic about the moment. I was prepared to talk about my experiences and my potential and ask good questions about the plans for Kiawah, but I didn't have to. Al spent much of the time showing me around and telling me about Kiawah's vision for the next fourteen years. He seemed content just to know that I was on the pro tour and that I had been recommended by Roscoe Tanner.

While I was there, I met Tommy Cuthbert. Right before my interview, he interviewed with Al for the resident golf professional position at Kiawah's Marsh Point Club. Tommy was a native South Carolinian, about my age, and was the head pro at Berkeley Country Club, an hour north of Kiawah. He was an accomplished golfer who, when he was 18, became the youngest golfer to win the South Carolina Open. He seemed like a nice guy.

I really enjoyed the day and wondered if Kiawah would be my future. It would certainly be different. Rather than my traveling to play in other cities, people would travel from other cities to play with me. Tennis would just be one component of the complex resort life, rather than the primary focus of everyone around me. All of the career-defining wins and losses of my playing days would take a back seat to my new successes, failures, challenges, and experiences. It could be wonderful … and terrifying. Al and I shook hands and I left.

I hoped that I would hear back from Kiawah soon. And I wondered how Tommy Cuthbert's interview went.

CHAPTER NINETEEN

Enjoy the Perks of Your Job

Meeting and Playing with Celebrities

On the plane back to Indianapolis from Charleston, I thought about the pro tour and the life I'd be giving up. Whether I went to Kiawah or elsewhere, I was really moving on. I knew I was making the right decision, but I laughed at the one thing I was sure I'd miss as a tour player: the perk of running into tennis-loving celebrities and politicians. There had been quite a few.

Charlton Heston

As one of America's most prolific leading men of stage and screen, Hollywood star Charlton Heston appeared in almost 100 films over the course of sixty years, including The Ten Commandments, Ben-Hur, and Planet of the Apes. In the early 1970s, I was invited to play doubles with him on his private court at his home in Hollywood Hills. His two highly-protective German Shepherds greeted me as I pulled up, followed quickly by Mr. Heston himself. I was so glad someone called off the dogs that I forgot to be in awe of my gracious host. Charlton's home was quite humble, considering the magnitude of his stardom, but for the Oscar he won for Ben-Hur that was staring at me from the mantle in his den. I was more comfortable on the court, although I remember pausing for a moment to smile when I realized that I was playing doubles with *Moses*. Charlton loved tennis, played a nice game, and I think he enjoyed our afternoon.

Burt Bacharach and James Franciscus

Actor James Franciscus and I played in a pro-celebrity tournament against composer and songwriter Burt Bacharach and Pancho Segura in 1972 at the La Costa Resort and Spa. At the time, Pancho was the resident professional at La Costa and he and Burt were the tournament's defending champions. They were favored to win again.

I enjoy these pro-celebrity events. The spectators don't really care who wins — they just want to see if the celebrities can play — the celebrities just don't want to embarrass themselves out there, and the pro players absolutely don't want to lose to celebrities. It's a fun dynamic. I am also in awe of people who can do more than one thing well.

Our match that day was quite competitive. James was ecstatic that the last point belonged to us, and Burt and Pancho were shocked we beat them. A few hours later Pancho challenged us to play again — this time for $5,000. James declined. He wanted to savor his victory.

Johnny Carson

I gave Johnny Carson a tennis lesson in Fort Lauderdale, Florida, in 1971. I was in between tournaments; Johnny was in between marriages. My friend and fellow tennis professional, Frank Froehling, had arranged for me to stay at an exclusive houseboat hotel called "Le Club International," which also happened to be where Johnny — a self-described tennis fanatic — was vacationing. Johnny's manager asked if I would give him a lesson. That was the first, and still only, time I've been interrupted during a lesson by a hostess walking on the court to give my student an alcoholic beverage and a kiss.

George Peppard

I remember actor George Peppard from his role alongside Audrey Hepburn in *Breakfast at Tiffany's*, the television series *Banacek* and *The A-Team*, and from playing doubles with him in a Pro-Am tennis tournament in Palm Springs in the early 70s. George wasn't a particularly good tennis player but he seemed to enjoy the game and was very nice. He gave me an expensive bottle of champagne to thank me for playing with him.

George Peppard and me in Palm Springs in the 70s

Alan King

Comedian Alan King was the headliner at Caesar's Palace in Las Vegas and the sponsor of the Alan King Classic Tennis Tournament hosted there from 1972 until 1985. It was a fun stop on the WCT tour. King was a passionate tennis player and he called his tournament a "carnival." The first year he offered $50,000 in prize money, doubled that the second year, and by 1985 the prize money was almost $500,000. This was an attention-getting amount of money back then.

In 1983, the owners of Caesar's Palace — King's longtime employers, who had given him permission to host the tournament — sold their interest in the hotel and grounds, and King didn't fare as well with the new owners. Around the same time, King's friend and pro tennis player Charlie Pasarell asked King to move to California and help him grow his small "Pilot Pen" tournament in La Quinta. Pasarell wanted King to help him build a new hotel facility. Together, along with partner Ray Moore, they created the enormous Indian Wells venue.

I met Alan a few times in Las Vegas when I played in his tournament. Pancho Gonzales was the "name" pro at Caesars, and boxer Joe Lewis was employed as a "greeter" in the casino. Years later I ran into Alan in the President's Suite at the US Open in New York. He was quite cordial and immediately remembered me from Las Vegas. I got the impression he really missed the "carnival" days.

Jeb McGruder

Jeb McGruder was a lawyer for President Nixon during the Watergate years. He was convicted for his involvement in the cover-up during the Watergate trial in 1973. I was asked to play doubles with him at a private tennis court in Washington, D.C. I was in Washington to play in the Washington Star Professional Tournament, an annual WCT event in July in Rock Creek Park. I played with McGruder just before he went to prison.

CHAPTER TWENTY

Follow Your Dream

Retiring from the Pro Tour

A week after I got back to Indianapolis, I got the call from Al Forest offering me the job. Roy Barth, Resident Tennis Professional, Kiawah Island Golf and Tennis Resort.

My only hesitation was that Colleen and I would be on the East Coast. My sister Patty's husband, Don Phillips, encouraged us to do it. "You can live anywhere in the world for two years as long as you are all together," he said, "and if you don't like it, you can always come back to Southern California." He made sense, especially the "all together" part. Since Jonathan was born, Colleen didn't travel with me. I missed my son and I missed Colleen, my best friend and traveling companion. Almost anywhere the three of us could be together sounded good. But there was more; this wasn't just any job. I had the opportunity to start a new tennis program at a destination resort in a beautiful new facility on a gorgeous island in an area with a year-round tennis climate. I was 28; the oldest Kiawah employee at the time was only 42. This could be a great chance to work with dynamic individuals. Maybe this was my dream job. Colleen and I decided to give it two years.

All that was left to do was pack up our house, hire someone to drive my Mustang to Charleston, and retire from the men's pro tennis tour. We hadn't been in Indianapolis that long and, after spending most of my pro career on the road, we didn't own much. I found someone to drive the car and packing was an easy proposition. Retiring from the tour was even easier; I just stopped showing up.

Really. That's how it worked then. In the age before network television tennis coverage (other than Wimbledon and US Open final), ESPN, the Tennis Channel, *Tennis Magazine*, endorsements, and social media, only the top ten or so players were household names, even fewer on the women's tour. There was no paperwork, no formal declaration, no boss to inform, no retirement party.

In 1976, there was nothing for me to do but stop: stop mailing in tournament registrations, stop arranging for practice courts, stop contacting hitting partners, stop booking plane flights, and stop making hotel reservations. The funny thing was, other than my closest tour regulars, nobody would notice I was gone. The tournaments would plug some other guy into my spot in the draw, just as I had been plugged in when I started. Because absence from a draw could also be due to injury or planned time off, players could have retired months or even years before I noticed.

There wasn't even a final paycheck. The first three years I was on the tour there was no ATP, so those years didn't count toward retirement. And, according to the ATP rules, I did not play enough pro years after the ATP was formed to qualify for retirement benefits at all. There was nothing.

Yet, there was a lot. I looked back on my tennis-playing life: three national junior titles, two-time All-American at UCLA, and seven years on the pro tour. I traveled to 22 countries and 42 foreign cities, I was ranked No. 8 in men's singles and No. 2 in men's doubles in the United States, and in the Top 40 in the world. I played the US Open eight times, once reaching the fourth round. I played Wimbledon four times, the French and Australian Opens each once, and I won one tour title. In singles, I beat Pancho Gonzales, Tom Okker, Vitas Gerulaitis,

Charlie Pasarell, Alex Metreveli, and John Alexander, and I played close matches against at least eight players who were ranked in the Top 10 in the world: Rod Laver, Björn Borg, Ilie Nastase, Tom Okker, Fred Stolle, John Newcombe, Stan Smith, and Tony Roche. In doubles, my partners and I enjoyed wins over at least five players ranked in the Top 10 in the world, including Arthur Ashe, Ilie Nastase, Dennis Ralston, Tom Okker, and Stan Smith. No matter what I did next, I'd always have that.

I would have loved to win the NCAA championship rather than be the runner-up, win at least one major tournament rather than exit in the third or fourth round, defeat Rod Laver rather than just take him to three sets, and prevail against Björn Borg in the US Open after winning the first two sets. I played competitive matches against the greatest tennis players of my era — and I lost more than I won — but in order to lose to these great players, I had to earn the opportunity to play them in the first place. Which I did. I am fulfilled by that.

Looking back now, the only regrets I have about my time on the pro tour were that I wish I had taken more time to see the sights in and around the cities I visited, talked to the top pros about their techniques, and taken more time to get to know my colleagues as individuals, not just as opponents. I would be fascinated to study how, despite our diverse backgrounds, cultures, families, and experiences, each of us was propelled to make the same career choices.

Coincidentally, the last tournament match I played as a pro before moving to Kiawah was in San Francisco against Roscoe Tanner. I thanked him for helping me start the next chapter of my life.

PART TWO

LIFE LESSONS FOR THE

BUSINESS OF TENNIS

CHAPTER TWENTY-ONE

Take One Point and One Day at a Time

Resident Tennis Professional,
Kiawah Island Resort

Colleen, Jonathan, and I moved to Charleston in April 1976, two weeks before Kiawah opened for business. Jonathan was ten months old and the three of us lived in a small hotel room until we found a townhouse to rent. Colleen quickly became friends with our new neighbors, Chris and Karen Weihs, who had a son, Tyson, who was about the same age as Jonathan. I got to know our new tennis community by practicing with the local pros and, as the resort was getting ready for its big grand opening weekend, I got to know my fellow department heads, including Tommy Cuthbert, the candidate who interviewed with Al Forest just before I did. Tommy had been hired as the Head Golf Professional and he and his wife, Beverly, were among our first friends in Charleston.

Kiawah Island Golf and Tennis Resort officially opened for business on May 2, 1976, to a weekend of gala parties and golf, tennis, and family-friendly events. High profile individuals, including South Carolina Senators Strom Thurman and Fritz Hollings, stopped by. There were nine tennis courts — two hard courts and seven clay courts — at the resort's new West Beach Tennis Club, 35 hotel rooms, two restaurants, a small shopping center, and numerous villas under construction in West Beach Village.

One of the weekend activities planned at West Beach was a tennis exhibition between Roscoe Tanner and Tom Gorman. They entertained the guests with a set of singles, and then I teamed up with Roscoe and we played doubles against Tom and a local Charleston teaching professional named Bob Joyner. After years of intense competition, followed by weeks of playing very little tennis, I appreciated being on the court for an afternoon of fun. I looked around. "My" new bleachers were filled with spectators around "my" new center court. It felt like the beginning of something wonderful.

Roscoe Tanner and me on Opening Day.
Kiawah Island Resort May 2, 1976
(photo courtesy Kiawah Island Golf Resort)

The Monday after the Grand Opening — my first week working at a resort open for business — the reality of what we had done set in. Colleen and I had been caught up in getting settled and being part of the big opening weekend. Once it was over, we realized this was it: we were still 2,500 miles from our families and friends. We only knew a few people in Charleston. The resort was in its infancy and we wondered if it would succeed. It was my first job that didn't involve playing competitive tennis. I knew what to do on the court, but the business of tennis? Not so much. I had a Bachelor of Arts degree in Economics from UCLA. Would that even help? I hoped so.

Kiawah's 35 hotel rooms didn't get me a lot of tennis-playing guests, but more rooms were on the way and the privately owned rental villas were being sold faster than the company could build them. The real estate agents were making all the money, taking orders for units and managing waiting lists until the next phases came on the market. Sparrow Pond Cottages, Fairway Oaks Villas, Shipwatch Villas, Seascape Villas, and Greens Lake patio homes — *I should have been a realtor!* As the projects were completed, I had more tennis-playing guests.

If I hadn't been married, I don't think I would have stayed in Charleston very long. It was a slow start — especially compared to the frenetic, competitive, travel-intense life of the pro tour we gave up — but Colleen and I hung on together and took one day at a time, hoping we had made a smart career move.

Within a few months we met more neighbors in Charleston, befriended some Kiawah employees, and got to know local tennis pros, players, and students. One of my first students, Charleston native Tommy Croffead, was referred to me by his brother-in-law, Jim Elliott, who was in the group sales department at Kiawah. Tommy was a good player and we became a friends, as did our wives. When Tommy and Patti introduced us to their cousins Eric and Renie Forsberg, who seemed to know everyone in Charleston, Colleen and I started to feel less "new." Both Tommy and Eric started playing tennis as adults and I enjoyed helping them with their games. I still missed Southern California, but we were slowly acclimating to life in Charleston.

To stay busy at work the first year, I started writing down the teaching tips I had been taught and those I absorbed on the tour. With Kiawah's help, my *Tennis Tips from Roy Barth* booklet, a gift to all resort tennis guests, was printed. I didn't realize at the time I was developing my own unique teaching method. In the years that followed, I taught hundreds of students and I was able to add thirty more pages of tips to my next two *Tips for Better Tennis* booklets.

My first Tip booklet from 1976 alongside the two editions that followed

I prefer being busy but the slow start at Kiawah was not altogether bad. Taking one day at a time in the first months in my new job was like playing an opponent for the first time. I would take my time to study his game, evaluate his strengths and weaknesses, and consider his plan, just as Arthur Ashe did when he played me. Then I would assess my own skill set and focus on what I had to do to be successful. Having that opportunity to grow as my job grew turned out to be beneficial. There wasn't much at Kiawah when we arrived, but I wasn't ready to manage too much.

CHAPTER TWENTY-TWO

Listen to What Others Teach You

Learning the Business of Tennis

As comfortable as I was teaching tennis and running clinics is how uncomfortable I was with the business side of my job. In my first budget meeting in early June, we discussed the numbers from May. My boss, Al Forrest, went around the room and addressed each of the department heads.

"Roy," he said, "well done. You made your numbers in May."

Why would he congratulate me? I had no control of the numbers and I didn't even understand the budget, let alone put it together. But I would have to be responsible next time. As a department head, I was expected to prepare a detailed annual business plan, including key assumptions, goals, challenges, major variances, staffing guide, capitals, and asset additions. I was also expected to create a reasonable budget and meet the forecasted revenue, expenses, and payroll for the current year, as well as form the budget for the next year.

At the end of August 1976, I started working on the 1977 budget. I used the actual numbers from 1976 and factored in the projected new Inn and Villa guest room units to forecast the 1977 numbers. Each month I recorded court hours, court fees, shop revenue, lesson income, and department expenses and compared them to the Inn and Villa room nights. I also had to justify everything I wanted to purchase. Before I could propose adding more courts or even buying a ball machine, I had to show enough projected revenue over the coming years to pay for them.

My numbers confirmed the expected: higher occupancy proportionally increased court hours, lesson revenue, and pro shop sales. In the first few years, when the Kiawah Island Inn Company managed all the accommodations, the occupancy numbers were readily available, but we still had to do all our calculations by hand. Years later, a computer did these calculations, making the budget process much easier, but department heads still had to understand what their numbers meant.

That first year, I was also given the responsibility for the clay-court maintenance. I had played on plenty of clay courts — some in better shape than others — but I didn't know what it took to maintain them. These courts were the "green" clay, not the European and South American red clay like at the French Open. I learned from my maintenance staff that our seven clay courts needed to be watered, rolled, and inspected daily for divots, mounding clay, and lines that were not safely tacked down. The courts also needed to be cleaned, leveled, and top-dressed periodically to be sure they met the highest standards of safety and playability. Managing court maintenance was not my favorite thing, but it was a crucial part of my job.

I believe I was hired by Kiawah because of my pro tour playing resume — that's what Al Forrest cared most about in my interview — but I kept my job because I learned to manage a successful tennis operation. I made some mistakes at first but decided it was OK if I didn't make the same mistake twice. And I received some excellent advice from Kiawah's director of construction, Tony Niemeyer.

"Be Kiawah's go-to guy for everything tennis," Tony counseled. "Be the expert in building new courts, maintaining the courts, organizing special events, teaching, hiring, merchandising, and promotion."

Tony inspired me to become that expert. I started by visiting other resorts in Charleston and Hilton Head. I walked around their tennis centers, took pictures, and noted what I liked and didn't like about their operations. I developed friendships with their tennis directors and benefitted from their experiences.

The most frustrating part of my research was seeing how busy these other facilities were; Hilton Head was packed with resort guests while Kiawah was quiet. Nineteen seventy-six was the height of the 70s tennis boom and Kiawah didn't yet have the lodging and amenities to compete. I could have done all the things Hilton Head was doing but I needed more guests.

I worked with what I had, continuing my on-the-job business education. I had to be an excellent tennis instructor and manage a first-class tennis program, but I also had to turn a profit. I could only succeed financially if the company succeeded; looking out for the company first and myself second was the right approach. In my first tennis camp program in 1977 — a group of women in their 40s and 50s from Charleston — Kiawah got the going court fee rate, I got my teaching fee, and we split the profit. It was a win-win.

Everyone at Kiawah was new to Kiawah, but they brought their expertise with them. Tony Niemeyer had already managed construction projects, my staff already knew how to maintain courts, and Tommy had already been a head golf professional. I had no experience in much of what my new job entailed. When I was younger I trusted those who knew more than I did, and there was merit in what they taught. In the early Kiawah days, I was grateful for the guidance from my colleagues.

CHAPTER TWENTY-THREE

Concentrate on One Challenge at a Time

Settling into a New Life, My Many New Bosses,
and My Second Child

After my first year at Kiawah, I also got a new boss. Al Forest resigned and George Taylor, the vice president of Kiawah Island Company, oversaw the resort operations until he could hire a new managing director. My agreement with Al Forest had allowed me to keep a small percentage of the gross pro shop sales, but George Taylor wanted that percentage to go to the shop manager as a sales incentive. It amounted to my giving up a few thousand dollars a year. Rather than make an issue of it, I decided to let it go. Learning which battles to fight in business was a good lesson for me. The retail side of the business was not my area of expertise, and I felt that I would be better served waiting to fight for an issue I felt more strongly about, like tennis instruction. I would eventually get the chance.

My first teaching challenge was to develop a good instructional program — the most important element of a successful tennis operation. I was excited about this. My boss, George Taylor, an avid golfer, suggested I create a Stroke-of-the-Day clinic, similar to the popular program the golf operation offered each morning. I also learned from visiting other resorts in the area that tennis guests want to meet and play with other guests, so we offered doubles round-robin mixers and put out a "Meet Your Match" signup sheet at the desk from which we could pair guests of similar ability.

Colleen and I had agreed to give Kiawah a try for two years, and it took about that long for the resort to attract enough vacationers to keep me busy. In 1978, Kiawah had a 150-room ocean-front inn, the Gary Player-designed Marsh Point Golf Club, a small shopping area called the Straw Market, the Sparrow Pond Cottages, and two restaurants. It wasn't a lot — and the resort was still growing — but it was finally enough inventory to spin off steady tennis business. I was still the only tennis pro, and I offered private lessons and clinics for adults and juniors, but I had to balance the on-court time with the off-court business responsibilities. It was a lot to do by myself but I much preferred being too busy than not busy enough.

Colleen and I decided to stay. We bought a house in Charleston and we welcomed our second son, Sandon Thomas Barth, into our lives.

Before the Kiawah resort, Charleston was a close-knit, primarily golfing community unaccustomed to welcoming new residents, and it was a challenge to acclimate, especially for Colleen. My life was consumed by work. I drove 25 miles to Kiawah six or seven days a week, and I worked long hours, which left Colleen to keep our home life afloat. She was a young mother of two in a small town where we had no family, we were just beginning to make friends, and I wasn't around that much. But if this transition from the tour to raising two kids in a new town was tough on her, she never let it slow her down. She focused on her new challenges, turned our house into a beautiful home, got the boys on the waiting list for the Mason Preparatory School — a coed private school in town — and joined a local tennis team in the Charleston League.

My third year at Kiawah I got another new boss. Scott Morrison, an experienced hotel manager with an outgoing and dynamic personality, replaced George Taylor, who went back to being the vice president of the Kiawah Island Company. Scott taught me how to keep records of each special program by organizing them in event-specific notebooks. These notebooks helped me tremendously over the years as these programs grew. I always knew where to find what we'd done previously, what everything cost, and my ideas for how to improve in the future. Scott also approved my request to hire another teaching pro.

I studied the tennis demand, the increased revenue, and the number of new rooms scheduled to open, and put together a proposal justifying a second pro. Scott praised my analysis and my new hire. It was exciting to be able to expand my tennis program, yet I was struck by the responsibility I now had for someone else's livelihood. I was used to having my family depend on my income, but now another family depended on my success. I took it seriously.

On the court, my morning Stroke-of-the-Day clinics started to fill up, private lesson demand increased, and we offered year-round Adult Mini-Camps and summer Junior Mini-Camps. I made it a priority to ask the guests about their experiences and tailor programs to meet their needs. It was great to have another tennis pro and guests who were invested in our tennis center.

And, as per his agreement with Kiawah, Roscoe Tanner continued to bring in touring professionals to play singles and doubles exhibition matches twice a year. In the early years, Kiawah hosted, among others, Stan Smith, Cliff Drysdale, Chris Evert, Vijay Armitraj, Tom Gorman, Bob Lutz, and doubles greats — and twin brothers — Tim and Tom Gullikson. These events were always popular with Kiawah guests, club members, property owners, and my staff.

We also added seven more clay courts to the West Beach Village over the next few years — giving me sixteen courts in all — and a few more teaching pros to keep pace.

West Beach area of Kiawah Island
(photo courtesy Kiawah Island Golf Resort)

As much as my parents loved the game of tennis, and hoped Patty and I would too, they never pressured us to play. But if we wanted to be on the court, they would be out there too, feeding balls, running drills, and playing points. When my father hired seasoned pros to take us to the next level because he felt it had become too difficult to teach his own children, I assumed Patty and I had gotten to the point where our skill level exceeded my father's ability to teach. As a father on the court with my own two sons, I learned it wasn't just about skill.

Colleen and I encouraged Jonathan and Sandon to learn to play tennis but, like my parents, we never pressured them or took for granted they would want to play. I taught them when they were little, and I certainly could have kept pace with their growing skill level, but I think kids reach periodic saturation points in their lives when they can no longer absorb even one more thing their parents tell them, no matter what the subject. My father must have felt this way when he hired Wilbur Folsom, Maureen Connolly, and Les Stoefen to work with Patty and me. I asked my teaching pros to work with my kids — although I still made a point of watching them from the pro shop window.

I am so glad both Jonathan and Sandon
enjoyed playing tennis.

Jonathan and Sandon were good students and natural athletes at Mason Prep and took to basketball and soccer as naturally as they took to tennis. Colleen got involved in their school activities and was eventually hired by Mason Prep as a teacher's aide.

In my work world, Kiawah was growing steadily but the upper management continued to turn over, each time requiring department heads to adjust to new styles, personalities, and rules. It was a challenge.

When Scott Morrison left, he was replaced by Hank Hickox, who, I think, was overwhelmed by the job on his first day and never recovered. He was a nice man but just seemed not to have the organizational skills to manage the 150-room Inn, villa rentals, and the golf and tennis programs. In the pre-computer days, my pro shop manager hand-wrote all the spring and summer clothing purchase orders and sent them to Hank through interoffice mail for his approval. He lost track of them. We had to rewrite the orders and send them to him again, delaying our delivery of season-specific merchandise. A month later, the original purchase orders surfaced on Hank's desk. This experience taught me the importance of keeping a copy of any essential original that leaves my office.

In 1982, I reported to Jon Comber, the vice president of resort operations — my fifth boss in six years. When Hickox left, Comber was promoted from the manager of the Inn to the resort's managing director. Jon was my first boss who wasn't older than me; we were both 35. Comber was now responsible for the Inn and Villa accommodations, food and beverage, golf, tennis, and the recreation operations. During his first months, the company finished developing West Beach Village. There was already golf at the Marsh Point Golf Club, tennis at the West Beach Tennis Club, guest rooms at the Inn, and shopping and eating at the Straw Market village when the company built Night Heron Park, which included a restaurant, pool, soccer field, bike shop, and more villas.

I liked Jon Comber. He was organized, a skillful decision maker, and extremely detail-oriented. He got things done. On his lunch break, he would walk the courts at the West Beach Tennis Center and then send me a memo telling me that a trash can was overflowing, or debris in the walkways needed to be blown. He taught me to look at the grounds and the courts the way he did — through the eyes of the resort guests. It was a valuable lesson then and it has stuck with me all these years.

Kiawah added East Beach Village next, which included Turtle Point golf course, Turtle Point and Turtle Cove Villas, East Beach Tennis Villas, a shopping area with a restaurant, and the new East Beach Tennis Club — my second tennis complex! In its first phase, East Beach included a well-stocked pro shop, five clay courts (one lit), three hard courts (one lit), and an innovative practice alley with a ball machine and an automated retrieval system. The long-range plan called for 19 clay courts (nine lit), three hard courts (one lit), and two practice alleys.

When I first came to Kiawah, the West Beach pro shop was almost completed, and I had no input in its design. The building was functional, but I expect it was designed by someone who had never run a retail operation. When the company was developing East Beach, Mark Permar, the director of Kiawah's forward planning department, assigned Jerry English, Kiawah's in-house architect, to work with me on the project. Together we partnered with Allan Bainbridge, an architect from Bainbridge and Associates in Atlanta, to create a building with a welcoming deck, generous retail space, an office for me (my first actual office), an office for the manager-buyer and head pro, and more storage. I enjoyed the process as much as the building we designed.

With the opening of East Beach, I managed two tennis centers with a combined 24 courts and two pro shops. I was now responsible for teaching tennis, managing the daily operation, maintaining all the courts, running two profitable pro shop retail operations, and controlling the department budget.

When the percentage of gross pro shop sale income was taken from me and given as an incentive to the shop manager a few years prior, I let the issue go. But now that I had to manage two tennis locations, which cut into my teaching time and profitable lesson income, I knew this was an issue worth fighting for. Comber agreed with my analysis and restructured my compensation package accordingly.

As my facilities increased, so did my staff. I was now responsible for two head pros, anywhere from two to six teaching pros depending on the season, a shop manager-buyer, two shop supervisors, three shop attendants, and two maintenance managers. Some days I felt like a full-time human resource manager. I challenged myself to strike a fair balance between praising an employee's efforts and being tough enough to push them to succeed. I learned to set specific responsibilities for each position and to make employees accountable. It meant a lot to me when my boss, one of my employees, or a resort guest acknowledged something I'd done well, and I wanted my employees to feel the same success. I just needed to recognize those opportunities.

And I went through a lot of yellow legal pads. Before day-timers — and anything electronic — were popular, I prioritized my daily checklist of my most important goals on a yellow legal pad. As I completed a task, I crossed it off my list. At the end of each day, I started a brand new list, rewriting what had not been completed and adding new items for the next day. If I waited until the morning to make my day's list, I'd inevitably be sidetracked by whatever greeted me when I arrived at work and I'd never get to the list, let alone the tasks. I also learned not to waste time. Just as my father taught me when I was in college, I gave myself timelines to get things done.

As the resort grew, I also earned how important Kiawah's support departments were to the success of the tennis department. While the game of tennis may be an individual sport, the business of tennis — especially at a resort — is all about teamwork. I made a concerted effort to develop a good working-relationship with the managers and staff in the reservations, human resources, accounting, hotel and villa operations, group sales, marketing, IT systems, and facility maintenance departments. In this effort, I was fortunate to work with some of the nicest, most accommodating, and most talented individuals. I owe much of the success of Kiawah's tennis operation to the relationships I fostered with these departments.

In short order I had a new house, a second child, new courts in one tennis center, a whole second tennis center, a large staff, an even larger resort, and five new bosses. Colleen had a new career, the kids started school, and we decided others should work with them on their tennis games. Lots of changes, but I managed them all by staying positive, doing my job, and thoughtfully absorbing each new relationship. Those six years could have been completely overwhelming if not for my focusing on one challenge at a time.

CHAPTER TWENTY-FOUR

Don't Burn Out

Learning to Manage
My Expanding Responsibilities

More courts and more staff meant I could host more events. In 1984, I ran the first Kiawah Island Junior Clay-Court Championship for boys and girls ages 10-18. We had 70 juniors — a respectable size draw for a new tournament — and it was a major undertaking for my staff and me. We challenged ourselves to make the first year a huge success in hopes of offering the tournament as an annual event with increased participation.

To manage my growing responsibilities, I had to be more organized, which meant working harder. I was stretching myself thin. Until Colleen mentioned it had been weeks since I'd taken a day off, I hadn't even noticed. She was worried about me. And with good reason.

Gradually, without realizing it, I was not focusing on each task with the clarity and purpose I was used to. If my staff came to work as unfocused as I'd become, they would be no good to the department. For the first time in a long time, I thought about how I had ended up in the hospital at the end of my sophomore year at UCLA. I had to deal with this stress the same way: by regrouping. But this time, I couldn't just look out for myself. I had a whole department to consider. With the help of the Human Resources department, I learned to schedule some regular days off, streamline my responsibilities, and delegate more efficiently to my managers without increasing their workload. I also started to play more social tennis on the weekends with my friends Tommy Croffead and Eric Forsberg — who were always fun — and travel off the island to play weekend tournaments and exhibitions. The change of scenery allowed me to clear my head and see what innovative things others were doing. I began to feel fresher, more motivated, and I got my focus back.

Just as on the tour, players can only push themselves so far before their games suffer. Taking breaks from the court — and from the office — allowed me to return motivated and energetic.

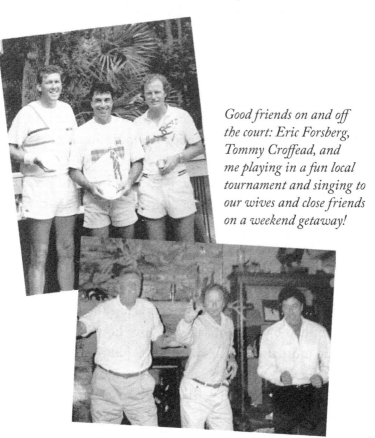

Good friends on and off the court: Eric Forsberg, Tommy Croffead, and me playing in a fun local tournament and singing to our wives and close friends on a weekend getaway!

CHAPTER TWENTY-FIVE

Understand Your Industry

Becoming Involved with the USTA and PTR

The United States Tennis Association (USTA) is the governing body of tennis in the United States. From its beginnings in 1881, the USTA has sought to grow the sport by promoting it to every level of player. Among its many responsibilities, the USTA trains and provides tournament officials, oversees the National Tennis Rating Program (NTRP), organizes league play for all levels of community tennis, creates a "pathway ... to develop world-class American players" through its junior development programs, oversees the Davis Cup and Fed Cup teams, and owns and operates the US Open and the Billie Jean King Tennis Center in New York.

The USTA is divided into 17 regions across the country and proudly serves more than 650,000 members. I love how highly inclusive it is. Most of the tournaments I played in as a junior were USTA tournaments. Years later, I was honored to be the president of one of its districts.

Separate from the USTA, The United States Professional Tennis Association (USPTA) and the Professional Tennis Registry (PTR) are the two different organizations from which a tennis teacher or coach in the United States can become a certified teaching professional. Both organizations require members to complete a certain number of internship hours and workshops to learn the teaching basics and stay current with the industry.

The USPTA, initially called the "Professional Lawn Tennis Association of the United States," was born in New York City in 1927. According to the USPTA website:

> *On Sept. 23, 1927, a small group of tennis professionals gathered in an upper-story room of the Spalding building in New York City. Their mission was to bridge the gap between the amateur ranks and a respectable career as a tennis professional. Their answer was to establish the Professional Lawn Tennis Association of the United States.*
>
> *The nascent organization sent out the following notice to all recognized tennis professionals:*
>
> *For some time there has been a very strong feeling among lawn tennis professionals that there is a need for some organization to protect and promote their interests, and to assist them in obtaining a proper and recognized status in the tennis world. A meeting was held on September 23 and it was decided to form an Association. An initiation fee of $10 will be charged to all new members. Dues are to be $5 annually.*

(Although the intentions are similar, this is not the ATP or the WTA, the professional men's and women's *tour players'* associations).

The Lawn Tennis Association name was changed to the USPTA in 1957 — and the annual dues have gone up from $5 — but the mission remains the same: to educate, certify, and maintain the high standards of tennis-teaching professionals and coaches across the country in on-court (skill development) and off-court (business management) positions.

From its new headquarters near Orlando, Florida, the USPTA serves its more than 15,000 members by hosting educational events and offering teaching tools, financial guidance, and job networking support.

Likewise, the Professional Tennis Registry (PTR) promotes the game of tennis by educating, certifying, and serving the professional tennis teaching and coaching industry. PTR founder, South African native Dennis Van der Meer, was a talented tournament player in Johannesburg who developed a reputation as a popular instructor. He came to the United States in the 1960s to continue his teaching efforts, only to find that the variety of teaching methods promoted by professionals was confusing to his students. He created the PTR in 1976 to standardize instruction worldwide. He developed the "Standard Teaching Method."

Today, the PTR is the "largest global organization of tennis teaching professionals … dedicated to educating and certifying teachers and coaches." The PTR claims over 10,000 U.S. members and 5,000 international members.

While similar in purpose, the differences between the USPTA and the PTR are significant. According to the USTA website:

> *The main difference between the organizations is how the programs are set up. The USPTA certifies coaches to teach at all levels and age groups from its initial professional certification and then allows coaches to progress based on experience and increased knowledge. The PTR targets its teachings at coaches working with specific age or talent levels and then offers specialism within that narrower range. Coaches can be a member of both organizations at the same time.*

Other differences include the makeup of the memberships and the groups' ultimate goals. The USPTA specifically certifies American teachers and coaches and is dedicated to improving the future of American tennis. The PTR has a diverse international membership and aims to certify teachers and coaches of all nations who will teach the players in their countries.

Occasionally these organizations, who serve the same industry and many of the same players, collide. Later in my career I would be right in the middle of some of these tensions.

I had been a member of the USPTA since 1978, but in 1984 I joined the PTR as well. I didn't necessarily need the teaching certification — although it is a fabulous program — but I liked the culture of the organization and the networking opportunities, and I wanted to play in the national PTR singles and doubles championship tournaments. And I especially liked the popular annual symposium held on Hilton Head Island, an easy two-hour drive from my house. The distinct multiculturalism inherent in the PTR attracted interesting speakers and seminars to the symposium, which complemented the on-court demonstrations, trade show, and tournament. This was a great opportunity for me to meet colleagues and talk up the Kiawah experience.

The first PTR symposium I attended taught me how much I didn't know. The industry was evolving to encompass more than the game itself and I was fascinated to hear speakers who specialized in sport science, sports psychology, and nutrition. That first year I partnered in the tournament with Jorge Andrew, a longtime member of the Venezuela Davis Cup team, and we won. Our playing styles were similar: Jorge was upbeat and his positive energy and encouragement were infectious. He also moved quickly around the court and had a strong serve, volley, and overhead. That victory was the first of 13 consecutive PTR titles he and I would win together as good friends and undefeated champions.

Over the years when one of us was not playing well, the other would take over and raise his level to win the match. In the last year we played together, we were down two match points at 2-6, 2-5, 15-40. Uncharacteristically, neither of us was playing well at the same time and we were facing a tough server: Sal Castillo, the No. 1 45-and-over singles player in the U.S. (Jorge and I were in our 50s). Somehow we didn't miss another ball, and we came back to win the match and pre-serve our undefeated status.

Jorge and his wife became U.S. citizens and Jorge taught tennis in Florida before moving to South Carolina. We are still close friends.

*Jorge Andrew and me at one of our many
PTR symposium tournaments.*

That same year I joined the PTR (1984) was also the year I met Lucy Garvin. She was in her second year as first vice president of the South Carolina Tennis Association (SCTA) — a district of the USTA's Southern Tennis Association — and she ran junior tournaments throughout the southern states. I was introduced to her by Jack Mills, the president of the SCTA, when they attended a meeting at Kiawah. We met when she came to play at West Beach, but her reputation preceded her. I already knew she was a long-time volunteer for the USTA, work-ing the tournament desks when her kids played. She eventually became a certified USTA official and a tournament director, and she even gave workshops on how to run a tournament. *She would be the perfect person to run next year's Junior Clay-Court Championship for me!* Hoping Lucy would offer to do it herself, I asked her if she knew anyone who might be interested in running the tournament. She agreed to do it. My event was in good hands.

Understanding and networking within the USTA, USPTA, and the PTR was just as important to my directing a tennis program as was my understanding and networking within the amateur, pro, and ATP ranks in my playing days on the pro tour. These were my professional associations, the authorities who governed tournaments, standardized teaching practices, protected players, and furthered the popularity of the game. My commitment to study and to contribute to these organizations was genuine. I grew up admiring my mother's passion for volunteering and I was happy to do my share.

CHAPTER TWENTY-SIX

Hang On Like a Crab

Surviving Big Changes at Kiawah

Things were coming together. We had been in Charleston for eight years, Jonathan and Sandon were nine and seven and doing well in school, and Colleen was busy managing our household, working at Mason Prep, and driving the kids to their various activities. I was running two busy tennis centers with increasing ease, and I had carved out a workable balance of playing, teaching, managing, and networking. We had close friends from tennis, church, and the kids' school, and I enjoyed a nice reputation in the tennis world of the southeast. I was 37 years old, in good shape, and in good health. Everything felt right.

So the day I was summoned off the court to attend an emergency meeting of all department heads, I was concerned. The meeting was called by Sal Alzouman, the president of the Kiawah Island Inn Company, Ltd., a subsidiary of the Kuwait Investment Company. Alzouman was a Kuwaiti citizen with a degree in business from Ohio State University, but that was all I knew about him and we had only met a few times. He had just come from a budget meeting with my boss, Jon Comber, in which he instructed Jon to cut *one million dollars* in payroll and expenses out of the resort's operating budget. Jon was adamant that such a deep a cut would negatively — and possibly irrevocably — impact the guest experience. Jon could not agree to do it and he resigned.

Without Jon, Sal appealed to the department heads directly. He said that we had one week to cut our departmental expenses by 15 percent and, if we couldn't, our jobs were in jeopardy. I went back to my office and studied my department's budget. What to cut? Court maintenance? Pro shop inventory? Staff hours? Bonuses? There were no good answers. I went down the list and took 15 percent out of each line item. It was painful to think how this would hurt the guest experience.

Sal hired Charlie Daoust, the manager of the Atlanta Hilton Hotel (also owned by the Kuwait Investment Company) to replace Jon Comber. I think Mr. Daoust was brought in specifically to cut expenses and reduce the payroll, and it didn't take long for his budget cuts to show, most profoundly in island maintenance. Restaurant windows were dirty, trash bins overflowed, debris lined the streets after a storm, and if something broke, it took forever to get it fixed. The number of house-keepers at the Inn was dramatically reduced, hotel reservations were being taken by one person instead of five, and many of the employees who hadn't been fired chose to quit. It was really depressing.

And it didn't take long for Kiawah's "dirty laundry" to hit the local paper. The *Charleston Post and Courier* printed the headline "Trouble in Paradise" over a beautiful photo of the ocean from the 17th hole of Turtle Point Golf Course. The article highlighted Kiawah housekeep-ers picketing outside the entrance to the resort. Dirty laundry indeed.

Charlie Daoust was 64 years old, significantly older than most of the department heads at the time. Whether it was the age differ-ence, his budget-cutting assignment, or his personality, he didn't relate well to the department heads. He had an unpopular job to do and he meant business. We did what we were directed to do or we were fired. Six months after the budget cuts started, half of the department heads who attended that first meeting with Sal Alzouman were no longer with the company.

Something was going on; this was not the way to run a first-class resort. We soon learned that the company was preparing to sell the island. I discussed the situation with Tommy Cuthbert, my good friend and fellow department head. We were hired at the same time and had been friends since before the resort opened. We relied on each other to get through the more stressful times.

Should we leave too? Our children were in school, our wives were friends, our families were involved in the community, and we didn't want to uproot all of that. We had been building our respective programs for eight years and were proud of what we had accomplished. We predicted Kiawah would eventually improve; we just needed to tough it out and stay positive, despite the negativity around us.

How long could this last? One year, maybe two?

It took three and a half years of this underfunded and depressing existence before the Kiawah Island Company was sold to Kiawah Resort Associates.

In college, my friend Allen Fox taught me that when a tennis match wasn't going well I should "hang on like a crab" because things could turn around. It worked when I came back from being down two sets and 2-5 in the third set against Clark Graebner at Wimbledon in 1968 and almost won the match. It worked when I played top-seeded Tom Okker in 1969 and I was behind 1-4 in the first set at the Pacific Southwest Professional Championship and I came back to win. And it worked at Kiawah.

When Kiawah Resort Associates (KRA) bought the island in 1988 for $105 million, they brought back my old boss Jon Comber to run the resort. (Lesson: maintain a good relationship with your boss, even as he or she is leaving; you never know when you might work with him or her again!) After three years of cutbacks, layoffs, and compromised service, Comber could raise the level of the resort again. Tommy and I were glad we had hung on. But there was more uncertainty to come.

CHAPTER TWENTY-SEVEN

Get the Most Out of Your Talent

New Ownership at Kiawah,
a Televised Pro Event, and a Big Vote

When UCLA Coach John Wooden noted that I had gotten the most out of my talent, he was referring specifically to my tennis game, but what stayed with me was the idea that personal success in anything is measured by doing the most with what you have. It was a lesson I needed at Kiawah and in my capacity as a volunteer.

To reduce their debt on its investment, KRA sold off the resort division to Landmark Land, a national real estate company specializing in golf properties, luxury hotels, and upscale communities. Landmark's parent company, Oak Tree Savings, helped finance many of Landmark's properties, including the Palm Beach Polo Club in Florida and the Carmel Valley Ranch, Mission Hills Country Club, La Quinta Resort, and PGA West Resort in California.

Landmark Land, in concert with PGA executives, decided to move the 1991 Ryder Cup from PGA West in California to Kiawah Island, and play it the last weekend in September on the yet-to-be-completed Pete Dye-designed Ocean Course. The pressure was on to finish the course in time for the tournament.

Under Landmark's ownership, Jon Comber was let go because Landmark wanted to bring in its own Director of Resort Operations, Chris Cole. I liked Chris and worked well with him. He was personable and very supportive of tennis, but my job was to focus on improving the tennis experience for all Kiawah's players, no matter who the owners brought in. It was how I used to approach a tennis match: focus on my performance no matter what those around me were doing. If my opponent was playing well, I didn't get discouraged. I kept going and waited for the level of his game to drop. Good things happened if I just concentrated on my game. That's how I got the most out of my talent on the court. It worked off the court too.

Focusing on improving the tennis experience for all Kiawah's players. Junior Camp at Kiawah in the late 1980s. Jonathan is standing, third from the right. Sandon, wearing glasses, is kneeling in the center. (photo courtesy Kiawah Island Golf Resort)

In September 1989, Hurricane Hugo devastated parts of the Charleston area and the beachfront communities. Kiawah suffered little structural damage, but millions of dollars in tree damage. Nearby, the Wild Dunes Resort on the Isle of Palms fared far worse. Wild Dunes had hosted the U.S. Men's Professional Clay-Court tournament in

1988 and 1989, but their tennis facilities could not be rebuilt in time to host in 1990. With my USTA connections and Chris Cole's support, we were able to sell Kiawah as the alternate venue. We hosted a great tournament and I was proud of my department for how it handled the responsibility. The resort looked great, the courts were in top condition, the shops were stocked, and my team worked well with the USTA directors and officials. Kiawah got a lot of exposure, including national television coverage.

My greatest talent off the court was bringing business to the resort. My most successful marketing pipeline was my volunteer work within professional associations, specifically the USTA and the PTR. My friendship with Lucy Garvin was a big part of that, and I had enormous respect for her diplomacy. She can listen to all sides of an issue and come up with a balanced solution. And she knows what works. When she felt the South Carolina Tennis Association (a division of the USTA) needed to be led by a teaching professional, she "worked on me" for six months until I agreed to accept a two-year term as president. I owe Lucy many thanks for that endorsement; it was the start of a wonderful journey of volunteer and networking opportunities.

Lucy Garvin (official referree) and me (director) at the Kiawah Junior Tournament in 1985

Volunteer positions, just like income-producing jobs, have their share of pressure-filled challenges. My USTA leadership role certainly did, and how I fared would impact my reputation in the industry and at work.

The SCTA offices are located near Columbia, South Carolina. In 1990, my second year as president, a group proposed that the organization build a tennis center complex in nearby Lexington, South Carolina, which would also house new SCTA offices. They envisioned a teaching and tournament hub to serve the Columbia tennis community. Apparently, the land would have been donated and the South Carolina Tennis Patrons Foundation would raise money for the complex.

I worried whether combining statewide USTA administrative oversight and day-to-day local facility operation was really in the best interest of the SCTA. How would it impact the other local tennis facilities already in the area? The SCTA board turns over every two years; perhaps that is not a good formula for consistent facility management. I wasn't sure.

I was lobbied hard from both sides, including being called off the court the morning of the big vote to take an "emergency" phone call to hear just one more unofficial impassioned argument.

To prepare for the binding vote, I consulted Robert's Rules of Order, the standard of parliamentary procedure. Tensions were running high and I had no experience presiding over such a venue. I learned that I could have a Sergeant-at-Arms present to maintain order (I immediately arranged for one), that anyone who wanted could speak one at a time for a few minutes (but with no questions or debate to follow), and that I could conduct either a public roll-call vote or a silent ballot vote (I chose a silent ballot vote).

The proposal to build the new complex was voted down by one vote.

Years later, a tennis complex was built on that site with private funds. It was called the Lexington County Tennis Center and its first director was my PTR partner Jorge Andrew. This was a win-win; I wasn't opposed to a facility, just the SCTA's ownership of it.

My volunteer experience as president of the SCTA was a distinct learning experience for its challenges and its opportunities. I was fortunate to serve as chairman of numerous USTA–Southern committees, become a member of many national committees, become captain of the Italia Cup (an international team of the top 35-and-older players), and be appointed vice chair and chair of the USTA Davis Cup Committee. These positions gave Colleen and me the chance to travel the world — this time as ambassadors of the game rather than competitors — and to promote the Kiawah experience. All good networking.

I have always been fascinated by what people are good at. In my playing days, others looked at me and wondered how I could make a living playing tennis, yet their talents intrigued me equally. I marvel at the "big boys" who put together massive real estate deals (the developers I know all happen to be men), the teachers who have the patience to teach a class full of kids, and the agronomists who keep hundreds of acres of golf courses green. And nothing was more humbling than the few times I played golf with Tommy. *I really should have gotten Tommy out on the tennis court!* Talent takes commitment and passion, and I consider myself fortunate that mine evolved as my career morphed from the game of tennis to the business of tennis.

CHAPTER TWENTY-EIGHT

Cultivate Important Relationships

Another New Owner, Another New Boss, and a Fed Cup Match

Just when things seemed to be running smoothly, Kiawah was thrown into another ownership transition. More change equaled more challenges to developing long-term working relationships.

In the late 1980s, the government had revised the rules and regulations for savings and loans. The Resolution Trust Company (RTC) — the regulating arm of the government for savings and loan companies — determined that Oak Tree, Landmark's parent company, did not meet the new government guidelines. At issue was the amount of money Oak Tree kept versus the amount it was loaning to its investment properties like Landmark. In 1990, Landmark came under investigation by the SEC for its accounting practices.

In the meantime, Kiawah was hosting the 1991 Ryder Cup competition — the top golfers from the United States against the top golfers from Europe — on the newly opened challenging seaside Ocean Course. Dubbed the "War by the Shore," this Ryder Cup competition brought worldwide attention to Kiawah and its amenities.

The RTC waited until the conclusion of the tournament and the celebration of the U.S. victory to take control of Landmark and all its properties nationwide. Chris Cole from Landmark agreed to stay on as director of resort operations to preserve operational continuity. However, the RTC restructured the organizational chart to give Greg French, the head golf professional at the Ocean Course, responsibility for golf, tennis, and recreation. I reported to Greg, who was a nice guy, but he didn't know anything about tennis.

In those years of uncertainty, Tommy Cuthbert and I kept a low profile and worked hard to keep our departments running no matter what was going on around us. With each ownership change, we feared the new owners would "clean house" and bring in their own people. We had been at Kiawah a long time but felt immensely vulnerable with each transition. Fortunately, that never happened.

Tommy Cuthbert and me at Kiawah

Outside of work, things were good. Jonathan and Sandon finished Mason Prep and attended Bishop England High School in Charleston, where they played on the tennis team, leading their school to win multiple South Carolina State Championships. Colleen remained at Mason Prep, assisting teachers and planning special events. Jonathan also started working with me at Kiawah, teaching tennis on the weekends and over the summers. He is a very outgoing "people person" and I enjoyed watching him interact with the resort guests.

Kiawah employees worked for the RTC for two years before RTC put all the Landmark properties up for sale. Potential buyers paid a non-refundable $50,000 just to be eligible to bid. In 1993, Richmond, Virginia billionaire Bill Goodwin purchased the resort for approximately $40,000,000, which included the Kiawah Island Inn (150 rooms), villa operations, two conference centers, all the restaurants, four golf courses (but not the Ocean Course), two tennis centers, all the recreational activities, the Straw Market, and the Town Center.

The government didn't put the Ocean Course up for sale until some wetland issues were resolved. Once it was for sale, Bill Goodwin outbid Kiawah Resort Associates and purchased the Ocean Course for roughly $27,000,000.

Tommy and I agreed that our patience and positive attitude had paid off. We thought we finally had an owner with a commitment to making Kiawah Island Golf and Tennis Resort realize its tremendous potential. We were encouraged by this relationship.

Mr. Goodwin kept Chris Cole as director of resort operations but, unfortunately for me, he didn't last. For the second time in my tenure at Kiawah, my boss resigned in a budget meeting. Mr. Goodwin asked Chris to reduce the payroll in the golf operation, which meant letting go some of the golf professionals Chris had brought to Kiawah. Chris didn't feel he could keep his job if they were going to lose theirs.

When Chris resigned, Mr. Goodwin notified the four head golf pros and me that he wished to meet with us each individually the next day. We were in the middle of the budget process and I had not received my first draft of numbers back from the accounting department. I needed them to prepare for my meeting with Mr. Goodwin. I called accounting and found out they hadn't yet entered the information I gave them. I panicked. I begged them to get me something I could use and agreed to wait in their office for it. At 11:00 p.m., they got me a first draft of my budget. I stayed up until 3:00 a.m. working on a variance report for my meeting with Mr. Goodwin.

Tired but prepared, I entered Mr. Goodwin's office in the morning and put my budget information on the conference table. "Let's not talk about the budget today," he said, "I'd just like to sit down and get to know a little about you." *What!?* After all that, we weren't going to discuss the budget! I'm sure if I hadn't been ready, he would have asked to see it. It's still better to be prepared.

Up until this meeting with Mr. Goodwin, my tennis department was part of Kiawah's golf division, as defined by the RTC. Mr. Goodwin decided that tennis would be better served as part of the Hotel-Villa department because tennis could help fill guest rooms and the rooms division could help sell tennis business. No such mutually beneficial marketing relationship existed for me with the golf operations. That night, Goodwin called Prem Devadas, the resort's managing director, and arranged for me to attend the Executive Committee meeting the next day.

I learned very quickly this new arrangement was not just in name only: it was a whole different management scenario and I'd have to adjust. I was to attend the Executive Committee meeting every week and be prepared to answer general and specific questions about my tennis operation and its budget. It took six months for me to get a decent night's sleep before these weekly meetings.

After my first week working for Prem, he called me to his office. "Do you want to continue to work at Kiawah"? he asked.

"Absolutely," I replied without even thinking, but the answer would have been the same if I had thought about it. I liked my job.

Prem seemed happy with my answer. I learned that Prem was surprised — and I think impressed — that as a manager I still taught tennis. He had worked with many hotel managers and department heads who didn't also do what they employed their staff to do. I managed two tennis centers with pro shop sales, 23 clay courts, eight teaching professionals, five in-shop personnel, and two maintenance personnel. I was responsible for instructional programming, special events, merchandising, and marketing. Yet I couldn't imagine doing my job without spending some time on the court giving lessons and running clinics. Not only was instruction my strength and passion, it was my most valuable tool for learning about the guest experience. That a Kiawah tennis guest could book a lesson with the former-tour-player-department-head, or at least see me on the court with others, was one of those marketing intangibles not to be undervalued.

I was equally impressed with Prem; working for him was the best thing that happened to me at Kiawah.

Around the time of this management transition, *Tennis Magazine* changed how it ranked the best resorts. It used to just name the "Top 50," and Kiawah was always in the list. Then it started ranking the best ten resorts, making the run for the top spots all that much more competitive. The first year, Kiawah was ranked No. 3 in the country, but Prem knew we could do better.

Kiawah: the No. 3 Tennis Resort in the country per Tennis Magazine
(left to right):
*Mike Hain (teaching professional), Prem Devadas (managing director of Kiawah Island Resort), John Gompert (head professional), Suzanne Bringman (shop manager/buyer), Peter Francesconi (*Tennis Magazine*), me, Mark Fletcher (shop attendant), Cynthia Keyes (teaching professional), Amy Drolet (shop supervisor), Tim Wood (maintenance supervisor)*

"What do we need to do to move up to No. 1?" Prem asked me.

A lot was riding on my answer. I believed Kiawah's excellent reputation and favorable ranking as a destination tennis resort was due to the caliber of the instruction we offered, but Prem's question was a great opportunity for me to get the amenities and equipment we needed to exceed our competition. I told him we needed benches, awnings, and electric water fountains for every pair of courts, and we needed lights for nighttime play. He got me all of that and challenged me to become No. 1. Prem seemed really committed to the tennis program.

Although we all craved that national ranking top spot, we just kept trying to build our program, one student, one guest, one event at a time. It was working.

I rarely took more than a day at a time off from work — tennis was a seven-day-a-week department and I enjoyed my job — but in 1995 I told Prem I needed to fly to San Diego for a few days to be inducted into the inaugural class of the Hoover High Athletic Hall of Fame.

I got the call a few months earlier. My high school was honoring 23 alumni who were not only good students who had excelled in their sport in high school, but they also had to, according to Hoover High, "play professionally within the sport for seven years, being a first-team college All-American or playing on an Olympic or U.S. National team."

The induction ceremony was in the school gymnasium, where our portraits hung on the west wall. Other inductees included Ted Williams, '37 (baseball), Ray Boone, '42 (baseball), Mickey Wright, '52 (golf), and Bill McColl, '48 (football). Most of the honorees were present at the ceremony except Ted Williams who, at 87, lived in Florida and didn't feel up to the trip. He did participate by phone, however, and for all his accomplishments, he really seemed to be touched by the moment.

I was quite flattered to be honored by my high school, especially as a member of the first class of inductees and alongside so many accomplished athletes. I took education seriously and did well, despite the time it took to travel to and play in so many junior tournaments.

The visit back to Hoover was made even more enjoyable when I saw my high school friend Pete Kofoed in the crowd. The school seemed smaller, and Pete and I were definitely older, but it was all very familiar.

A few years later, I was again inducted into a hall of fame. This time, it was the South Carolina Tennis Hall of Fame for being "an outstanding contributor to tennis history in South Carolina." For someone who never considered moving to the East Coast, and thought twice about accepting the job at Kiawah, I was overwhelmed by this honor. I owe all the credit for this recognition to Lucy Garvin. She encouraged me to become involved in the USTA and I am forever grateful to her.

The South Carolina Tennis Hall of Fame museum in Belton, South Carolina, is about as far from Kiawah as one can get and still be in South Carolina. The building is a beautifully renovated train depot and its highlight is the museum's portrait gallery of inductees. Each portrait is painted by Belton native and accomplished sports artist Wayland Moore. I was most proud that my family, including my parents, were with me as I received this honor. My parents traveled from San Diego — it was quite a long trip for one night — but I was so glad they were there. I always valued my opportunities to publicly thank them for giving me the gift of tennis.

South Carolina Tennis Hall of Fame portrait, 1997. This black and white photo doesn't do justice to the painting's vibrant colors.

In 1998, Prem and I worked together to bring the quarterfinal round of the women's Fed Cup competition between the unseeded United States team and the No. 2-ranked Netherlands team to Kiawah. Along with the U.S. team of Monica Seles, Lindsay Davenport, Lisa Raymond, and Mary Jo Fernandez, and their captain, Billie Jean King, came international television coverage for the island. This was a huge coup for Kiawah, and a 5-0 win for the U.S. team.

1998 Fed Cup team at Kiawah
(photo courtesy Kiawah Island Golf Resort)

Prem and I also negotiated to bring the Family Circle Professional Women's Tennis Championship tournament to Kiawah. It had been hosted at the Sea Pines Resort on Hilton Head almost every year since its inception in 1973, and it was looking for a new home beginning in 2001. We held extensive talks with the tournament owners but came to an impasse with $250,000 still on the table.

Prem could not justify losing $250,000 each year to host the tournament, despite the attention it would bring to Kiawah. We dropped out of the negotiation. As much as I might have enjoyed the exposure, it would have been incredibly stressful to manage the facility operations for the tournament every year during our always-busy Easter season. Prem's decision probably added ten years to my life. Fortunately, the tournament — which is now called the Volvo Car Open — ended up at a wonderful new venue on nearby Daniel Island and still brings hundreds of tennis-loving fans to the Charleston area every year.

Some of the best relationships in my life have taken work. Among them, my rapport with Prem Devadas. I went from being completely intimidated by him, to our recognizing our mutual respect, to his becoming a trusted colleague. Mr. Goodwin was a bottom-line-driven owner who respected me and supported the tennis operation even though it was not a big revenue source. My high school in San Diego and my adopted home state of South Carolina each voted me into their sports/tennis halls of fame after recognizing my tennis accomplishments and my integrity on and off the court. I am blessed to have cultivated so many nice relationships.

CHAPTER TWENTY-NINE

Focus on What You Can Control

Kiawah is Still a Tennis Resort

In the late 1990s, Kiawah's golf business started to decline. The golf industry had built too many golf courses and the tee time inventory exceeded demand. Mr. Goodwin had invested millions in purchasing and upgrading Kiawah's five golf courses, and the decline in golf revenue for the resort was devastating. My friend Tommy Cuthbert, the director of golf, really felt the pressure. He wasn't responsible for the number of courses, yet it was his job to sell the tee times. I saw the stress he was under and I think it really took a toll on him.

Mr. Goodwin and his marketing department thought Kiawah needed an extra edge to distinguish itself in the golf world, so they decided to change the name of the resort from the Kiawah Island Golf and Tennis Resort to the Kiawah Island Golf Resort. Just like that — in one grand gesture — everything my department worked so hard for, our collective identity, was literally erased and functionally downgraded. It was a huge blow to my program, my staff, and Kiawah's tennis members, not to mention to me personally and professionally.

I was not naïve. The tennis operation had never been a priority in the resort's marketing program — not like the five-star hotel, the villas, golf, recreation, and the beach — and it had never been a major income producer for the company. But the name change would hurt the tennis marketing effort. It wasn't just that the word "tennis" was not in the name, it was that it had been *removed* from the name. Even though the internal underlying motive was to elevate golf, the public perception was that the tennis program was no longer good enough to define the resort. I couldn't believe this would help golf as much as it would hurt tennis.

Should I have left the resort over this?

If I were going to leave, I would have left years earlier when Sal Alzouman cut our budgets down to unworkable numbers, the resort looked awful, and many of my colleagues left. I had already toughed out slow growth at the beginning, rapid management turnover, ownership changes, sudden department head resignations, and the hefty budget cuts.

Should my decision be different because my department was targeted directly?

I thought about my job. The reality was that despite the name change and the external perception that tennis had been downgraded, internally Mr. Goodwin was just as invested as ever in me and the tennis program. Most importantly, I had been there 23 years, I had found the niche my father advised, and I really enjoyed what I did.

I thought about my family. Colleen was busy at Mason Prep and with our church. Jonathan attended the College of Charleston and worked at Kiawah teaching tennis with me in the summers. When he graduated from Charleston, he came to work with me full time. Sandon studied and played tennis at Clemson University, only a few hours from Charleston. I loved going to watch him play, and I loved how easy it was for him to come home to visit. Did I really want to change all that?

And I thought about my staff. I was responsible for them. The department now had to work harder to maintain the same business revenue for the company who had just yanked its visibility. It reminded me of playing with last-minute court changes, ongoing crowd distractions, and rain delays. The only thing we could control was how we performed, and we had to make our game the best it could be under the circumstances. My employees deserved better than my abandoning them at this critical time. Leaving was not an option.

I decided to deal with the name change the way I dealt with an umpire who made a bad call: I wasn't going to argue with him or walk off the court. I was just going to accept it, keep playing, focus on what I could control, and try to win in spite of it. It would be a challenge to keep pace, though. We needed some new initiatives.

CHAPTER THIRTY

Gain Confidence through Mini-Goals

The Roy Barth Teaching Method,
5-Star Service, and Resort Rankings

The Kiawah name change hit the morale of my tennis department hard, but we couldn't let that deter us. I thought back to what helped me gain confidence in the face of difficult challenges on the tour: creating mini-goals. We didn't have to dwell on the "big picture" name change — it didn't at all diminish what my department offered — we just needed to define and conquer smaller goals to continue to distinguish ourselves.

Define Consistent Instructional Methods

Why do guests come to Kiawah to play tennis? They don't come just for the courts, the accommodations, the beach, or the food — many places have those. And all top resorts offer instructional programs for juniors and adults of all levels and offer to pair guests of similar ability. Some even sponsor professional exhibitions and tournaments as Kiawah did. But I believe tennis enthusiasts come to Kiawah for our superior instruction. I figured out how to make it unique.

I worked with my head professionals, David Boyd and my son Jonathan, to develop teaching templates for each stroke. We determined what the top players in the world in each generation have done the same, and then we broke down each stroke into four key foundation points in proper sequence.

Then we trained all our teaching professionals to teach these same foundation points the same way. My staff not only possessed solid skills — I didn't want my guests to beat my pros and go home and brag about it — but they also embraced our teaching style. If we all taught the same key foundation points, rather than contradict what a guest had been working on with a pro or coach at home, our guests could take lessons or clinics from any of us on any day or any visit and continue to improve. This is what brought tennis players to Kiawah at first, and it's what prompted them to return year after year.

I channeled my lessons from Maureen Connolly and Les Stoefen, who taught me as a competitive junior, and from Glenn Bassett, who coached me in college. Their lessons of the 50s and 60s — the timeless fundamentals of the game — resonated with the Kiawah guests of the 90s and 2000s, and I had a unique instructional program.

Improve Staff Efficiency

My department improved the tennis center experience off the court as well. When Kiawah hired Teresa Keller, a trainer of five-star service, to train the hotel employees, the other managers of the resort also benefited. I already had training checklists for each tennis shop employee, but Teresa helped me set mini-goals for each staff member to make them accountable and advised me how to praise and review them more effectively. We expanded our retail inventory in both pro shops with new brands, and we further refined the court maintenance and landscaping standards. I embraced the five-star hotel standards for the tennis operation. We were, after all, all in the hospitality business.

Identify New Marketing Opportunities

I got more personally involved in marketing. When I was under the golf-villa "umbrella," I depended on the company's overall marketing to bring in tennis business. Jack Case worked in Kiawah's marketing department and took an interest in what Kiawah's tennis program had to offer. Together we developed a few ads for *Tennis Magazine*, TennisResortsOnline.com, and other tennis-related publications. He also helped me produce a DVD from my book *Tips for Better Tennis*. I had always been "out and about" as the face of Kiawah tennis — visiting other resorts, playing in tournaments around the country, attending USTA and PTR events — and it served the department well, but I made a renewed effort to network more, both inside and outside the company. New business could come from anywhere.

The DVD format may be old technology, but the foundation points of the game are timeless.

I had already achieved one of my earlier mini-goals: bringing a nationally televised tournament to Kiawah. In 1990, Chris Cole helped me bring the Men's Professional Clay-Court Championships to the island, and in 1998 Prem helped me bring the Fed Cup match to Kiawah. While events of those caliber are rare, smaller mini-goals were certainly within reach. Over the next few years, I arranged for Kiawah to host the USTA Leadership Meeting with 120 participants (three times), the USTA National Staff Training Conference with 150 participants (twice), the USTA Southern Section Summer Meeting with 100 participants (twice), the USTA South Carolina Annual Meeting with 100 participants (four times), and the Wilson Racquet Sports National Sales Meeting, to name a few.

Secure Top Rankings

My other mini-goals were about rankings. I'd been chasing rankings most of my life — first to be ranked in the Top 10 as a player, and then to get Kiawah ranked as a top tennis resort in the country and in the world. I ended my days on the pro tour happy with my highest rankings, but I was still determined to earn Kiawah the top spot. I was getting closer.

Recognition by the USTA Southern Section was certainly more than a mini-goal, so I was honored to be inducted into its Hall of Fame. The Southern Section of the USTA includes the nine most southeastern states, except for Florida, which is a section unto itself. My extended family, including my mother, my Aunt Mary, and my cousin Becky from California, attended the induction ceremony. I was glad my mother got to hear me publicly recognize Wilbur, Maureen and Les — the coaches she and my father hired to teach me — and to meet my friend and mentor, Lucy Garvin.

My tennis department and I came through the name change with dignity. I still can't believe removing "tennis" from the name of the resort helped golf as much as it hurt tennis, but my job was to succeed in spite of that.

CHAPTER THIRTY-ONE

Enjoy the Perks of Your Job

Meeting and Playing (More) Celebrities

In 1999, actor, director, producer, and American icon Robert (Bob) Redford lived at Kiawah for six months while he directed the famous golf movie *The Legend of Bagger Vance,* starring Matt Damon, Will Smith, Charlize Theron, and Jack Lemon. He filmed the movie on Kiawah's golf courses, in the city of Savannah, Georgia, and in other Lowcountry locations.

Bob booked court time with me once a week to hit and get a good workout. He struck the ball quite well and kept it in play so I got a good workout too. It took a few sessions for me to get used to his schedule though: he was routinely 40 minutes to an hour late. Tommy Cuthbert said Redford was just as late for his golf lessons. Tommy and I called it "Redford Time" and planned to catch up on our paperwork while we waited for him. During our workout, Redford's staff would sit in his SUV outside the pro shop waiting to drive him to Savannah to film the "downtown" parts of the movie. I laughed thinking about his film crew out there on location adapting to Redford Time.

Despite his being eleven years my senior, Bob and I had a lot in common. He grew up in Southern California — in Santa Monica, about two hours from my home in San Diego — where he started to play tennis at age 14. He hung out at the public tennis center in the afternoons, holding on to the fence and watching the UCLA team practice. A few of the players offered to teach him to play. He was a quick learner and went on to play in the same tournaments I played in as a junior (Long Beach, Santa Monica, Ojai, etc.), ten years before me. He asked if I knew Bob and Norm Perry, the UCLA brothers who taught him the game. I knew them well.

Bob invited Colleen and me to watch the filming of a *Bagger Vance* scene. That week, Kiawah was hosting the South Carolina Tennis Association meeting so I invited our friends Bob and Lucy Garvin and Charles and Helen Jeter to come along.

"Be at the Ocean Course at 10:00 p.m.," Redford told us.

We were not sure if he meant 10:00 p.m. our time or 10:00 p.m. Redford Time. No matter, we'd certainly wait.

The scene being filmed that night featured Matt Damon playing fictional golfer Rannulph Junuh, Will Smith in the title role of the caddy, and J. Michael Moncrief as Hardy Greaves, the young protege and child version of the older narrator played by Jack Lemmon. In the scene, darkness is falling as the players approach the last few holes of the highly competitive four-day tournament. Junuh prepares to hit his ball by clearing a blade of grass nearby, which accidentally causes the ball to move.

"It moved. I have to call a one-stroke penalty on myself," Junuh announced to Bagger and Hardy, the only two people who saw it happen.

"No!" pleaded Hardy, "Don't do it. I won't tell a soul. Cross my heart. Ain't nobody gonna know."

"I will," said Junuh, "and so will you."

Of all the scenes filmed at Kiawah, I was present for one about honor among athletes in their sports. I still wonder whether Bob Redford purposefully invited me to that scene.

Bob was a gracious host, even as he was working, and we had a great time. As tennis players, my guests and I agreed that if we thought playing golf takes too long, *filming* golf takes even longer. Yet *Bagger Vance* remains one of my favorite movies.

Thinking about Robert Redford's visit reminded me that leaving the pro tour didn't mean I'd lost the chance to run into celebrities who enjoyed the game. It seems teaching tennis at a luxury resort and coaching pro teams gave me the same opportunities.

Marlo Thomas

Marlo Thomas and her husband, television talk show host Phil Donahue, came to Kiawah in 1978, hoping to relax and enjoy some anonymity. Marlo, the daughter of actor-comedian Danny Thomas, is probably best known for her role as Ann Marie in the television series *That Girl* (1966-1971), and for her work furthering her father's legacy of helping sick children at the Saint Jude Children's Research Hospital in Memphis, Tennessee.

Marlo and Phil usually vacationed in Europe, where they were not as well known, but at that time Kiawah was only two years old, minimally developed, and low-key; they thought they might escape there. I gave Marlo a few tennis lessons. Her on-court personality was much like I anticipated from her public persona: she was fun to teach — outgoing, energetic, and quite determined to improve. Unfortunately for Marlo and Phil, other Kiawah guests recognized them and interrupted their dinners to ask for autographs, forcing them to choose room service for the remainder of their stay.

Robert Mugabe

Robert Mugabe was president of Zimbabwe from 1987 to 2017. In my capacity as vice chair of the USTA Davis Cup Committee, Colleen and I had traveled to Harare, the capital of Zimbabwe, in February of 2000 for the first round of Davis Cup matches between the U.S. and

Zimbabwe. Mugabe attended the matches.

Colleen and I met Mugabe and his wife, Grace, at the pre-match "official draw" event. He was dressed quite regally, way more formally than one usually dresses to watch a tennis match. Mugabe was a controversial figure. He was lauded for freeing Zimbabwe from British rule but vehemently opposed for the dictatorial way he managed the country, which included allegations of corruption, human rights abuses, and crimes against humanity.

Sitting in the same indoor stadium with him was unsettling. Not only were there soldiers with automatic weapons stationed in each aisle, but I found it difficult to look at him and not to think of the accusations of abuses to his people. There was so much opposition to Mugabe at that time that assassination attempts were not uncommon and we feared for USTA president, Judy Levering, who sat next to Mugabe during the competition. Fortunately, there was no incident.

On the court, Captain John McEnroe and his U.S. team of Andre Agassi, Chris Woodruff, Rick Leach, and Alex O'Brien played Zimbabwe brothers Byron and Wayne Black and Kevin Ullyett. After Agassi won his singles match in a close third set tie-break, the countries were tied at two wins apiece. In the fifth and deciding match, Chris Woodruff was down a set and a service break to Wayne Black, and feeling bad about it, especially because he had lost his earlier singles match to Byron Black in straight sets. At the next changeover, McEnroe delivered to Chris Woodruff what I can only describe as an animated "chewing out." (Imagine that!) When Chris returned to the court, he turned his game around and won the next three sets. Victory U.S.A.!

Before returning home, Colleen and I took a side-trip to Victoria Falls — a waterfall described as one of the "Seven Natural Wonders of the World" — on the Zambezi River, which separates Zimbabwe from neighboring Zambia. February is considered within the Falls' "flood season" and the views were incredible, almost like going back in time to before modern civilization.

Ernest (Fritz) Hollings

Ernest (Fritz) Hollings was a native Charlestonian and former South Carolina Governor (1959-1963), U.S. Senator (1966-2005), and Democratic presidential candidate (1984). He was also an avid tennis player. In 2011, Peter DeVito, Fritz's good friend and tennis partner, brought the 89-year-old Fritz to Kiawah to take a lesson with me. I watched them play doubles together. Peter called Fritz "the Statue," because "he just stands there and makes me do all the running."

Fritz's reputation as a thoughtful but salty political personality made me think he would be difficult to teach. I found just the opposite; he was friendly, eager to improve, and respectful of my teaching ability. He took my instructional manual, *Tips for Better Tennis*, and told me later he'd read it cover to cover. Peter took a photo of Fritz and me and we signed each other's copy. Peter told me that Fritz kept my signed photo of us on his shelf in his home office.

Senator Fritz Hollings, 89, and me at Kiawah in 2011

Rick Santorum

Rick Santorum was a former senator from Pennsylvania, Republican presidential candidate in 2012 and 2016, and CNN panelist. Rick is the brother of my good friend Dan Santorum, the CEO of the PTR. I played golf with Rick and Dan on Kiawah's famous Ocean Course in 2000. I met Rick again in 2012 after he participated in a nationally televised presidential debate at the Citadel in Charleston.

Lloyd Bridges

Roscoe Tanner brought touring pros to Kiawah for tennis exhibitions and clinics. Bob Moore, Kiawah's director of marketing, brought celebrities to Kiawah for the same reason. In 1982, actor Lloyd Bridges came to play, along with actor Dick van Patten and his son, actor and touring pro player Vince van Patten. Lloyd Bridges was a prolific actor on the stage, big screen, and television for more than 60 years. He was also an avid athlete. He and Roscoe played against Dick and Vince in a charity event to raise money for the Children's Fund at the Medical University of South Carolina. I don't know whether the four players or the spectators had a better time. While the ball was in play, Lloyd was a worthy opponent, but before and after the points he was a fan-favorite crowd pleaser, always with a big smile.

Roscoe Tanner, Lloyd Bridges, and me in a Pro-Am at Kiawah in 1982

CHAPTER THIRTY-TWO

Maintain a
Positive Attitude During Illness

Two Surgeries, One Ranking, and a Sanctuary

In 2003, my friend Tommy Cuthbert was still a staple of the Kiawah staff, but he was no longer the director of golf. The stress of the job itself, coupled with the immense pressure he felt from the owners in the late 1990s to book tee times in a waning golf market, took a toll on him mentally and physically. He suffered from frequent stomach problems, tired easily, and was losing weight. He just wanted to do what he liked best: teach golf. At Tommy's request, he stepped down as director of golf and moved to Kiawah's dedicated teaching facility full-time. As the new director of golf instruction, Tommy spent his days in one place, rather than running around the island or preparing for meetings. He really enjoyed working with guests one-on-one to improve their golf game. He seemed much happier.

Kiawah hired Roger Warren to replace Tommy as director of golf. Roger was the general manager of Seven Bridges Golf Club in Woodridge, Illinois, and he was the president of the PGA Illinois Section. He was also the 1998 Illinois PGA golf professional of the year.

Over the next few years he moved up the ladder to become first vice president and then president of the PGA.

Two thousand four started the way I expected but didn't end anywhere close to what I would have anticipated. Kiawah was poised to complete The Sanctuary, a five-story, 255-room, $110 million-dollar luxury "seaside mansion" hotel and spa in the East Beach Village area of the island, within walking distance of the East Beach Tennis Center. From our courts, we watched it — and heard it — being built for two years. In total, The Sanctuary was eight years in the making, at times needing to address significant challenges from state environmental groups intent on preserving the wetlands along the intended beachfront site. Once the issues were resolved, Prem and Mr. Goodwin hosted a press conference announcing the hotel's development, complete with floor plans, conceptual renderings, and even a raised platform on the beachfront site for guests to walk up and experience the view from the lobby elevation.

In the first half of 2004, we watched the activity around the hotel go from busy to frenzied. Full-grown trees were brought in and planted along the entryway. Truckloads of furniture, fixtures, and equipment arrived every day. New staff members reported for training. It was an enormous project.

The Sanctuary Hotel, East Beach, Kiawah Island
(photo courtesy Kiawah Island Golf Resort)

In the midst of all the Sanctuary construction and outdoor beautification, Prem walked over to the East Beach Tennis Center and looked around. A half million dollars later, we had new landscaping, walkways, and a new deck outside; the building was painted inside and out; and we got new carpeting, display racks, and a new point-of-sale system. I guess our 1982 look just wasn't going to cut it next to the new luxury hotel.

I took advantage of the renovations to add a few personal touches to the shop: a "history wall" of Kiawah's tennis program, and two of my favorite teaching mantras. One wall says, "To be successful in tennis, as in life, you must be focused and pay attention to the details." And the space over the door out to the courts promotes the "Point of Impact."

The tennis department's instructional mantra painted over the door to the courts in my newly renovated East Beach Pro Shop

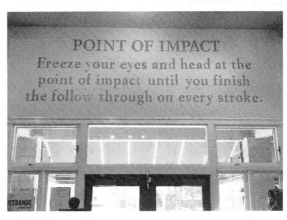

The Sanctuary Hotel opened on August 20, 2004, and was every bit as beautiful as advertised. This was Prem Devadas' project: a turn-of-the-century, grand hotel with every world-class amenity. He got what he wanted. This was the largest addition of accommodations to open at Kiawah at one time, and I readied my tennis center for the increase in business.

Later that year, I learned that Ron Bohrnstedt, my lifelong friend, teammate, and roommate at UCLA, had double bypass heart surgery. He had worked at Sawgrass in Ponte Vedra for a few years after retiring from the tour and then became the director of tennis at the Greenbrier in White Sulphur Springs, West Virginia, where he remained for the next 20 years. He also served on the Board of Directors of the USTA and was a vice chairman of the Davis Cup committee. In 1999, he moved back to Florida, this time to the Orlando area, to become the head coach of the men's tennis team at Rollins College. He was also one of the fittest guys I knew, and not just for someone 57 years old. He told me he felt no symptoms and only learned about his blocked arteries at a routine company physical.

Within a week of hearing about Ron, I learned that Brian Cheney, my friend from junior tennis and co-recipient of the Sportsmanship Award at the National Boys' 18s tournament in 1965, needed a stent to keep a partially blocked coronary artery open in hopes of preventing a heart attack. At 56, he played almost daily and was an active participant in senior leagues. He, too, had no symptoms of heart disease.

I was sure I was OK — my whole life I'd only suffered from blisters, cramps, and one stress-induced breakdown, but that was years ago. Even though I took cholesterol medicine, I felt fine. I made an appointment to see my doctor anyway.

On October 25, 2004, I checked in at the Medical University of South Carolina at 5:30 a.m. for double bypass heart surgery. In the time the waiting room clock advanced an hour, I felt I aged a year. Around 9:00 a.m. an anesthesiologist came to administer my IV drip. He asked me what kind of "cocktail" I'd like. I guess that's anesthesiology humor.

I laughed, but not at that.

"What's so funny?" Colleen asked.

"I was just thinking about my report to the Executive Committee I asked Theresa Silo to read for me at today's meeting. She should be reading it to everybody right about now."

"What did the report say?"

At this moment I am having open heart surgery at MUSC. I want to make sure you hear the great news from me: Tennis Magazine *just ranked Kiawah Island Golf Resort the No. 1 Tennis Resort in the United States. That's my report.*

The anesthesiologist didn't seem to care about my big announcement to the Executive Committee, but it meant a lot for me to tell them. *At least if I don't make it through the surgery, they will know I knew the good news before I died. That will make them feel better.*

"Cocktail time," the anesthesiologist declared. I felt cold, then tingly, and then numb.

I spent four days in the hospital after my heart surgery. From the moment I woke up in the recovery room, I was in excruciating pain and was instantly sorry I had agreed to the operation. I had been feeling *fine!*

The thought of the No. 1 ranking from *Tennis Magazine* buoyed my spirits. We had been working toward this recognition for years and I knew how elated my colleagues, especially my tennis staff, would be. The coveted No. 1 *Tennis Magazine* ranking is not just based on the tennis facility, staff and instruction; it is based on the whole guest experience, which includes accommodations, food service, the fitness center and spa, the overall service, and the price. Prem was quite effusive in his praise.

> *We are very proud to be ranked as the finest American resort at which to play tennis … This achievement is a testament to the hard work of our Director of Tennis Roy Barth and his team of talented and dedicated professionals.*
>
> *– Prem Devadas, Kiawah's Managing Director*

Just as satisfying as the recognition was the headline in the local paper: "*Kiawah Island Golf Resort Named No. 1 Tennis Resort in the Country.*"

Ten days after my double bypass heart surgery, I had a brain tumor removed from my left frontal lobe. Despite the initial post-bypass surgery pain, I was grateful that I had issues that could be fixed and doctors who could fix them. My childhood friend Johnny Sanderlin wasn't so fortunate but his plight inspired me to keep a positive attitude about illness.

CHAPTER THIRTY-THREE

Learn from Those Around You

Inspiration from the "Greats" of My Job

I returned to work in 2005 in a limited capacity and started to get my life back in order. Three months after my brain surgery, I was cleared by both my neurologist and my cardiologist to hit tennis balls. I felt weak but elated to get my life back. I was 57, but there were moments when I felt 157.

My staff had done an excellent job running both tennis centers in my absence. In fact, in that time, Kiawah was awarded the 2005 "Private Facility of the Year" award by the PTR as:

> *... the tennis facility that demonstrates a commitment to the promotion of tennis and is supportive of PTR members. Areas of consideration: hosting PTR educational activities; community service, tournaments, exhibitions, charity and sectional events.*

It's funny to return to work after a long absence to find everything running smoothly. I briefly wondered about the legitimacy of my role if my staff could adapt so seamlessly, yet I was profoundly gratified I had trained a staff able to manage the department on its own. They learned from me, and that made me proud.

The Sanctuary Hotel was attracting new interest to the island, which brought in the increased tennis business I anticipated, and the No. 1 national ranking added to our visibility. The courts were in great shape, our tennis programs were well-attended, the tournaments were well run, and my unique approach to instruction was continuing to bring in guests serious about improving their tennis skills. I remember thinking how nice it was that Kiawah finally had a dedicated owner-management team in place and what a difference that kind of longevity made.

And then half of that team, Prem Devadas, announced he was leaving.

I guess after you develop and open a world-class destination like The Sanctuary, your career star is rising and day-to-day resort operations seem mundane. It was the right time for Prem to find his next challenge. He partnered with Sheila Johnson to form Salamander Hospitality. Salamander owns, builds, and manages luxury hotels and resorts in Virginia, South Carolina, and Florida.

I learned a lot from Prem, and I would miss him, but of course I wished him well. I recalled how intimidated I was when I first met him and how flattered I was when he admired my ability to manage the department and still teach.

Roger Warren, the director of golf, was promoted to replace Prem as resort managing director. I reported directly to Roger. Roger is a "numbers guy" as well, so I started keeping an Excel spreadsheet of the special events I brought to Kiawah over the last few years, including USTA-sanctioned tennis tournaments, non-sanctioned tennis events, and tennis meetings. In addition to the court fees, lesson income, and pro shop sales — which I would be tracking anyway — I charted the income generated by my tennis guests in venues other than tennis: guest accommodations at The Sanctuary Hotel and Villas, and food and beverage functions. This spreadsheet showed the specific impact the tennis business had on the other revenue centers. I found the information fascinating but also necessary to protect the tennis operation.

The spreadsheet proved invaluable in a budget meeting when Roger Warren surprised me by asking why the tennis operation wasn't more profitable for the company. I responded confidently: "We make money for the company for which we get no credit."

"Can you show me the numbers?" Roger asked.

Two hours later I emailed the lodging and food and beverage numbers to Roger, clearly showing the tennis-specific income over the previous three years.

I would never have thought to track this additional information this way if not for the lessons I learned from Prem. He would have applauded my initiative and enjoyed that my hard work paid off.

CHAPTER THIRTY-FOUR

Celebrate the Milestones in Your Life

A Tennis Center, a Learning Center,
and the Loss of a Good Friend

Some milestones in my life caught me by complete surprise. Others I fully anticipated still left me in awe. Some I'd been chasing for years. And one I didn't wish for at all.

In 2005, I ran into Vijay Amritraj, a former touring professional and ATP board member, at the US Open in New York. He told me that I "owed him big time." Apparently he had prevailed in his fight to award retirement benefits to the ATP's "founding fathers" from 1972. He convinced the ATP board to credit us for the years we played on the tour before the ATP was formed. By adding my first three professional pre-ATP years to my four professional official ATP years, I became eligible for retirement benefits based on my seven years on the tour. (In 1972, the only benefit that I remember receiving was free warm-ups from Adidas!). Thirty years after retiring from the pro tour, I started receiving monthly retirement checks.

The year 2006 marked my 30th anniversary as director of tennis at Kiawah, which meant I had already been recognized by the human resources department five times — once every five years — for my employment milestone. Since Tommy Cuthbert and I had been at Kiawah from the beginning, we were the longest-serving employees at each of our five-year luncheons.

The longest serving Kiawah employee overall is M.C. Heyward. He was hired as a "gopher" in 1974 for Kiawah's senior vice president, Frank Brumley, when the Kiawah office was in downtown Charleston. When the resort opened in 1976, M.C. became a bellman at the Kiawah Island Inn. Over the years, M.C. has held numerous jobs — including driving the island's shuttle van and delivering the mail — but he became famous for hosting southern-style oyster roasts at Mingo Point on the river for the resort guests. Thanks to M.C., these oyster roasts, complete with live entertainment, are Kiawah's longest-running event. At M.C.'s 40th year anniversary with Kiawah, the company hung a plaque at Mingo Point commemorating M.C.'s devotion to these gatherings.

I got the memo about my 30th anniversary luncheon around the same time I received a summons for jury duty in Charleston County. They were both scheduled for the same week in January.

Teresa Keller from Kiawah's human resources department left me a voicemail message. "Roy, I haven't heard back from you about the anniversary lunch, but you are coming, right? I really hope you are going to be there. Call me back as soon as you can to let me know you are coming."

I called her back. "Well I don't know if I'll be there because I'll need to call the courthouse number the night before to see if I'm supposed to report the next day. But I'll be at the luncheon if I can."

"I really need you there, Roy," she said. "Maybe you can call to get your jury duty week postponed, or maybe Kiawah can get the courthouse to reschedule it for you."

I guess she really wants me there.

I called the courthouse the night before the start of my jury week and learned I did not have to report. I went to the luncheon. Teresa looked relieved.

When I saw Mr. Goodwin — whom I couldn't recall ever having

seen at one of these events — and Roger Warren, the president of Kiawah, and then Colleen, and Tommy's wife, Beverly, I thought how nice that they all showed for our 30-year recognition.

The program began as usual: the HR department called up each anniversary class, starting with the five-year employees. When it was time for the 30-year employees — just Tommy and me — I was sitting in the back reviewing my notes. Teresa called us up to the front, acknowledged our tenure, and Tommy and I each spoke, thanking the resort for the opportunity to work there, thanking our departments for their dedication, and thanking our wives for their support. The company gave Tommy and me each a flat-screen TV as a gift. It was a much nicer TV than the one I had bought myself with the $300 prize money I won after I defeated Charlie Pasarell in the Pacific Coast Championships in 1969, but it made me feel just as accomplished. Thirty years is a long time in one job; it was nice of them to acknowledge it.

"Please remain seated," Roger Warren said as he walked to the lectern, "there's more to do."

I thought Tommy and I had heard all the accolades we were going to hear that day about our service to Kiawah, but I was wrong. Roger announced that Kiawah's golf teaching facility was being renamed the "Tommy Cuthbert Golf Learning Center," and he unveiled the plaque with an etching of Tommy's likeness that would be located at the entrance to the center. Wow! I was so happy for Tommy, sitting there with his wife, both tearing up, that I almost missed the second part of the announcement: "… and the East Beach Tennis Center will now be called the 'Roy Barth Tennis Center.'" There was a plaque for me, too. I couldn't believe it. I hugged Colleen. My legs felt weak as I walked to the podium to shake Roger's outstretched hand. Now *this* was a Kiawah name change I could be happy about.

Within a few days a new "Roy Barth Tennis Center" sign replaced the familiar "East Beach" sign outside the pro shop. I laughed as I thought, "Oh great, now if anyone has a complaint, they will know who to ask for by name."

Months later, a father and young son came off the courts toward the pro shop. The son took his time reading the sign.

"Dad," he asked, "who is Roy Barth?"

"This tennis center is named for him. That's him right over there," the father said, pointing toward me as I stood behind the shop counter.

"You mean he's still alive?" the boy asked.

Yes, I am still alive.

Unfortunately, my friend and colleague of 30 years, Tommy Cuthbert, was not. Tommy died of non-smoker lung cancer in June 2006, just five months after the 30-year award. He was 58. He and Beverly sat at that luncheon knowing his legacy was unfolding in front of him as he was dying. I believe Kiawah would have honored him posthumously, but I'm so glad he had even a short time to enjoy this milestone honor. Colleen and Beverly remain close friends.

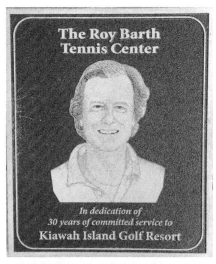

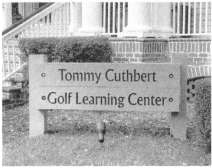

Without Tommy, I was officially the lone second-longest-serving Kiawah employee, behind M.C. Heyward. That's a milestone I really didn't want, at least not that way. Not long after Tommy died, TennisResortsOnline.com, the popular, comprehensive, web-based resource for tennis vacations, ranked Kiawah Island Golf Resort the "No. 1 Tennis Resort in the *World*." It was bittersweet success. I know the first person who would have come over to the tennis courts to congratulate me would have been Tommy.

CHAPTER THIRTY-FIVE

Honor the Role Your Parents
Played in Your Success

USTA "Family of the Year" Award

The Roy Barth Tennis Center. I was proud to have my name out front, especially my last name. My extended family was a significant part of my success at Kiawah, both in their unwavering support of my efforts, and in their own commitment to the game of tennis.

The USTA noticed that too. That year, we were named the "2006 Ralph W. Westcott USTA Family of the Year."

> *This honor is awarded annually to the family who in recent years has done the most to promote amateur tennis, primarily on a volunteer basis. All members of the family should participate in some way, either as players or by offering their services in running programs or tournaments or in junior development activities. The selection of recipients is made by the USTA Awards Committee from nominations submitted by the 17 USTA Sections. The Award is presented at the Annual Meeting & Conference.*

The Annual Meeting and Conference that year was in Tucson, Arizona, in January 2007.

I was there, but my success as a player, coach, teacher, and past district president was just a small part of this collective award. I could not have been prouder to see my family honored this way. My *whole* family.

Colleen was there. Lucy Garvin had taught Colleen how to run a tournament desk and Colleen was an integral part of running Kiawah's junior tournament each year. And if there was a separate award just for the number of miles any parent logged driving children to and from practices and tournaments, Colleen would have won that too.

Jonathan was there. He had been working with me at Kiawah since 1993, first just in the summers and then full-time when he graduated from the College of Charleston. In 2006, Jonathan was Kiawah's assistant tournament director, and he and I were ranked No. 5 in the country as a father-and-son team for having reached the quarterfinals in three national father-son tournaments together. In 2004, Jonathan married Meredith Moore, an accomplished tennis player who played No. 1 singles and doubles at Furman University and whose team won its conference title all four years she was there. Together Jonathan and Meredith won the national Husband-and-Wife Indoor Doubles Championship titles in 2005 and 2006. Meredith was there too.

Sandon was there. He attended Clemson University in South Carolina and played varsity tennis on their conference-winning team. He also earned himself a national men's amateur ranking in singles and in doubles. In 2002, Sandon was the assistant coach of the men's and women's tennis teams at the College of Charleston.

My sister Patty was there. Even though Patty, who was retired and living in Newport Beach, California, had given up tennis at age 15 after winning a national junior title, she still deserved to be part of the Roy Barth Family Tennis Award. Had she not won a few tennis trophies when she was ten, eight-year-old me might never have been jealous enough to want to win trophies too. Patty's husband, Don Phillips, who had encouraged Colleen and me to try Kiawah for two years back in 1976, was there too.

Father Thomas Dove, our friend and priest, was there. He married Colleen and me in Los Angeles in 1971. We consider him family.

My mother was there. At 87 years old, my mother flew from San Diego to Tucson to be part of her family's celebration. She would never have missed it, although I'm glad she could fit it in her busy schedule. At age 80, she had reached the final of the USTA National 80s Doubles Tournament, and in 2003, at age 83, she and her friend Jane Howard won the gold medal in the Senior Olympics in Salt Lake City. She enjoyed good health and competitive bridge games and had only stopped playing tennis within the last year.

I suggested to my mother in advance that she make some notes in case, as the matriarch of the family, she wished to say a few words. I hoped she would. When we were seated, she told me she had left her notes in her room but, since the Family Award was the last award on the program, she had plenty of time to write new ones. When she did get up to speak, she was in her element. She put her elbows up on the lectern, moved the microphone into place, and proceeded to thank everyone for everything — from Franklin Johnson, the president of the USTA, who my mother knew from his childhood days in San Diego, for "growing into such a nice young man," to the banquet facility staff for the food and the beautiful nametags. She told me coming to Tucson for this award was the best time she ever had.

Sadly, my father could only be there in spirit. He died in 2001, at age 84, two years after having double bypass heart surgery. But his legacy was well represented. He played tennis his whole life, taught my mother, my sister, and me to play, and was a lifelong staple of the San Diego tennis community. I loved playing in the father-son tournaments with him and, as much as he would have loved for us to win a title together, I think he'd have been even more gratified to know that, just like him, I was lucky enough to play father-son tournaments as the dad too. He introduced us to the sport that fulfilled us individually and brought us distinction as a family. In my remarks, I dedicated my Family Award to him.

The USTA committee probably thought it was awarding three

generations of Barths, but there were four generations present. At that award ceremony, Jonathan's wife, Meredith, was pregnant with their first child.

USTA 2006 Family of the Year Award
Father Dove, Don Phillips, Patty Phillips (my sister), Sandon, my mother Pat,
me, Colleen, Jonathan, and Meredith. (photo courtesy USTA)

That award brought my whole bi-coastal family together for the last time. In December of 2008, my mother had lunch with her sister, as she often did, and later that afternoon had a massive stroke. Her friend Jane Howard called to tell me. She died two weeks later.

I think of my mother as extraordinary. She never met anyone she didn't like, which is astonishing considering how many partners and opponents she had on the tennis courts and all the years she served as president of the Balboa Tennis Club. She was always a positive person in spite of the sadness I know she felt at never fulfilling her desire to be a teacher. Years earlier, the San Diego public school system rejected her application because she suffered from slight hearing loss in one ear. I feel bad for the many children who missed having her as their teacher.

In her later years, my mother crafted beautiful delicate angel-shaped pins out of tiny seashells and gave them out at church to anyone who said something nice about someone else. The members of the church called her the "Angel Lady." At the funeral, the ladies from the church gave angel pins to everyone in attendance, which included my high school friends Don Parker and Pete Kofoed. I still have my pin.

With my mother's passing, I became the patriarch at age 61. Jonathan and Meredith had a one-year-old daughter, Madelyn, and I found, as many first-time grandparents must, a new capacity to love another human being. I got the daily reports about everything she did and how brilliant she was, and I was overwhelmed with the joy of watching my son be a father. Madelyn represented the fourth generation of tennis-playing Barths and the second generation of Barth kids to be raised on the Kiawah courts.

I recognize how fortunate I am to have had loving parents, and to have a sister, wife, children, and grandchildren I adore. Most important to me is that they know they are what make my accomplishments matter.

USTA 2006 Family of the Year Award (photos courtesy USTA and USTA Southern Section)

CHAPTER THIRTY-SIX

Treat Your Partner and
Opponent with Equal Respect

Vying for Space Under Golf and Next to the Pool

In 2009, I had been at Kiawah for 33 years, just more than half my life, and as the expression goes, "the more things change, the more things stay the same." The resort division was being restructured again and I was about to get another new boss. Roger Warren and Mr. Goodwin, the owner who had wisely taken tennis out from under the golf umbrella in 1993, put tennis back in the golf division in 2009. Rather than report directly to Roger, as I had for four years, I would now be reporting to Brian Gerard, the director of golf.

Brian had been at Kiawah since 1986, when he was hired right from college as a cart attendant. Over the years he worked his way up to be head golf pro at Turtle Point, then head pro at the Ocean Course, and then director of golf. Brian admitted he didn't know anything about tennis, but he looked forward to learning.

Golf and tennis are no more the same business model than they are the same game. They are both played by striking a ball with pinpoint accuracy and accelerating through the swing, and they both have "inventory" — tee times and court time — that is lost if not sold, but golf will always bring in more revenue than tennis, it will always take up more space than tennis, and it will always garner more resources and attention at a club or resort that offers both. I never understood the management model that has the golf operations overseeing the tennis operations, yet there I was again.

As a stepchild of golf, tennis seemed insignificant, but I'd been in this position before and my tennis program was still the No. 1 tennis resort in the world according to TennisResortsOnline.com. Tennis players knew we were doing something right. I taught Brian that while golf makes its money from tee times, tennis makes its money from instruction, meetings, camps, and tournaments. I continued to improve the tennis operation by looking for opportunities to attract more of these group events, including bringing a national sales meeting for Wilson Racquet Sports and the USTA's national leadership meeting to The Sanctuary Hotel during the slow season. We also increased participation in the five Ladies Tennis Weekend packages during January and February to over 200 women.

The tennis operation was busy. As much as I still marveled at how I was managing two busy tennis centers, I remembered how much easier I had it just managing one. Not only did I used to have a consolidated staff, my maintenance equipment was only in one place, I purchased for only one retail outlet, and I didn't spend valuable time traveling between two centers. With two tennis facilities, the resort guests often arrived at the "other" location for lessons, clinics, and tournaments. I learned a valuable lesson from this thinking though: take a minute to be grateful for what you have because it could always be worse.

Kiawah's buildings and amenities were in constant motion. In all my years at Kiawah, I learned a lot about capital investment, building inventory, and predicting future demand. As buildings age, they can only be renovated so many times before the numbers support complete replacement. At the same time, demand for amenities changes and the resort needed to adapt to stay relevant. When compared to The Sanctuary, the original Kiawah Island Inn seemed dated and unappealing. Its gardens and rocking chair porches were guest favorites but the hotel itself, which was built in the 70s, wasn't old enough to be nostalgic and wasn't new enough to earn five stars. Mr. Goodwin decided to close the Inn along with its two restaurants and older-style pools to make way for new development. This change would mean the guests who rented villas in West Beach would no longer have a nearby place to swim.

To preserve the appeal of the West Beach rental villas, Roger Warren, with the approval of Mr. Goodwin, replaced four of the West Beach tennis courts with a new pool and moved the recreation and pool administration into the newly outfitted West Beach Tennis *and Pool* Center. Yikes! It was a little crowded in there. We lost courts, retail space, half the "desk," and a lot of revenue. But we managed. I couldn't believe I longed for the two shops to operate the way they had before. I was especially fortunate that Jonathan was the head professional of the West Beach tennis operation. He managed the inconvenience admirably.

I was proud of how Jonathan had taken to the job overall. He handled everything well. His business talent was marketing and communication; he's naturally outgoing and approachable, and people like him. The financial analysis and number-tracking did not come as easily to him, but he worked hard to master those skills.

Jonathan and I both understood that within the resort, and especially during the recent changes, the golf department, the recreation department, Mr. Goodwin, Brian Gerard, and others were not our "opponents." We were all "players," vying to find our place in the ever-evolving Kiawah equation. Just like on the pro tour where my partner one day was my opponent the next, success at the resort — a microcosm of the larger business world — demanded concession, cooperation, and mutual respect among the players.

As busy as he was managing West Beach, Jonathan still found time to enjoy playing and he kept his game in top shape. In 2009, he and I won a national father-son title in the National 60-and-Over Father-Son Championship in Sarasota, Florida. I finally won a father-son title — a National USTA title! My father would have really loved that.

That year, Jonathan and Meredith had a second daughter, Mckenzie. I was a proud "Pee-Paw" of two wonderful girls.

Spending time with Madelyn and Mckenzie

CHAPTER THIRTY-SEVEN

Develop Character:
It's More Important than Winning

California on My Mind

Neither Colleen nor I pressured Jonathan to play tennis, teach tennis, or manage a tennis operation at Kiawah or anywhere, any more than we discouraged Sandon from doing the same. Sandon was a talented player at Clemson, part of the team that won the Atlantic Coast Conference title in 1997, and an excellent assistant coach at the College of Charleston. He also dreamed of playing in Europe and worked hard to make that dream come true. He and Ryan Bauer, his friend and teammate from Clemson, qualified for the International Tennis Federation's "Futures" pro events and played in France, England, and Scotland.

In 2009, Sandon married Sanaz Ghazal, a Harvard graduate who played on Harvard's tennis team for four years. Sanaz attended Yale Medical School, did her residency at Massachusetts General Hospital and Brigham and Women's Hospital in Boston, and returned to Yale for her fellowship. Sanaz is a practicing obstetrician and gynecologist and specializes in reproductive endocrinology and fertility.

Sandon still plays tennis, but he chose a non-tennis career. After Clemson, Sandon received a Master's in Public Administration from the College of Charleston and now works for Medtronic, selling medical supplies internationally. Sandon is an active Clemson alumnus who contributed to the development of the new indoor-outdoor tennis complex. Clemson acknowledged Sandon's generosity by naming the new outside court No. 3 after him.

Court 3 at Clemson: The Sandon Barth Court. Dedicated in 2018.

Sandon and Sanaz live in Irvine, California. The West Coast!

The day Sandon told me he and Sanaz were settling in Southern California was the day I gained a newfound respect for my parents. Sandon was moving 2,500 miles away from Charleston, away from Colleen and me, away from his brother, and away from where he grew up. He would not be a presence in our everyday lives, and he would miss watching his nieces grow up. Selfishly, I was sad.

But I knew what I had to do: the same thing my parents did in 1976 when I chose Charleston over Southern California. My parents never made me feel bad for settling on the East Coast, but now I know how much character it took for them not to express their disappointment. They would have loved to be a daily presence in our sons' lives. I needed to show Sandon and Sanaz the same consideration. I was happy for them but sorry for the many miles between us.

In 2010, Colleen and I flew to California to prepare to sell my mother's house — my childhood home — on Cooper Street in San Diego. I took a break from moving furniture and went to Morley Field.

This wasn't the first time I'd been back there. After my father died, my mother, sister, and I dedicated a bench at the courts with his name on it in his memory. Whenever I visited my mother or went back after she died to sort through boxes of memories stored in the basement, I found solace in a few minutes at my childhood tennis courts. I didn't take my racquet; the visits were not about playing. I'd walk around, get lunch at the concession stand, sit on the "Robert Barth" bench, soak in the California sunshine, watch the players, and enjoy the memories. It was peaceful. Occasionally, I'd even see someone I knew from the old days, one of the "regulars" who never left.

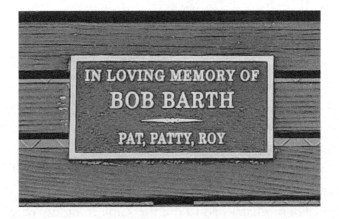

Plaque on the Bob Barth bench at Morley Field
(photo courtesy Geoff Griffin)

That day in 2010 offered a chance meeting I'll always cherish. I arrived at the courts, got my hamburger, and sat down on the Barth Bench. In the distance I saw a spirited men's doubles game and immediately recognized one of the players. It was David Sanderlin, Johnny's older brother. David lived about 25 minutes away and told me he usually played closer to his house, rarely at Morley Field.

I knew that his mother, Owenita, who had taken Johnny and me to Chattanooga on the Sky King train in 1960, had passed away in 1995, but I didn't know if his father was still living. He was. George Sanderlin was 95 and still lived in the same house in Granite Hills where Johnny grew up. I hadn't seen him since Johnny's funeral in 1963. I wanted to, especially just after Johnny died, but my parents thought it would be too hard on his family to see me. And since Johnny and I hadn't gone to the same school and we lived a half-hour apart, I was unlikely to just run into them. And then I left San Diego to go to college. I did send them a Christmas card every year though.

I'd thought about George over the years; running into David that day was a blessing. It might be my last chance to see his father. I called George to ask if Colleen and I could visit. As soon as I arrived at the house, all the memories of my friendship with Johnny came flooding back: the asphalt court where we practiced, the miniature golf course he built, the posters of our tennis heroes on Johnny's bedroom wall, and his many trophies, including the one we won together in Chattanooga.

"I wish Johnny was here to see you," George said. The sadness had never left him.

I was 63 years old and I felt a lump in my throat. What a wonderful friend I lost all those years ago.

I've often wondered what Johnny's life might have been. We may have won more national junior doubles titles, we would have gone to UCLA together, and we might have turned pro at the same time. Johnny may have stayed on the tour longer than I had and maybe gotten further in the major tournaments. He may have even won a few. Or, better yet, we could have won a major together. Maybe he would have chosen a non-tennis career. He liked to draw plans of houses so maybe he would have been an architect. Or even a math professor. He would have been successful in whatever he did. I'm sure we'd still be friends in our 60s though, and we'd be happy about each other's life choices. I imagined Johnny coming with his wife and kids to visit Colleen and me in Charleston, where he and I would partner in a doubles' exhibition at Kiawah. I would introduce him as my oldest and best friend. One can always make new friends — and I have — but it's impossible to make new old friends.

He was the best.

Visiting with George Sanderlin in 2010
in the same house where Johnny grew up

CHAPTER THIRTY-EIGHT

Benefit from Your
Strengths and Weaknesses

The End of My Playing Days

I returned to Charleston and to Kiawah feeling a little nostalgic. Selling my parents' house and seeing 95-year-old George Sanderlin reminded me how long ago those San Diego childhood days were. Thank goodness my wonderful and sometimes sad experiences there — especially learning to appreciate my strengths and staying positive when weakened by illness — would always be with me. I was going to need those lessons yet again.

When PTR founder and president Dennis Van der Meer retired in 2010 for health reasons, a nine-person PTR governing board was established; my good friend Jorge Andrew was one of the original nine members. In the board's second year, I was invited to join. At my first board meeting I was nominated and then voted in as treasurer. For a guy who struggled with economic theory in college and didn't understand the budget he was responsible for when he started at Kiawah, I was able to bring my years of on-the-job budgeting education to help streamline the PTR budget process. *No one is more surprised than me that financial analysis turned out to be a strength!* After five years as treasurer, I was nominated and then voted in as president of the PTR.

My increased volunteer responsibilities for the PTR were well timed because I was about to be sidelined from the court. I was playing singles against Langdon Brockington, a good friend and one of my teaching pros, when my left leg felt weak. An MRI revealed spinal stenosis: nerve damage due to compression in the L4-L5 vertebrae. I made an appointment to see Dr. Patel, the surgeon who did my brain surgery six years earlier. Dr. Patel told me he could do a partial laminectomy to move the vertebrae away from the compressed spinal column, but there was no guarantee that the nerves would regenerate. I had the surgery.

A year later, I was back in Dr. Patel's operating room for him to correct a cervical spine issue. This time two discs in my neck were pressing against my spinal cord. Dr. Patel said he could ease the pressure by removing the flattened discs. He also told me that without the surgery, further injury to my neck — from a car accident, for example — would most likely leave me paralyzed. With the surgery, I'd be less vulnerable.

I was lucky to recover from both surgeries, but I had to accept that the wear and tear my body endured my whole career was catching up with me. I was fortunate not to have been hobbled by injuries as a junior, in college, on the pro tour, or while teaching, but all that high impact finally took a toll. Undaunted, I recovered and returned to work. Dr. Patel seemed happy with my progress.

With those surgeries behind me, I was able to enjoy some moments I would have hated to miss.

In 2013, I was inducted into the San Diego Tennis Hall of Fame, which is housed at the new Balboa Park Tennis Club. I am honored to be celebrated there alongside Maureen Connolly, Wilbur Folsom, Les Stoefen, Pancho Segura, Michael Chang, Dodo Cheney, and others. In my remarks at the ceremony, I recalled the wonderful memories of my years playing tennis with my parents and sister at Morley Field and Balboa Park. Those courts provided hours of joy for me and my family, and every lesson I learned there is part of who I am as a person, not just as a player. I also recognized my high school friend Don Parker as well as my old friend and opponent Carlos Carriedo. I joked that I never forgave Carlos for beating me in the 16s Hard-Court Nationals in 1963. That got a big laugh.

That year I also served as vice chair of the USTA Davis Cup, Fed Cup, Olympic and Paralympic committees, and I served on the board of the PTR.

But the best part of 2013 was the birth of Sandon and Sanaz's first child, my grandson, Navid. What a cute kid. I especially treasure the pictures I'm in with Sandon and Navid. Three generations of Barth men. In those moments, I miss my father the most.

A few years later, Sandon and Sanaz had a second child, a daughter, Mina. Ever since 1976, I've wished California and South Carolina were not so far apart, but never as much as when I had grandchildren on the West Coast. I love Sandon and Sanaz and I'm so proud of the life they have created for their family, but selfishly I would prefer they live closer to the rest of us.

Sanaz, Sandon, Mina, and Navid

In 2015, I was presented with the USTA Southern's highest award — the Jacobs Bowl — which honors a volunteer who has exhibited outstanding service to USTA Southern. More than the award, which was extremely flattering, 2015 also marked my 30th year as a volunteer for both the USTA and the PTR. Not only are these organizations dedicated to excellence in competing in and teaching the game I love, they offered me the privilege of working side-by-side with incredibly talented individuals.

The "Four Musketeers" (clockwise from top right): Lucy Garvin as president of the USTA, Dan Santorum as CEO of the PTR, Jorge Andrew as president of the PTR, and me as (former) president of the USTA South Carolina Tennis Association.

Just as my position with the USTA Southern District came with its share of pressure-filled challenges, so did my PTR leadership role.

After more than 30 years of attending the yearly conferences and playing in the PTR tennis tournaments, and five years of serving on the board as treasurer, I was installed in 2015 as the president of the PTR.

The USTA (the governing body of tennis in the United States) and the USPTA and PTR (the two teaching certification organizations) have always enjoyed an amicable relationship. After all, they are all in the business of growing the popularity and maintaining the high standards of the game. Yet their overlapping interests, combined with their distinct differences, has led to large and small contentious moments driven by power, politics, and money. Why should the tennis industry be any different from any other industry? The relationship among these three entities was called into question during my tenure.

In 2015, the USTA proposed more stringent certification standards for all teaching professionals in the United States and offered the USPTA and PTR the designation of official "USTA Accredited Association" as incentive to adopt the new guidelines. The USTA even proposed merging the USPTA and the PTR into one entity to better roll out and manage the new certification requirements. Each organization has its own ideas about who this would benefit and whose culture would be enhanced or compromised. There was no consensus and discussions were often contentious.

This proposal tested my leadership. I am generally in favor of exploring change to keep current, weighing the pros (literally!) and cons, doing a cost-benefit analysis, engaging consultants and lawyers, and considering the effect on the individuals involved — in this case, many thousands of members. Sometimes though, after all the research, the best decision is not to make the change at all, or to only agree to some of what was proposed. This was our resolution.

The PTR and the USPTA endorsed the USTA's mission to raise the standards of teaching professionals — including more hours of internship and workshops — even if it might cost each organization a few members, but the groups opted not to merge. I am pleased that even through the passion-filled arguments from all parties, the end-result — which everyone agreed would be beneficial — was a higher standard of all certified teaching professionals in the United States. These changes are still in the works. Current members will be grandfathered in but, starting in 2021, new members of either association will be subject to the more stringent certification requirements.

Through these often-stressful negotiations, I again found myself relying on the strength of the lessons from my playing days. I kept my emotions under control, I respected the position of each side, I stayed focused, remained positive, and never bowed out. And I enjoyed the team dynamic of working with my talented colleagues toward a mutually acceptable goal — just like in doubles.

Even after all the years of development at Kiawah, the quaint roads on and off the island have remained pretty much unchanged. I have driven the same 17 miles on these roads to and from work for over 40 years. Although Bohicket Road is a four-lane road for a few of the miles, Main Road is still only a two-lane road, with no room to pull over for most of my commute. If I ever get behind a slow-moving vehicle, or the car in front of me is waiting to make a left turn, there is nothing I can do but wait. These are minutes — maybe hours — of my life I will never get back.

One afternoon in 2016, I left bright sunny Kiawah Island and drove north toward home. The sky in front of me started to turn shades of deep purple and I knew I was driving into a Lowcountry storm. These storms come up quickly — usually late in the afternoon — can be quite violent for a few minutes, and then move on like nothing ever happened.

A mile or so later, the rain was coming down so hard I couldn't see the road. I wanted to pull over and wait it out but there was nowhere safe to do so. I slowed to about 15 miles per hour, focusing only on the tail lights of the car in front of me. Colleen called to see if I had left work yet. I answered the phone — keeping both hands gripped to the wheel — and told her I was right in the middle of the storm but I was fine. The guy in front of me slowed and signaled to make a left turn. I slowed and stopped along with him but the guy coming up behind me at 35 miles per hour didn't see me stop.

"I've been hit!" I told Colleen.

Colleen called Jonathan, who was still on the island. And then she called the police. The man who hit me banged on my window and asked if I was OK. He was soaking wet but appeared unharmed.

"I think so," I said, moving my arms and legs enough to be sure I still could. My neck felt sore but I was not in pain.

The police wrote up the accident report and Jonathan took me home.

Over the next few weeks, my neck got progressively stiffer. I went from teaching with a stiff and painful neck, to not teaching at all, to not being able to get out of bed. I made an appointment to see Dr. Don Johnson, an orthopedic surgeon and founder of the Southeastern Spine Institute in Charleston. He needed to sedate me so I could turn my neck comfortably to get into the proper position for the x-ray.

"Roy, this does not look good. You have a blood clot in your C2-C3 vertebrae, close to the brain stem, and you need to have this looked at by a specialist. I want you to see the best neurosurgeon in Charleston. He's at MUSC. His name is Dr. Sunil Patel."

I laughed. The same Dr. Patel who did my brain surgery in 2004 and my back surgery in 2010? The same Dr. Patel who told me in 2011 I needed cervical spine surgery because without it the impact from a car accident could paralyze me? (Good call!) I wondered if he had a "frequent surgery" card where the tenth surgery is free. I had to be getting close.

"Nice to see you, my friend!" Dr. Patel said with a big smile and strong handshake. We discussed my x-ray and MRI. This time Dr. Patel was not suggesting surgery. Rather, he proposed we wait a month or so to see if the blood clot would dissolve on its own. In the meantime, he recommended I do some low-impact exercise to increase flexibility, like walking laps in the pool or riding a recumbent bike. The blood clot did eventually dissolve on its own, and I was able to move my neck again without pain, but only very slowly. That was the good news.

The bad news was that my tennis-playing days were over. I couldn't run or turn my head fast enough to get into position during a live point, but I could still hit balls and teach, with some modifications. Rather than lead intensive drill sessions, I did the Stroke-of-the-Day clinic, which didn't require me to cover so much of the court. I could break down the details of each tennis stroke, which I really enjoy, and help students improve. Sometimes even a small modification can make a big difference in someone's game.

Teaching "leverage" in a forehand Stroke-of-the-Day clinic
(photo courtesy Kiawah Island Resort)

I don't think only aging athletes regret the degenerative process their bodies experience, but maybe it's sooner or more pronounced when you've spent your whole life pushing the limits of your physicality. Recognizing that your body will never again work in the same way you depended on it to make a living is a harsh reality. But my lifelong commitment to being in shape, healthful eating, limited alcohol, and decent sleep allowed me to play professionally, enjoy teaching and play for fun, and likely helped me survive and recover from these serious health issues. I'm just thankful to still be able to be out on the court.

Two thousand sixteen was also the year Colleen retired from Mason Prep. After 30 years and many roles, most recently as a teacher's aide for fifth through eighth grades, she was ready to step down. Colleen has always been an enthusiastic multi-tasker and dedicated herself to the school and its many programs from the time our boys were little. *Are they really grown now with children of their own?* In her retirement, Colleen has renewed her love of fitness and gardening, and she and our lawn have never been in better shape.

Even without Colleen, there are still Barths at Mason Prep. My granddaughters Madelyn and Mckenzie are students, and my daughter-in-law Meredith is on the faculty. Meredith teaches science and physical education, sharing her passion for learning and sports while stressing the importance of teamwork and communication. And Colleen does return to Mason Prep occasionally, but just to join the afternoon carpool line to pick up Madelyn and Mckenzie and take them to their after-school activities. I'm sure they love their time with "Mimi."

After five major surgeries and a serious car accident, I feel fortunate to have developed new strengths: I'm happy with my pared-down teaching curriculum, I've learned to like walking laps in the pool and exercising indoors at the fitness center, I appreciate the slower pace of my responsibilities, and I'm teaching my grandchildren to dance. Really! In the late 1950s when I was 12 and Patty was 14, she made me practice dancing the California version of the Carolina Shag with her, and I've loved to dance ever since. Anyone in my family can teach the kids to play tennis, but I'm the only one they will dance with.

And I must stay healthy. Sandon and Sanaz had a third child in February 2020 — my fifth grandchild, Kamran Ghazal Barth — and he too will need to learn to dance.

Sandon and his family in 2020: Navid, Sanaz, baby Kamran, Sandon, and Mina

CHAPTER THIRTY-NINE

Respect the Past
but Focus on the Present and the Future

How the Game has Changed in My Lifetime

One of the many gratifying aspects of my long and varied career in tennis is that others seek my perspective and opinions on the game. I am often asked 1) whether I like how tennis has changed over the years, and 2) who I think would win if players in their primes from different generations played each other. My first thought is that the game is fundamentally the same it has always been and my life lessons seem timeless. But the question is valid; technology and style of play, fitness, prize money, opportunity, and the declining interest in doubles have decidedly changed *parts* of the game, making the hypothetical "era-vs-era" match question interesting but impossible to answer.

Technology and Style of Play

When I started playing, my parents brought me a junior Dunlop Maxply wooden racquet. There were not a lot of choices. All racquets were made of laminated wood, had a head size of approximately 85-98 sq. in., and were strung with nylon. (The junior racquets were two inches shorter and a little lighter than the adult wood racquets.) By today's standards, the adult wooden racquets were heavy and not stiff enough to create or absorb a lot of pace.

My first racquet: a Junior Dunlop Maxply. After I outgrew this racquet it got passed around to my cousins. When everyone outgrew it, my aunt gave it to my mother, who had it framed for me. It still has my name on it.

In 1967, Wilson introduced the revolutionary T2000 racquet. It was made of steel, which made it lighter and stiffer than wooden racquets; it had a longer throat and a smaller head (76 sq. in.) than wooden racquets; and its strings wrapped around the metal frame — as opposed to threaded through a wooden frame — which created a trampoline effect and allowed balls to "fly." While Jimmy Connors had tremendous success playing with the T2000, others found its accuracy unpredictable.

Yet the idea that new racquet materials could be engineered so players could use less energy to swing faster and hit harder inspired racquet manufacturers to keep inventing. What emerged was graphite, a composite of carbon (80 percent) wrapped around fiberglass (20 percent) to give the racquet stiffness and power without adding weight.

In 1969, Arthur Ashe started working with Head to create the graphite Edge racquet, and the next year Ashe won the Australian Open playing with it. In 1975, Ashe won Wimbledon again using a newer version of that Head racquet named for him: the Head Arthur Ashe Competition 2. This racquet had an iconic, metallic, flat-profile design. I've heard of tennis enthusiasts who still have these racquets; they don't play with them anymore but they just can't seem to part with them either.

Also in the early 70s, the Wilson Sporting Goods Company developed a line of graphite Pro Staff racquets. Chris Evert and Pete Sampras won numerous major titles with these.

In 1978, sixteen-year-old Pam Shriver beat No. 1-seed Martina Navratilova to reach the final of the US Open playing with the over-sized (107 sq. in.) green-trim aluminum racquet made by Prince Sports. Shriver lost to Chris Evert, but the racquet was a winner among club and league players who found the larger sweet spot quite forgiving and capable of generating considerable power.

By 1980, most new racquets — in all head sizes — were made from graphite combined with other space-age materials including Kevlar, titanium, and fiberglass, and were designed to make lighter, more powerful racquets. Today's racquets are just newer iterations of that same technology.

Over the years, players have not only used these scientifically engineered racquets to hit harder, but they have also used them — in conjunction with a modest-to-extreme grip change — to alter how the ball spins off the racquet, specifically to hit with "topspin." This is a significant change in the game over my lifetime.

Topspin is forward ball rotation generated by swinging low to high and allowing the strings to "brush up" on the back of the ball. A well-hit topspin ground stroke clears the net comfortably, drops deep into the court, bounces, and takes off toward the back fence. The harder a ball is hit with topspin, the harder it is to return.

I was taught to hold my junior Dunlop Maxply wooden racquet with the "eastern" grip — as though I was "shaking hands with it" — and hit "flat" (no spin) ground strokes in a low-to-high swing path. The emphasis was on control, not power. To volley, I turned my grip slightly counter-clockwise to the "continental" grip, and counter-clockwise even further to the "eastern backhand" grip to hit the "flat" one-handed backhand. This was pretty standard for the equipment and style of play at the time.

It was possible for us to hit topspin with our heavy wooden racquets and our eastern grips, but we couldn't generate much power. The same shot today hit with a lighter, stiffer, graphite racquet is much faster and has significantly more power but, since the court is still the same size, the ball can easily fly long. To control the forehand topspin with these new racquets, players 1) rotate their grip clockwise to a "semi-western" position and sometimes even further to a "western" grip position (counter-clockwise for left-handed players) and 2) swing low-to-high with considerably more racquet head speed. The pronounced topspin they create brings the hard-hit ball down into the court. The strings and strokes in my day just couldn't create such dramatic ball movement or absorb that power.

Björn Borg and Guillermo Vilas embraced this style of play in the 70s. They preferred to stay in the backcourt and generate heavy forehand and backhand topspin ground strokes, content to engage in long rallies and hit penetrating topspin winners. As they continued to win major titles, the world's coaches started to teach this style to juniors.

I think juniors who learn this "power and heavy topspin" style focus too much on ball-striking at the expense of strategy, finesse, and the foundation points of the game. I prefer an all-court player willing to employ different speeds, spins, and strategies to win points from the backcourt as well as at the net.

"Analytics," the study of data and statistics, could use the same balance. In my playing days, I only saw matches "charted" a few times by a player's friend or father sitting in the stands counting the number of first serves in, double faults, and forehand errors. As a touring contract professional on the WCT, I created my own form of analytics: my "mini-goals." I made priorities of attacking the net off every short ball and keeping my feet in constant motion, and I tracked my success rates for both. *And I did it all in my head — while I was playing!* Today analytics are tracked electronically and studied by everyone. Teams of coaches, statisticians, agents, broadcasters — and even chips embedded in racquets — collect, collate, and analyze a player's every move and match-specific trends.

Are analytics progress? Only if used with the player's natural tennis instincts during a match. Once the match starts, it is the player — not even the most advanced statistics — who hits the ball and makes the in-match strategy decisions. The sports term "analysis paralysis" is relevant; overthinking in the heat of competition can cause a player to "choke" or tighten up rather than be relaxed and go with sound tennis instincts. Fortunately, the game hasn't changed so much that the human element has been eliminated.

I think the best advancement in technology, however, is the "Hawk-eye" electronic line-calling system. High-tech cameras record every shot from every angle and synthesize the images to produce one clearly-defined flight path and one precise point of impact(!) with the ground. Hawkeye is lauded not only for its accuracy, but also for having greatly reduced the number of animated, momentum-shifting, match-delaying discussions between players and umpires over line call disputes. I have been the recipient of some really bad line calls in my career. I think Hawkeye would have helped me tremendously.

Fitness

In a 2013 interview in the *Sports Business Journal*, Donald Dell, former player, Davis Cup captain, and current sports agent and lawyer, was asked, "What has changed the most in tennis?" His answer:

> *The athletes in tennis are much more physical. You take the top five players ... if it rains at the US Open, they are in the gym — men and women. In my day, we'd go to a movie. McEnroe, Gerulaitis: Those guys, they wouldn't know a gym if they walked by one.*

Although today the top players would be playing under roof when it rains at the US Open, Dell was absolutely right about the fitness part. I never experienced the off-court fitness intensity of today's players. At UCLA, Hall of Fame Coach Glenn Bassett had us spend the first half hour of tennis team practice stretching, running sprints, and doing agility drills. Then after two hours of play-action drills and match play, he would have us run two miles. That was the hardest I ever worked out in my life. In the pros, I stayed in shape doing my own tennis-specific, on-court drills when I practiced, and I played a lot of physically demanding matches. Some tournament clubhouses had gyms with free weights and basic treadmills. I don't know if anyone used them; I never did.

I am currently in favor of enhanced off-court training. If a player isn't already fit enough to tough out a grueling five-set match, off-court training may make the difference. Yet I am puzzled by how many injuries I see, especially among junior players. Are they working their bodies too hard? Are the junior coaches pushing their players to emulate the professional players? Today's game may be more physical than the game I played, but so much more is known about physiology and conditioning. It seems there should be fewer injuries.

Prize Money, Endorsements, and Expenses

Perhaps the most dramatic change in tennis since I played on the tour is the increase in prize money. When I lost to Roy Emerson in the fourth round of the US Open in 1969, I picked up my check for $1,000. It barely covered my hotel bill for the ten nights I stayed in New York City, let alone my air transportation back to California. In 2019, a player who reached the fourth round earned a check for $163,000.

In 1973, I took Björn Borg to five sets on a blistering hot day in the first round at the US Open and lost. My prize money for the effort was $100. In 2019, a first-round loss at the Open earned $58,000. The year I played Borg, John Newcombe won the singles tournament and earned $25,000. In 2019, singles winner Novak Djokovic earned $3,850,000.

Today's prize money isn't even a player's only source of income.

Endorsement deals for clothing, shoes, and racquets are quite lucrative, as are appearance fees and commercials. In my day, Stan Smith had contracts with Adidas clothing and shoes and Wilson racquets. Arthur Ashe had contracts with Le Coq Sportif clothing and Head racquets. The other Top 10 players at the time also had clothing, shoe, and racquet deals, but they were miniscule — *I mean miniscule* — compared with today's arrangements.

Even with all of the jaw-dropping earnings, the business end of today's tennis career comes at a price, literally. Today's pro players are like companies with a long list of employees to pay, including assistants, coaches, trainers, and agents. They also enter into contracts, hire lawyers, and are obligated to make appearances and maintain a presence on social media. The prize money depletes quickly. For the world's top players, there is still plenty left over and it's a great deal for those who are talented enough to get there. But for the lower-ranked and younger players whose expenses are substantial and whose income is dependent on results, this stage of a tennis life can be very challenging.

Are these players better off than I was? Hard to say. My dream was to play professional tennis and travel the world, and I was good enough to earn the money to cover my travel expenses. That was the life I chose. For all that needs to happen behind the scenes today before players can walk onto the court prepared to play, much more depends on their substantial prize money than depended on my meager income.

Wimbledon Prize money, 1970, when £1 equalled about $2.40.

PRIZE MONEY

EVENT 1   The Gentlemen's Singles Championship
Total prize money £22,700

The Winner	£3,000
The Runner-up	£1,500
The losers of the Semi-Finals each	£800
The losers of the Quarter-Finals each	£450
The losers of the Fourth Round each	£220
The losers of the Third Round each	£165
The losers of the Second Round each	£125
The losers of the First Round each	£100

EVENT 2   The Gentlemen's Doubles Championship
Total prize money £3,200

The Winners	Per Pair £1,000
The Runners-up	£800
The losers of the Semi-Finals	£400
The losers of the Quarter-Finals	£200

EVENT 3   The Ladies' Singles Championship
Total prize money £12,350

The Winner	£1,500
The Runner-up	£750
The losers of the Semi-Finals each	£400
The losers of the Quarter-Finals each	£225
The losers of the Fourth Round each	£150
The losers of the Third Round each	£125
The losers of the Second Round each	£100
The losers of the First Round each	£75
(Byes who lose in second round count as first round losers.)	

EVENT 4   The Ladies' Doubles Championship
Total prize money £1,800

The Winners	Per Pair £600
The Runners-up	£400
The losers of the Semi-Finals	£200
The losers of the Quarter-Finals	£100

EVENT 5   The Mixed Doubles Championship
Total prize money £1,600

The Winners	Per Pair £500
The Runners-up	£350
The losers of the Semi-Finals	£175
The losers of the Quarter-Finals	£100

GRAND TOTAL OF PRIZE MONEY £41,650

Junior Academies

Much like the discussion about great players from different eras competing against each other, the question of how my career would have been altered by today's junior experience is purely hypothetical. Would I have left home to live at a regional, national, or international junior tennis academy and taken high school classes online? Would I have attended a local tennis academy and been home-schooled? Interesting to think about.

Opportunities for young players are much more concentrated than they were in the 50s and 60s. I attended public school in San Diego and came home each night to do my homework. There were no other options. Tennis was my passion, but I had to fit it in around my "regular kid" life. Other players of my era had similar experiences playing in neighborhood parks, rec centers, and local tournaments to develop their talents, perhaps for much longer than they might today. At even the slightest display of potential, kids much younger than we were are enrolling in all-consuming tennis academies.

In my experience — Southern California in the 60s — the top players would develop their games by seeking instruction from local top professionals. I was fortunate that Wilbur Folsom, Maureen Connolly, and Les Stoefen lived in the San Diego area. But I also needed to find players who would challenge me: juniors my age, men in their 30s, and other students of my coaches. Les Stoefen also taught hard-hitting Kathy Blake and arranged for us practice together. (Kathy Blake not only made it to the semifinals of the US Open mixed doubles in 1966 with fellow tour professional Butch Seewagen, she later married Wayne Bryan and gave birth to twins Bob and Mike Bryan, the most successful men's doubles team of all time.) While this approach to learning and playing took individual initiative, it must have worked. Most of my generation of pros came through their local ranks this way.

I'm pretty sure I would still choose the life I lived, even if the intensive academy experience would have meant a few more wins in my career. I can't imagine not having the friends I had in public school — I might never have known Don or Pete — or not playing high school basketball, or maybe not even going to UCLA. I would have missed the non-tennis things we did as a family, and spending time with my grandparents. I had all that *and* got to play college and pro tennis.

That said, I do support the academies where the teaching is top-notch and talented opponents are readily available. The opportunity for these kids to learn the game and develop the discipline it takes to play is quite valuable, and I think the investment in the next generation of top players is important to keep the game viable. But, where I fit tennis around my "regular kid" life, these kids are fitting "regular kid" lives around tennis, and I worry they are missing out on their one childhood, especially if they don't make it to the top of the game. And most of them won't make it.

Ideally, I would have liked a little of that experience. I can imagine attending public school in San Diego with my friends and also being a regular at a local academy where all of the best pros and junior players worked together after school and on weekends. It was close to what I had learning from Wilbur Folsom, Maureen Connolly and Les Stoefen at Morley Field and Balboa Park, but I only had that because my parents and I arranged it. Still, no complaints.

A healthy balance between family life and concentrated tennis still appeals to me and has emerged as a new feature at Kiawah. My son Jonathan, who always wanted to run a junior academy on Kiawah, partnered with Bruce Hawtin, a native Australian who ran an academy in Charlotte, North Carolina, to open the Barth-Hawtin Junior Tennis Academy at Kiawah in 2019. Bruce brought a few juniors from his academy, and Jonathan brought a few college-bound juniors with whom he had worked to make up the inaugural class. Some students attend local schools in Charleston, some are taking accredited high school courses online, and others live at home and come to the academy during school breaks and summer vacations. Those enrolled year-round are staying in the supervised Academy Villa on Kiawah Island. These kids are committed to their schoolwork and their tennis; I am happy to see this balance.

Opportunity and Missed Opportunity

While the number of tennis academies is increasing, the opportunities to play tennis in college, and the number of scholarships available to do so, are decreasing. This is unfortunate. My college playing years were some of the best years of my life and my scholarship made them possible.

Perhaps because of the academies, and because some tennis phenoms are turning pro while they are in high school, the excitement of college tennis has dwindled. Some schools are dropping their men's tennis programs altogether, citing the expense of facilities for only ten or twelve players compared to sports with much larger teams. In other instances, regional conferences have folded, leaving schools without intercollegiate competition. My friend Johnny and I used to dream about playing varsity tennis for UCLA. Do kids do that anymore?

My college days were a wonderful transition from child to adult, as they should be no matter what the academic or athletic focus. College taught me to balance classes, practice, matches, and friends, and to stay healthy doing it. Even the total overwhelm of my sophomore year was a valuable college lesson. It would be a shame if some of these developmentally important experiences are lost.

When I played on the junior circuit, on my college team, and even on the pro tour, local tournament organizers of the smaller venues used to find private housing for players. I have fond memories of my hosts, especially those with whom I'd stay every year. They were tennis enthusiasts, often members of the host club, interested in the pro tennis life, and they went out of their way to make sure I had everything I needed for a comfortable and successful week. Not only did I always send a handwritten thank-you note, but years after I retired from the tour, I still kept in contact with many of these families.

Today, tournament organizers of USTA and professional events reserve rooms for players, officials, and coordinators at nearby hotels. It's less work than finding private homes and more efficient to have everyone in close proximity. Individuals can choose to stay in private homes but they must make the arrangements themselves.

I worry that players giving up family life to live in an academy, not going to college, and staying in hotels rather than private homes are missing key opportunities to enjoy non-tennis social situations. No matter their ultimate tennis success, this is a cost.

Another opportunity that has changed over the years is the opportunity to watch tennis. The upside is the abundance of live and encore programming on the Tennis Channel, the networks, and even YouTube videos. At any hour of the day I can watch a match, a documentary, feature programming, a specific player, or even a particular shot analysis. This exposure highlights a variety of matches and talent and offers expert commentary and instruction. Some television providers even broadcast the early round outer court matches from the major tournaments.

The downside is the opportunity to attend live pro tennis events. Sadly, many men's tournaments have left the United States for Europe, Asia, and South America, where tennis is more popular and big name sponsors are stepping up. In 1975, my last year on the tour, there were 27 pro tournaments in the United States. In 2019, there were ten. Fortunately, there are also a few weeks of World TeamTennis matches, the occasional Davis Cup tie, and Challenger tournaments (the pro level just under the ATP Tour) in about 20 American cities each year for fans to see the action in person. When I was a kid, I looked forward to watching the pros play at the Pacific Southwest Professional Championship at the Los Angeles Tennis Club each year. Aspiring young tennis players and adult fans alike should get a chance to see the pros up close, even if it means traveling a little further to do it.

Less Emphasis on Doubles

Of all the changes I have seen over the years, the one I find most unfortunate is the emphasis on singles at the expense of doubles. The popularity of doubles starts with the pros; if they don't play doubles, college players and juniors seem less interested.

In my playing days, all the top singles players played doubles, and usually mixed-doubles as well. At the 1969 Wimbledon, Margaret Court, Billie Jean King, John Newcombe, and Tony Roche all played singles, doubles, and mixed doubles. Once we traveled to the venues and secured lodging, we needed to capitalize on our earning potential by entering as many draws as possible. But more importantly, we really enjoyed playing doubles. My success hitting angled volleys, overheads, chipped returns of serve, lobs, and the serve-volley combination all came from playing doubles and improved my singles play. John McEnroe used to say he played doubles as practice for singles. He excelled at both.

Doubles is an exciting dynamic of considerable technical skill combined with camaraderie, teamwork, strategy, and on-court communication. Rocky Jarvis and Johnny Sanderlin were my best friends and junior doubles partners; playing with doubles specialist Bob Lutz was an education in court positioning and movement as a team; Steve Tidball and I enjoyed our successful four-season partnership at UCLA; Tom Gorman and I traveled the world together on the pro tour and became ranked No. 2 in the United States; and I made a friend in the very-different-from-me Torben Ulrich on the WCT Tour. In each of these partners I had someone with whom to share a win — or a loss.

Today's top singles players don't play much doubles. If they did, their major win numbers would certainly increase. The prize money is incidental, the chance of injury great, practicing with a partner takes time and effort, and their highest priority is earning tournament-qualifying singles ranking points. Ironically, recreational and club players play more doubles than singles, yet so much less attention is paid to doubles in tournaments and in the media.

As chairman of the USTA Davis Cup Committee from 2009 to 2012, I studied how many of the 17 USTA sections offered doubles in sanctioned junior tournaments. Only 29 percent. This was surprising. In many tournaments, the singles consolation round (also called the "back draw") has taken the place of doubles because it's easier to schedule, it doesn't involve finding partners, and it is much less work for the tournament director. Many pros don't want to make the effort to host a doubles draw and the kids miss out on a great experience. To its credit, the USTA is trying to do more to encourage doubles play by creating a combined singles and doubles ranking and offering weighted bonus points (15 to 25 percent depending on the USTA section) based on success in doubles.

Doubles was such an important part of my career and I think it bodes well for all juniors to learn it. We have always offered doubles in Kiawah's junior tournaments when other tournaments opt for the singles consolation draw instead.

For a game that hasn't changed that much over the years, tennis has sure changed a lot.

Do I sound old? Am I one of those guys who just longs for the good old days? I don't think so.

In the more than 60 years I've played, competed, taught, and managed in the tennis world, most of what I've seen is progress, even if some trends could benefit from a little balance. I play with and recommend graphite racquets — although I've kept my smooth flat ground strokes and style of play. However, I can teach players who choose the power and heavy topspin style; the foundation points are the same. I am interested in the electronically tracked performance data, but only as background for the player to consider during competition. I've joked with Donald Dell that I'd now know a fitness center if I walked by one. In fact, I go in one regularly. I watch the Tennis Channel quite often, I try to get to the US Open every year, and I encourage others to do the same. And I will always promote doubles for fun and to learn skills to improve the overall game.

CHAPTER FORTY

Follow Your Dream

Emeritus

"Good afternoon, Mr. Barth, it's nice to see you again. How is your book coming along? Please enjoy your walk in the pool and let me know if there's anything you need."

I'm still getting used to my schedule these days, and it's been more than two years. I teach one or two hours, four mornings a week, and I stay after the clinic to spend some time talking with the guests. I have more time to chat now than I had before. Afterwards, I head over to The Sanctuary and walk laps in the indoor pool or use the recumbent bike in the fitness center. The pool is therapeutic and indulgent, and it feels like I'm playing hooky from work. I am flattered by how hospitable the staff is all over the island. The Sanctuary is one of the finest luxury hotels, and guests should expect gracious hospitality, but I am not a guest. Sometimes I forget I've been at Kiawah since before the resort opened, longer than almost anyone else, including Mr. Goodwin and Roger Warren. I forget my name is on the sign in front of the tennis center. I feel like a celebrity — or perhaps a relic — when I go to the pool.

I drive off the island around 2:00 p.m., leaving the paperwork, budgets, reports, purchase requisitions, and meeting notes behind. I'm not responsible for them anymore, but they are in good hands. In the late afternoons, I work on various projects, write, read, check in on Madelyn and Mckenzie's after-school activities, or maybe nap. I am glad I did not retire completely.

As of January 1, 2018, I am Director of Tennis, Emeritus.

Unlike when I retired from the pro tour in 1975, I hadn't lost focus or concentration on my game at Kiawah. I continued to meet the considerable challenges of my job in my ever-evolving department and I could have kept going. Nor did I wish to change how I was living, as I did when Colleen and I decided not to raise our son while traveling on the pro tour. I was happy with our life, our house, and our friends in Charleston, and I had long since forgotten we belonged back in Southern California. That was where I grew up, and I had a wonderful life there, but Charleston had been my home for over 40 years. I set lofty goals for myself at Kiawah and in my volunteer commitments, and I reached them. In the process, I came through life-threatening surgeries whose outcomes could have compromised my faculties, my ability to play and teach tennis, and my independence. I was doing well. I just felt it was time.

In 2017, after 41 years as the director of tennis at Kiawah, I decided to step down, but not fully retire. I told Brian Gerard in June I would remain in my current position until the end of the year. The next day, Brian interviewed my son Jonathan for my job. After publicly posting the position and interviewing other candidates in the fall, the company offered the position to Jonathan.

My mother taught me to write thank-you notes to the families who housed me on the tour because they had opened their homes to me and cared about my well-being. At the end of my years at Kiawah, I felt as though Mr. Goodwin had done the same. In my note I told him how much I enjoyed working for the company, how honored I was that the tennis center was named for me, and how I was grateful that, while I knew his priority had to be the business of golf, he still found the resources — financial and marketing — to support the tennis program.

In Mr. Goodwin's response, he wrote:

> *I want to personally thank you for all that you have done for Kiawah and especially your efforts in managing the tennis operations. You have much to be proud of, and we were fortunate to have you on our team.*

There had been some tough times, and I had a few offers over the years promising more money elsewhere, but I knew my family and I had a good situation at Kiawah. I am glad we stayed.

January 1, 2018, my last day as the director of tennis, was Jonathan's first day in that role. It was an emotion-filled changeover.

January 1, 2018. Jonathan taking over the job I've had for 41 ½ years (photo courtesy Kiawah Island Golf Resort)

I thought about my father a lot that day. I recalled how his father, my grandfather Bruno, denied my father succession to his engineering firm because he didn't want to show favoritism to his son. Jonathan earned the job on his own (as I am certain my father earned his father's legacy), but unlike my grandfather, I was elated that my son would succeed me. Of course in my case it was Kiawah's decision, but I would have been heartbroken if Jonathan wanted to be in this business and I forced him to work elsewhere. I think my father would have been happy how things turned out for us.

The title "emeritus" is often used in academia; professors who retire from lecturing remain associated with their college or university to further their research and be remembered favorably. I am honored that Kiawah allows me to continue to contribute to its tennis program.

Just as I started the director job with only one tennis center, so did Jonathan. From 1976 until 1982, West Beach was Kiawah's only tennis facility. Since 1982, when the East Beach Tennis Center opened, I managed two separate tennis facilities. When the five-star Sanctuary Hotel opened in the East Beach Village in 2004, Kiawah planned to redevelop the aging West Beach Village to include a new Cougar Point golf clubhouse with a pro shop, bar, and restaurant; a villa check-in center; and a new 150-room five-star hotel with indoor/outdoor pools, spa, restaurants, shops, and a boardwalk. The planned multi-use conference center with underground parking and corporate offices was slated to be built right over my West Beach Tennis pro shop and courts.

I had been exposed to building construction, renovation, redevelopment, and re-use for over 40 years at Kiawah, and I thought I was pretty hardened to the necessity of it all, but I found myself quite emotional when the West Beach Tennis Center was torn down. It was my first real office, my first management opportunity, and the site of all of Kiawah's tennis firsts: exhibitions, tournaments, clinics, and guest pros. I felt sad about its demise.

But there was a distinct upside: tennis would once again be consolidated into just one facility. With the addition of ten new clay courts (eight lit) in the East Beach area, the Roy Barth Tennis Center — with a total of 22 courts and one dedicated automatic ball machine practice court — would become Kiawah's flagship tennis complex.

The East Beach area of Kiawah Island Golf Resort in 2019.
The Roy Barth Tennis Center is in the foreground;
The Sancutary Hotel, beachfront,
and Atlantic Ocean are in the background.
(photo courtesy Kiawah Island Golf Resort and Osprey Productions)

While this change moved courts further from the guests in West Beach, it made running the whole tennis operation much more efficient. I told Jonathan that if I had had to manage only one tennis center all this time, I probably would have lasted another ten years.

Kiawah Tennis is in good hands with Jonathan at the helm. As I'd hoped, the transition was rather seamless. Jonathan grew up on the Kiawah courts and worked there full-time since graduating from college; the staff didn't have to get used to a new boss (as I did so many times); and the regular resort guests were comforted by the continuity of their familiar programming and instruction. As a father, I was touched that my son thought enough of my job to want it for himself.

And I smile every time I see my granddaughters, Madelyn and Mckenzie, on the Kiawah courts. It seems Jonathan has asked his pros to work with his children. It's a familiar approach in my family.

In May 2019, *Forbes Magazine* printed an article entitled, "The Man Behind Tennis Resorts Online," in which travel writer Everett Potter interviewed Roger Cox, a long-time columnist for *Tennis Magazine*, about the tennis resorts he ranks at the top of his list. This question and answer about Kiawah are particularly gratifying.

> Potter*: Kiawah Island Golf Resort in South Carolina is the number one ranked tennis resort this year. What makes it number one?*

> Cox: *On the face of it, it may seem strange for a resort with golf in its name to rank so highly for tennis. In fact, though golf-centric, Kiawah has cared about tennis since it opened in 1976, when it hired former ATP touring pro Roy Barth to head its programs and eventually named its tennis center for him. More than four decades later, Barth still has an active emeritus role, though he has seamlessly passed along the day-to-day operations — and tennis director's title — to his son, Jonathan, who has himself been a fixture at the resort for two decades. About the same time, the resort nearly doubled the size of the Roy Barth Tennis Center to 22 courts — all but three of them Har-Tru, or green clay. The tennis gets very high marks for its staff, instruction, and programming, and so do the creature comforts off court.*

I am quite proud of what this banner represents.
I would never had dreamed this when I started at Kiawah in 1976.

I am as humbled by this review and its high-profile placement as I am by another recent tribute I treasure. In 2019, I was inducted into the Intercollegiate Tennis Association Men's Tennis Hall of Fame for my years on the UCLA tennis team. I was the 22nd UCLA Bruin to be so honored. This award was especially meaningful because my father played for UCLA in 1938. He would have been really pleased about this.

In 2020, I was again privileged to learn of another honor. After my long-time PTR membership, which included serving on the board, five years as treasurer, and three years as president, I was chosen to be inducted into the PTR International Hall of Fame.

I admit to being overwhelmed by these recognitions. I didn't volunteer to receive awards. I volunteered because I enjoyed the people I worked with on the committees. Together, we shared a love of the game and a passion to see our sport continue to succeed at the highest levels.

I do hope these honors will serve a pay-it-forward purpose: showing my grandchildren the importance of volunteer work. Even when the kids were little, my sons and daughters-in-law brought them to award ceremonies when appropriate. Of course I was happy to have them share my celebrations, but I am more gratified that they might remember the experience and recognize not that I got an award, but the pride I felt in having contributed. Whatever their interests, I hope when they get older, they will contribute similarly to their communities.

In my semi-retirement, I have more time to spend with friends and family and do the two things I love almost as much as playing tennis: teaching tennis and talking about tennis.

I am still teaching the Stroke-of-the-Day clinics, helping Jonathan detail the training program for newly hired pros, and working with students at Jonathan's academy for highly competitive junior players. I've always loved teaching adults and, even though years ago in Indianapolis I didn't quite embrace working with juniors, I have come to really enjoy that particular challenge. Perhaps I'm just a more seasoned teacher now, or maybe it's that I taught my own kids, or even that Jonathan is running this program. Today I can fully appreciate what these kids are pursuing, and I hope my insights add value to their effort.

When I talk about tennis, some people are interested in stories from my years on the tour, others in specific people or matches, and others in the business of the game. Whether the story is about how Arthur Ashe would prepare for a match in another country by learning a few words in the native language; or how "hanging on like a crab" applied to tennis, business, and life; or how my greatest incentive to play might have been that my sister won a trophy, their response is eventually the same: "You should write this stuff down."

Even my son Sandon, who has listened to "tour stories" all his life, heard me tell one he'd never heard before and suggested that "you need to put these stories in writing."

Were you really in London in June of 1973 and not allowed to play at Wimbledon?

Good for you for staying after Kiawah removed the word "tennis" from the resort's name. I don't think I could have done that.

Thank goodness Colleen didn't accept that other guy's proposal. (Yes, thank goodness! In 2021, we will celebrate our 50th wedding anniversary.)

Colleen bought me a new laptop, and I started typing. Maybe someday my grandkids and their kids will read these stories and learn about my life. When their genealogy project for school is assigned, they will have a head start. I kept typing.

My parents. San Diego. Junior tournaments. Johnny. Type. Type. Type. UCLA. My first Wimbledon. Colleen. The pro tour. Type. Type. Type. Becoming a parent. Kiawah and all its changes. The USTA and the

PTR. Surgeries. Semi-retirement. When I finished typing, I had more than a collection of life stories. I had a collection of life lessons: Focus on One Challenge at a Time. Cultivate Important Relationships. Learn from Those Around You. Gain Confidence through Mini-Goals. Tennis can be a metaphor for business and for life. At least that's how I see it.

And now to "teaching tennis" and "talking about tennis," I can add a third thing I love almost as much as playing tennis: writing about tennis.

Balboa Park Tennis Club was torn down to make room for more San Diego Zoo parking, but the city approved designating six courts at the Morley Sports Complex in Balboa Park as the Balboa Park Tennis Club. The pro tour I knew is long gone, replaced by a world of physiotherapists, high-tech tennis centers named for my contemporaries, extreme prize money, social media, "Hawkeye" technology, more tiebreaks, and graphite racquets. The best players of my generation who are still living are the older guys they show for a minute on TV, sitting in the stands at the major tournaments. Stan Smith is probably better known for his popular sneakers than for what he accomplished wearing them.

Even the Kiawah I experienced early on isn't the Kiawah of today — but I still have my straightedge and sharpened pencil if I need to make a spreadsheet! The steadiness of ownership and top management in recent years almost made me forget how tumultuous it once was. Tommy Cuthbert and I had been there for 25 years or more before we ever felt our jobs weren't on the line every day. Mr. Goodwin still owns the Resort, and Roger Warren still manages it. Brian Gerard is still the director of golf, and Kiawah's tennis program is still ranked the No. 1 Tennis Resort in the World by TennisResortsOnline.com (Kiawah has earned this distinction 12 times from 2006 to 2019). The facilities are beautiful and ever-evolving. It's come a long way.

I spent a few days at the 2019 US Open, where I sat in the USTA President's Box with my friend and past USTA president Lucy Garvin.

I was one of 730,000 people attending the tournament over its two weeks. Tennis is still popular. It's still exciting. It's still fun. It's still both my work and my hobby. And, every year I've come to the Open since 1966 — whether as a player or a spectator — I've gotten together with my college roommate and good friend Hank Goldsmith. He's never taken me to the same restaurant twice.

Hank and me in New York in 2019. Our getting together is a highlight of my visits to New York.

There's a wonderful scene toward the end of the 1989 baseball fantasy movie *Field of Dreams* in which writer Terrence Mann (played by James Earl Jones) explains to Ray Kinsella (played by Kevin Costner) why Ray should not sell the farm on which he built a baseball field. He explains that great players from the past have to come play, and nostalgic fans will come to watch:

> *… And they'll walk out to the bleachers, and sit in their shirtsleeves, on a perfect afternoon. They'll find they have reserved seats, somewhere along one of the baselines, where they sat when they were children and cheered their heroes. And they'll watch the game … The one constant through all the years, Ray, has been baseball … Baseball has marked the time. This field … this game … is a part of our past, Ray.*

I'm Roy, not Ray (although I was called "Raaaay"), and I play tennis, not baseball, but fictional Terrence Mann's passion is not wasted on me and my real life. The one constant through all my years has been tennis.

The movie suggests the fans will watch the "baseball men" from high up in the bleachers on a perfect afternoon. I can see my game from there too, and it's a wonderful perspective. To my left is what I've left: my name on my beloved tennis center. To my right is what's right for my future: my children teaching their children to play. And there's Colleen, proudly sitting in my player's box. I can still see my parents playing doubles together, my sister Patty winning her first trophy, and my friend Johnny's effortless strokes. I hear Maureen Connolly telling me to "relax and hit out" when the match gets tight, Les Stoefen encouraging me to watch the point of impact, and Glenn Bassett complimenting my volleys. I am coming back from two sets down at my first Wimbledon. I am hitting again after recovering from life-threatening surgeries. I am cheering my heroes.

And I hear the umpire say, "The point goes to Mr. Barth."

Commit to Making Contact

In March 2020, I finished my story and I looked forward to sharing it. I was ready to settle into my semi-retirement work schedule and think about my next project. Then, like everyone else, I was sidelined by the COVID-19 pandemic. Kiawah was forced to close for a time. All tennis — local, regional, and professional — was cancelled. I was devastated by the daily fatality count. I worried about my family and friends. I couldn't visit my grandchildren. At 72 years old, I was considered "high-risk."

This book project became a catalyst for reconnecting. After spending two years recounting the events of my life, I was inspired to catch up with some of the friends I'd celebrated.

I thought about Johnny's older brother **David Sanderlin** and how lucky I was to have seen him that day at Morley Field in 2010, in part because it prompted my last visit to see his father. David's wife, Arnell, answered the phone. David was too ill to speak; he'd been suffering with Parkinson's disease and multiple myeloma. I told Arnell about my book and how I had hoped to share it with David. David died three weeks later.

I called David's sister, **Frea**, to offer my condolences. The last time I spoke with her was at Johnny's funeral in 1963, and here I was calling to pay my respects to her other brother. She was the much older sister of my best childhood friend — she was married and had a child when Johnny and I were 13 — but she remembered me. Speaking with her was like having Johnny and David back for a few minutes.

Wilbur Folsom, my first coach from Morley Field, died in 1968 at the age of 59. He was survived by his wife, Ruth, and their seven children. I called **Bill Folsom**. We reminisced about Morley Field in the sixties and talked about Wilbur and how he was portrayed in the NBC movie, Little Mo, about Maureen Connolly. Bill said Martin Milner portrayed his father honestly and the movie was quite accurate. I hope to have lunch with Bill the next time I'm in San Diego.

I spoke with **Hank Goldsmith**, my freshman roommate from UCLA, a few times over the summer. Because no fans could attend the US Open, 2020 was the first in many years Hank and I did not meet in New York for dinner. We already have plans for next year though.

Bob Lutz, one of my junior doubles partners and best junior opponent, reminded me that we used to shoot hoops together, sometimes just after we'd contested a grueling tennis match. We were fierce competitors but all these years later, our shared memories make us sentimental allies. He invited Colleen and me to visit with him and his family on our next trip to California. I look forward to that.

I had forgotten my high school friends **Pete Kofoed** and **Don Parker** worked part time when we were in college. One year they were ushers at the Beverly Hills Theater. According to Don, Pete did all the work while Don ate all the popcorn. I was too focused on tennis then to think how fun those jobs could have been. The story made for a good laugh.

I'm still "hanging on like a crab" to my mentor **Allen Fox**. He was a graduate student who helped my game when I was a freshman. He played on the tour, he remained in the tennis business all these years, and he has written books about the game. No matter the distance between us or the time between calls, I value his guidance.

I speak with **Lucy Garvin, Jorge Andrew,** and **Dan Santorum** quite often about USTA and PTR matters but my book inspired me to reminisce with them about older days.

I spent a few days with **Steve Tidball,** my doubles partner in college, just before the pandemic. I envy that he is still competing. He was scheduled to play in the national 70-and-over doubles tournament this summer. Good for him. My pro tour doubles partner, **Tom Gorman,** had planned a trip to Kiawah. I hope he will reschedule.

There have been other wonderful conversations and I am committed to more. To be aging and be home seems the perfect time to bridge the years and the miles to share memories.

I hope you've enjoyed reading my story as much as I enjoyed writing it. Think about the people who have been important in your life and reconnect with them before it's too late, even if it's been years since you've spoken. The effort is well worth the reward.

Roy
September 2020

APPENDIX

QUICK REFERENCES, BONUS RESOURCES, AND MORE PHOTOS!

My Tennis Professionals and Coaches

Wilbur Folsom

Control Your Swing
> Don't swing like you are hitting a baseball. Get to the ball quickly and then set up and hit a smooth, controlled swing.

Hit to the Open Court
> Make your opponents run; wear them out and keep them off balance.

Maureen Connolly

Don't Burn Out
> Take a break from tennis. During the off-season, play other sports and participate in after-school activities. This will energize you.

When Hitting Ground Strokes…
> Swing low to high, allowing your palm to lead the racquet head

through the hitting zone. This keeps the ball on the strings longer for more control and power. Practice hitting the ball on the run, finishing your hand in the direction of the intended target.

Never Let Up

Don't feel sorry for an opponent during a match. Letting up even a little might allow them to work their way back in.

Les Stoefen

Focus on the Point of Impact (watch until you finish the follow-through)

Keeping your eyes and head frozen on the point of impact as you follow through to the intended target enables you to hit the ball in the middle of the strings and keeps you from telegraphing where you are hitting. The bigger the point, the longer you watch the point of impact.

Hit a Volley with a Short Karate Motion

Use your hands — not your arms — when volleying; it's a short, relaxed motion. Cock your hand(s) up and back and line up the butt of the racquet with the incoming ball so the racquet head is above the ball. Then chop forward and down like a karate chop, directing the ball with the edge of the racquet. The short and efficient stroke leaves little room for error. Less motion equals fewer mistakes.

Hit a Consistent Serve

Keep your arm up until you can see the ball toss above your hand. Freeze your eyes at the point of impact. Keep your wrist loose as you accelerate through the serve. Visualize the ball going three feet over the net (this makes you hit up-and-out on the ball, not down).

Glenn Bassett

Preparation is the Key to Success
> I thought I worked hard to prepare for matches in junior tennis, but at UCLA I found I could work a lot harder. It paid off in long matches.

Hit and Move
> Never stand and watch your shot; either move back to the middle after hitting a ground stroke or move forward after hitting a volley and overhead.

John Wooden

Success Is Getting the Most out of your Talent
> UCLA's legendary basketball coach believed that if you tried as hard as you could in competition, you were successful — win or lose.

Prioritize Conditioning and Confidence
> Short, intensive, play-action drills with constant movement help conditioning and confidence.

The Great Players
of My Era

_____

Arthur Ashe

Study Your Opponent's Game
> Avoid their strengths, play into their weaknesses. Change pace, direction, tactics.

Toss the Ball in the Same Place on Every Serve
> No opponent can correctly anticipate where your serve will land if you have a consistent toss.

Look Like a Winner
> Arthur was quoted as saying, "Regardless of how you feel inside, always try to look like a winner. Even if you're behind, a sustained look of control and confidence can give you a mental edge that results in victory."

Billie Jean King

Make Sacrifices and Be Willing to Take Chances
  To be a good player, you must make sacrifices, including dessert!
  (Billie Jean didn't eat dessert for four months leading up to play-
  ing Wimbledon.) She was willing to take chances, break off from
  the USTA tour, encourage fellow women players to play on the
  Virginia Slims tour in 1970, and create the WTA tour in 1973.

Pressure Is a Privilege. Embrace It.
  Like most great champions, Billie Jean played her best under
  pressure.

Rod Laver

Focus on the Ball, Not the Opponent
  Whether your opponent is your good friend from the club or the
  world's No. 1 ranked player, focus on your game and not theirs.
  Your game is the only thing you can control.

Back Up Your Talent with Practice
  I saw Rod Laver and Roy Emerson practice for two and a half
  hours on a backcourt during a WCT tournament in Louisville,
  Kentucky, when the outdoor temperature was over 100 degrees.

Björn Borg

Constant Footwork
  Borg was in constant motion, always moving when the ball was
  in the air coming toward him.

Take Away the Angle

If your opponent is winning points on the run with wide-angle shots, hit your approach shot down the middle, removing the angle.

Play Percentage Tennis on Big Points

I didn't, and I should have. I went for a winner down-the-line against Borg and missed it by an inch. I should have returned his serve down the middle of the court and given him the chance to miss the volley. I should have put the pressure on him, not on myself.

Roy Emerson

Work Out on Half a Court

It can be difficult to find practice court times during tournaments. Many times, I had to practice on a half a court to prepare for indoor professional tournaments. Half court drills, if done properly, can give you and your practice partner a great workout. Roy Emerson used every foot of half the court.

Attack Second Serve

Attack with authority from your opponent's slower second serve to set up your next shot.

Ken Rosewall

Use Your Opponent's Power to your Advantage

Shorten your backswing on your ground strokes and play off the speed of their shot.

Keep Your Opponent on the Run

Take the ball early on the ground strokes and run your opponent side-to-side. Create opportunities to attack and go to the net.

John Newcombe

Work on Serve-Volley Combination

John had a very smooth and rhythmic service motion, with a toss out in front of him that enabled him to be closer to the net on his first volley than most professionals. A good serve-and-volley combination is a great option to have on big points.

Develop Reliable Weapons

Go to your best stroke under pressure. Newk had his big serve and forehand ground stroke. I had my steady return-of-serve, precision volleys, and accurate forehand.

Know Your Opponent's Weaknesses

Choose the strategic shot at the key points of the match. Newk taught me that if an opponent had a weak second serve, I should move over in the alley into the backhand corner, daring the server to gamble and try to serve an ace down the middle. Narrowing the target increases the chance of a double fault.

Tony Roche

Change Up Speed on Ground Strokes

Develop a powerful flat or topspin forehand and a slice.

Embrace a Windy Day

On a windy day, attack the net at every opportunity rather than try to hit passing shots and lobs.

Jimmy Connors

Focus on Every Point
> Jimmy was a tough competitor; he played every point as though his life depended on winning it.

Get Low on Ground Strokes and Volleys
> You gain power and control by being able to hit the ball earlier from a low position using your legs.

Ilie Nastase

Embrace Variety
> The more options you have — touch, quickness, change of pace, change of strategy — the smarter you can play.

Defend! Defend! Defend!
> You can wear down your opponent by just running all the balls down. Consistency alone can frustrate your opponent and force errors. (It certainly did during my long five-set match against Ilie in the US Open in 1973. He wore me down just by making me work extremely hard to win a point.)

Stan Smith

Set Goals
> Set your goals high and work hard to reach them.

Play the Right Game
> Adjust your game to accommodate what each surface demands.

Charlie Pasarell

Know Your Opponent's Strengths and Weaknesses
Charlie had a great forehand, so I avoided it; I served to his back-hand and hit my first volley to his backhand. He tried to run around them to hit forehands, but the hard courts were just too fast for that.

Make the Most of the Return-of-Serve
When playing a big server, focus on getting every return-of-serve back in play. Don't give the server any "free" points. Make him "pay" on his second serve.

Richard "Pancho" Gonzales

Relax the Serve Grip
Pancho was a guest on *The Tonight Show* in 1970. Guest host Alan King asked Pancho what makes his serve so great. Pancho explained how he relaxes the grip on his serve, enabling him to bend his arm more freely, giving him more power and control.

Practice Your Second Serve
You're only as good as your second serve. Practice that too!

Fred Stolle

Disguise Your Shots in Doubles
Set up for one shot but hit another at the last second. (This takes practice, but it is effective.) Example: disguise your second serve return lob by transferring your weight forward — as if hitting a ground stroke return — and then hit the lob. Keep your head still as you are hitting the ball so as not to telegraph the lob.

Jan Kodes

Practice your Approach Shot/Volley/Overhead Sequence
> To play a great ground stroke player, like Jan Kodes, you must be able to attack, hit volleys, and hit overheads well. You are not going to beat him at just his ground stroke game.

Pancho Segura

Keep a Record of Your Opponents' Strengths and Weaknesses
> Tailor your strategy for each match and make the smart shot on big points.

Strategize Serving and Volleying in Doubles
> Hit the first volley down the alley to prevent your opponent at net from crossing toward the middle and intersecting your cross-court volley.

Rafael Osuna

Combine Quick Hands and Feet To Balance Lack of Power
> With quick hands and quick feet, you can use your opponents' power against them.

Practice Strategic Volleys
> Powerful volleys and touch-angled volleys are different shots and equally important to master.

Frank Sedgman

Mix Up Your Serves
> Develop both a wide serve and a down-the-middle serve, and mix them up to keep your opponent off balance. Frank kept me guessing by mixing up the direction of his first serves.

Vitas Gerulaitis

Show Confidence
> Walk out onto the court showing confidence whether you feel confident or not. Your look of self-assurance is not lost on your opponent.

Don Budge

Be Willing to Make Sacrifices
> Being good takes practice and practicing means giving up other opportunities. (Don never drank alcohol during the season.)

Improve Your Game During Off-Season
> The off-season is not a vacation; it's the time to improve your game.

Jack Kramer

Develop Two Weapons
> Rely on your two "go-to" shots at crucial points of the match. Mine were my forehand ground stroke and my volley.

Learn to Set Up an Effective Approach Shot
> Take advantage of receiving a short ball by hitting it down the line

and going to the net. Anticipate the location of your opponent's passing shot based on where you hit your approach shot and based on your knowledge of your opponent's strengths and weaknesses.

Chris Evert

Play Like You Practice
> Be just as competitive in practice as you are in tournament play.

Stay Composed
> Don't outwardly show frustration; give your opponent the impression nothing bothers you.

Harold Solomon

Keep Steady Players Guessing
> When playing a steady backcourt player, keep him guessing. Attack the second serve and come to net; serve and volley once in a while; take lobs in the air; and hit low, wide, slice ground strokes to draw him into net.

WHAT I LEARNED FROM

My Tennis Journey

Top Ten Overall Tips

1. **Position your Body**
   You can't be too low.

2. **Move! (Constantly)**
   Hit and move — don't stand and watch.

3. **Direct the Ball**
   Finish with your hand(s) in the direction of the target.

4. **Stay Relaxed**
   Keep a relaxed grip during racquet preparation.

5. **Line Up the Butt of the Racquet**
   Line the oncoming ball with the butt of the racquet on volleys and ground strokes.

6. **Focus on the Point of Impact**

   Freeze your eyes and head at the point of impact on every stroke.

7. **Conquer the Serve/Overhead**

   Position yourself sideways to the target. Relax your grip. Arm up, spring up, eyes up!

8. **Understand Racquet Head Speed**

   Swing slower to faster on ground strokes and the serve.

9. **Practice Hand Leverage**

   Your hand should lead the racquet head into the point of impact — it's the key for power and control.

10. **Take Short Steps**

    The closer to the ball you are, the shorter steps you should take.

WHAT I LEARNED FROM

My Tennis Journey

Top Ten Doubles Tips

1. **Use the Lob**

   Lob high when opponents have control of the net.

2. **Get your First Serve In**

   Concentrate on getting 80 percent of your first serves in.

3. **Shift as Team**

   Move together at net to the side where ball is hit.

4. **Play Percentage Tennis**

   Volley down the middle on high first volleys, create short angles if the volley is at your feet, and aim for six-feet zones on overheads, etc.

5. **Mix Up Return-of-Serves**

   Mix up returns by hitting down the alley, hitting crosscourt, or lobbing.

6. **Be Positive**

   Encourage your partner with positive body language.

7. **Focus on the Point of Impact**

   Exaggerate watching the point of impact in pressure situations.

8. **Clear the Net**

   Visualize hitting a volley three feet over the net on a put-away.

9. **Prioritize the Warm Up**

   Warm up before walking on court for your match.

10. **Move Toward Net**

    After each volley, move one step toward the net.

My Tennis Journey

Match Day Preparation

1. **Wake Up on Time**
   Wake up at least three hours before your match to allow your body to be fully awake.

2. **Eat Smart**
   Have a light meal before each match.

3. **Schedule Time to Warm Up**
   Warm up enough to break a sweat: hit with a partner, hit against a wall, or jump rope.

4. **Pack to Win the Match**
   Pack the basics in your bag: extra racquets, sports drink, energy bars, towel, wrist bands, hat or visor, tape, overgrip, Band-Aids, extra shirts, etc.

ARTICLES

Tennis Magazine

Over the years I contributed some instructional articles to
Tennis Magazine. Despite the passage of time, these foundation
points still represent the fundamentals of the game.
Here are a few of my articles.

IMPROVE WITHOUT CHANGING YOUR STROKES

BY ROY BARTH, with Robert J. LaMarche

A s a tennis teaching pro, one of my main duties is to dispense stroking tips to my students. Provided the players are dedicated enough to practice these stroking changes, they're almost certain to see improvement.

But I also know that players like you are constantly searching for advice that will help you raise the level of your game quickly without making any stroking changes. On the following pages, I outline five of my favorite tips that often result in immediate improvement in the key areas of footwork, pow-

er, relaxation, concentration and control. Try them and your opponents will think you've spent a month at tennis camp!

The author is a former U.S. top 10 player and is currently director of tennis at the Kiawah Island resort in South Carolina.

FOOTWORK
PIVOT WHILE THE BALL IS IN THE AIR

If you've reached a point in your tennis development where you're playing often and your strokes are solid but you don't feel you're improving, your footwork may need some attention. Why? Improper footwork causes inadequate preparation for all strokes.

One of the most common problems I see among club players is that they wait for the ball to bounce on their side of the court before they move their feet. You know the result: a late swing, with impact occurring behind the body. The ball usually flies off to the side of the court.

To immediately improve your game, pivot sideways on your feet while the ball is in the air, just after your opponent has made contact (see illustration, *left*). Then move quickly to reach the ball. That way, you'll meet the ball earlier, giving you more power and control on your shots. You will also find yourself in a more balanced hitting position.

POWER
USE YOUR LEGS TO DRIVE THE BALL

In clinics, whenever I ask players how they can generate more power on their shots, I'm always told you have to swing harder. But a hard, or fast, swing has a big disadvantage—it puts a lot of unnecessary strain on the arm.

Often-overlooked sources of power are your legs. After you've pivoted sideways and gotten in position to hit the ball, bend your knees and stride aggressively into the shot. (*right*). Your driving, forward weight transfer will put more of your body into the stroking motion, producing greater pace.

RELAXATION
KNOW WHEN TO SQUEEZE YOUR GRIP

Lighten up! Many players grip the handle too tightly, which locks the wrist and limits control.

The solution to the problem starts with the backswing for any stroke. First, keep your grip relaxed as you take the racquet back (*left*). Firm up your grip gradually in the forward swing until you make contact. Then, relax your grip.

Adjusting grip pressure this way will allow you to hit with more power and control while reducing arm fatigue.

█ RELAXED
█ FIRM

CONCENTRATION
WHEN NOT TO WATCH THE BALL

Most tennis players have been taught to watch the ball at all times during a point. But there is a time when you shouldn't: immediately after you've hit the ball.

A lot of players can't resist the temptation to lift their heads at contact to see how good their shots are or how their opponents are reacting. The result is a lifting motion of the upper body that causes frequent mis-hits.

If you freeze your eyes at the point of impact (*below*) for a split second after the ball leaves your racquet strings, you'll hit every shot more squarely.

CONTROL
IMAGINE SWINGING IN SLOW MOTION

In the excitement of a fast-paced rally, it's easy to lose control of your shots. Unknowingly, you probably speed up your stroking motions, thereby reducing your accuracy.

In situations like this, you have to pull in the reins and take control of your game once more. How can you do that? Use your imagination.

That's right. You've seen how TV broadcasts of sports events use slow-motion replays to show an athlete's movement. The replays make the motions look smooth and controlled. The next time you find yourself playing in a slapstick rhythm during a match, visualize yourself hitting in slow motion. Your control is likely to return quickly. ◢

ILLUSTRATIONS BY ED ACUÑA

USE "HAND LEVERAGE" TO POWER YOUR GAME

BY ROY BARTH, with Norman Zeitchick

f you were taught to lock your wrist on your strokes, you're missing out on an easy way to gain extra power and control on your shots. I call it "hand leverage." By holding your racquet hand at the proper

The author, a former U.S. top-10 player, is the director of tennis at Kiawah Island Resort in South Carolina.

angle with a wrist that's firm and flexible, not locked, and letting your wrist rotate naturally through impact with the ball, you can add substantial pace yet increase control.

On all shots—ground strokes, volleys, overheads, serves—let your hand lead the racquet face into the ball. I'm not talking about merely laying back your

wrist and slapping at the ball. That produces "flippers"—weak, uncontrolled shots. When the butt end of the racquet leads the racquet head into impact, you gain extra acceleration of the head as your hand rotates through on your stroke.

If you keep your hand relaxed, then your wrist will naturally rotate through at the point in your

GROUND STROKES: LINE UP THE BUTT OF THE RACQUET

To gain hand leverage on ground strokes, the butt of the racquet should lead the racquet head throughout your stroke. Set the angle of your hand on your backswing (far left) and line up the butt of the racquet with the height of the oncoming ball so you can swing through the stroke instead of merely slapping at it. Maintain this angle on your stroke up to and through impact with the ball (above left and right). Relax your hand so it rotates through as you are hitting the ball. Slightly squeeze the grip at contact, but do not lock your wrist.

VOLLEYS: USE A KARATE-CHOP MOTION

The butt of the racquet must lead the racquet head for good hand leverage on the volley, too. Keep your wrist cocked up and back, with the racquet face slightly open, as you line up the shot (above left). Line up the butt of the racquet, not the racquet head, with the oncoming ball. Then employ a hammer motion with your arm and hand, like a karate chop, to hit the shot, directing the ball with the bottom edge of your hand (above right). If you merely align the racquet face with the ball, you'll only block the ball back and lose pace and control. Your stroke should be a quick and precise motion. Again, do not lock your wrist.

OVERHEADS & SERVES: KEEP RACQUET COCKED

The hand should lead the racquet head on the stroke up to and through contact with the ball on both the serve and the overhead (below). If you cock your racquet behind you in the proper back-scratch position, the butt end of the racquet will naturally point toward the ball. Keep your hand relaxed and your wrist loose on your swing.

swing when your hand anatomically can no longer lead the racquet head. You will carry the ball longer on your strings, gain more "feel" on your shots and increase your control. The ball's path will be directed by the follow-through of the racquet head.

Hand leverage may be an advanced stroking technique, but there's no reason beginners can't learn to hit this way, too. For example, most beginners are taught to volley with a locked-wrist, piston-like punching motion. Yet you can't get enough power or feel that way. You can always fall back and use the piston action on the volley if you have trouble with hand leverage, but why not learn a better way from the start?

Check out these pointers to make the most out of hand leverage. See for yourself if it's not a better way to hit your strokes. You'll get more power and control with less effort, and you'll raise the level of your game whether you're a beginner or advanced player.◖

5 WORLD CLASS MOVES
IMPROVE WITH THE SAME STROKES

BY ROY BARTH, with Cindy Hahn

Changing strokes can be devastating to your confidence. Once you think you've got a solid topspin forehand, your pro changes your grip so you can add depth, and now you're spraying balls all over the court.

So, it's not surprising that the request I get most often as a teaching pro is, "Help me get better—but don't change my strokes." What's more surprising is this: It's not impossible. In their quest for an Andre Agassi forehand and Ivan Lendl backhand, amateurs—and teaching pros—often overlook the subtle elements, beyond stroking, that are a part of every pro's game. By teaching my students the five lessons below, I help them improve drastically while leaving their strokes—and confidence—intact.

The author, a former U.S. top-10 player, is director of tennis at the Kiawah Island Golf & Tennis Club in South Carolina.

BEND YOUR KNEES

Do your ground strokes float long? Do your serve and overhead lack power? Are your volleys weak? If so, the problem may be that you are not bending your knees.

If you stand straight up on your ground strokes, your low-to-high swing actually will be high to higher, which will cause the ball to fly long. If you bend your knees and start your stroke from a low position, the ball will travel on a lower trajectory over the net,

and land inside the baseline.

On serves and overheads, you can gain more power not by swinging harder, but by bending your knees, then launching yourself into the strokes. You'll be able to achieve more power with less upper-body effort.

If you bend your knees when you volley, you'll be in position to spring forward into the ball. This will enable you to contact the ball early, and will give you more power and control.

KEEP YOUR FEET MOVING

How many times have you stood admiring the overhead you just hit, then been rudely awakened when your opponent blasts the ball back at you?

The pros keep their feet moving before and immediately after a shot, ready for their opponent's reply. So should you. If you've been pulled out of the court for a wide ground stroke, scamper back to the middle. After overheads, move to the net in preparation for a volley. After volleys, move one step closer to the net, and recover your position if you are pulled wide.→

PHOTOGRAPHY BY JIM MORIARTY

PREPARE WHEN THE BALL IS IN THE AIR

Sometimes players with solid ground strokes wonder why they aren't improving. Often, the answer is in their racquet preparation. Many players wait for the ball to bounce before beginning the backswing, but that's too late. If the ball is coming quickly or you're playing on a fast court, you won't have time to swing through and meet the ball out in front of your body.

By taking the racquet back while the ball is in the air, you'll have time to hit the ball out front, which gives you more power and control.

TAKE A FLUID SWING

Another way to gain power without swinging harder—which often results in more errors—is to eliminate the unnecessary pause in your swing. Most club players take the racquet back quickly during ground strokes, serves and overheads, then stop before hitting the ball. This causes them to lose momentum and rhythm. Instead, take the racquet back slowly, then increase the speed as you swing through the point where you would normally pause. The momentum you'll gain will result in increased power.

HIT ON THE RUN

Most club players still are operating under the old edict, "Stop, set, swing." On some shots, that's not the best technique.

Running through the appropriate shots allows you to get into better position, generate more power and avoid the imbalance that occurs when you suddenly hit the brakes.

For instance, it's impossible to stop and set when you're sprinting to hit a wide forehand. You don't have time. And when you're playing serve and volley, you don't want to stop your momentum to set up for the volley. By running through the volley, you catch the ball higher in the air and arrive closer to net. 🎾

DOUBLES CLINIC

On Guard

Adjust your ready position against big hitters. BY ROY BARTH

oubles is a fast-moving game, so it pays to know how to protect yourself. I learned this when I played on tour against Arthur Ashe, whose blazing backhand would frighten anyone at net. To be ready for one of Ashe's biasts, I abandoned the traditional ready position, with the racquet straight up and down, in favor of an open racquet face, as I would hold it when hitting a backhand volley. You should adopt this stance against big hitters, too. That way, if one of your opponents drills the ball at your chest, you'll be in position to block it with a backhand volley. I've also found that holding the racquet this way doesn't slow you down on forehand volleys. You can turn your shoulder and hit a ball to your right (or if you're left-handed, to your left) just as quickly from this position. This worked wonders for me throughout my doubles career. Protection and simplicity: How can you beat that? ●

Roy Barth, a PTR Master Pro, is the director of tennis at Kiawah Island Golf Resort in South Carolina.

The traditional ready position leaves you vulnerable to body blows.

This alternate stance makes reaction volleys easy.

ILLUSTRATIONS BY KEITH WITMER

ADDITIONAL PHOTOS

From My Collection

More of the People and Moments
that Make Up My Story

My father and me in 1953

My father and me in 1965

FATHERS
AND SONS

Jonathan, my father, Sandon, and me in 1986

My father and me in 1988

Jonathan and Sandon in 2016

Sandon and Jonathan in 1987

Sandon, Kamran, and Navid in 2020

Colleen and me in 2000

Mina and Colleen in 2020

Patty and my mother in 1960

Madelyn, Mckenzie,
and Meredith in 2019

THE
WOMEN
IN MY LIFE

Sanaz and Mina in 2020

The 70's may have had crazy clothes
and lots of hair but it was a great decade
for Colleen and me, and for tennis.

With Pete Kofoed and Don Parker at our
Hoover High Graduation in 1965

Johnny Sanderlin in 1962

Eric Forsberg and me
at Roland Garros 2002

Pete Kofoed, Don Parker, and me in 2010, the day
before I sold the house I grew up in.

THE BEST
OF FRIENDS

Eric Forsberg, Tommy Croffead, and me
at a wedding in 2018

Hank Goldsmith and me at the
US Open in 2010

Steve Tidball and me as the
No. 1 doubles team at UCLA in 1968

Steve Tidball and me at the
UCLA-USC reunion in 1988

WORK/PLAY

with Lucy Garvin and Jorge Andrew at
the USTA South Carolina
Hall of Fame reception in 2017

with Billie Jean King and
Dennis Van der Meer in 1995

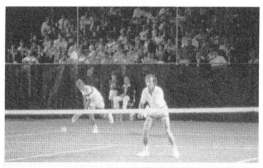

Playing doubles with Roscoe Tanner in 1982

Morley Field Courts in San Diego

Ralph Morton Championship, 1959. I am kneeling,
fourth from left. Patty is standing, second from left.

REPLACES BUCHHOLZ 1/8/71

Roy Barth Joins Pro Tennis Tour

By DAVE GALLUP

Roy Barth, who has produced one of the three best adult men's tennis records in a long line of San Diego-reared talent, has signed with World Championship Tennis, Inc., it was announced yesterday in Dallas, Tex., by Mike Davies, WCT's executive director.

Barth, 23, was ranked eighth in U.S. men's singles in 1969, and he and Steve Tidball of Van Nuys were accorded fourth ranking in doubles. Barth and Tidball won the 1969 Pacific Coast Sectional Doubles tournament at the La Jolla Beach and Tennis Club, upsetting the famed tandem of Stan Smith of Pasadena and Bob Lutz of Los Angeles.

It was the Barth-Tidball team's second conquest in the space of six months over Smith and Lutz, duplicating a triumph in the Pacific Southwest Championships in September, 1968.

HAD BIG WINS

Foremost among Barth's singles achievements in 1969 were victories over Charles Pasarell, Tom Okker and Lutz. In the U.S. Open at Forest Hills, he progressed to the fourth round before losing to Roy Emerson.

Though his success in 1970 was less spectacular, Barth did reach the finals of the Wimbledon Plate (a consolation tournament among first-round losers) and the finals of the West of England Plate, a similar competition, in Bristol, England. He also defeated Ray Moore, the South African, at Forest Hills.

As a junior, Barth won the National Boys 13 doubles championship in partnership with the late John Sanderlin, and in 1963, Roy won the High School division of the San Diego Ink Memorial Championships.

WENT TO UCLA

After his graduation from Hoover High, where he also played varsity basketball, Barth matriculated at UCLA and played three years of varsity tennis there. He defeated Lutz three times in Pacific 8 dual team matches.

In joining WCT, the 5-foot, 9-inch, 150-pound Barth will replace Earl (Butch) Buchholz of St. Louis, who is forced to leave the organization because of an ailing arm.

"Buchholz was able to play for only seven weeks of the 1970 tour," said Davies ... arm wa... ... to our ... even ...

"We s... year has been dif... Barth w... Roy because he has ... ing ...

taken a very big step up in class and it has taken him awhile to adjust but we know he is going to fit into our ... ture nicely."

Other members ... include Rod Lave... wall, Roy Em... Newcombe, Owe... Bill Bowrey, Ton... Fred Stolle of Au... ham Stillwell, M... Roger Taylor ... Pancho Gonzal... Ashe, Bob Lutz, ... sen, Dennis Rals... Holmberg of the ... Tom Okker of Ho... Gimeno of Spain... of Yugoslavia, C... and Ray Moore ... rica, Bob Carr... Pierre Barthes o... Torben Ulrich of ...

$201,453 FOR LA...

Laver pocketed ... biggest incomes ... 1970, winning ... $201,453. Rosewal... with $140,455. E... with $96,845. New... with $77,251, G... with $77,365, Roe... $67,232.

WCT, financed ... mar Hunt milli... bought out the N... League, operate... MacCall, a wealt... es insurance age... as captain of thr... Cup teams.

Barth's only peers in San Diego's male adult tennis history are Bill Bond, who won No. 10 U.S. singles ranking in 1961, and Noel Brown, a Point Loma High School graduate who was No. 9 in 1952 and '53. Bond, a La Jolla High School graduate, played three years of varsity tennis for University of Southern California and shared the National Collegiate Doubles crown with Ralston in 1961.

ROY BARTH
... newest contract pro

CLIFF DRYSDALE HOSTS CLINIC-EXHIBITION FOR ANNIVERSARY AT KIAWAH

Cliff Drysdale, former U.S. Open Doubles Winner and Singles Finalist, Wimbledon and French Open Singles Semi-Finalist, and currently commentator for ESPN's tennis telecast, hosted a Serve Clinic and Accuracy Contest for juniors and adults at Kiawah Island, commemorating its 10th Anniversary Celebration. In addition, he also participated in a Doubles Exhibition playing with Roy Barth, director of tennis, against Kiawah's teaching pros.

The stands were filled with enthusiastic spectators who later enjoyed a social with the players.

Roy Barth Makes Service Count At Award-Winning Kiawah Island

By Roger Cox

On May 1, 2006, Roy Barth celebrated his 30th year as the tennis director at Kiawah Island Golf Resort near Charleston, S.C. Over those three decades, he has survived multiple owners, hurricanes, open-heart surgery, and a brain tumor, and yet still shepherded Kiawah to a ranking as the No. 1 tennis resort in the U.S. in Tennis magazine and No. 1 in the world on TennisResortsOnline.com.

Barth-Tidball are really two people

By Cary Passeroff

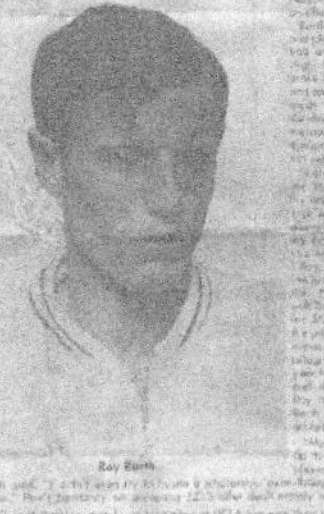

Roy Barth

Steve Tidball

IN THE PRESS

Kiawah's Roy Barth inducted into his fourth tennis hall of fame

BY JAMES BECK SPECIAL TO THE POST AND COURIER
MAY 21, 2019

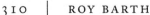

'Clay' puts steel in Barth

By Alan Grayson
Sports writer of The Christian Science Monitor

Forest Hills, N.Y.

Roy Barth is a tennis player with a set schedule. But somehow or other he's running well ahead of it.

Barth had one objective when he returned to the United States from Wimbledon and after four weeks' play on European clay courts. He wanted to advance his claim for a place in the top 10 next year.

He's already done that. He's emerged as Jack the Giantkiller, 1969 version. And in four domestic tournaments he's won a total of $1,925.

Those four weeks on clay made me think," explained Barth, who currently ranks No. 13 in the United States. "It really affected my strategy, because on clay you have to out-maneuver your opponent. As a result my groundstrokes became more solid.

"After I lost to Tom Edlefsen in four sets in the first round at Wimbledon, all I hoped to do in Europe was to win enough to pay my fare over and back. Then I found I could have stayed over there all summer, making about $500 a week. But I really wanted to get back where the tough competition was going to be.

"So I came back and practiced on grass for about two or three days before the Southampton Invitational Tournament," Barth continued. "I found that my game still had the steadiness I'd developed on clay, and I was able to come up to the net and do the thing I like to do best—volleying.

Strong in doubles

Hitherto Barth has been best known for his doubles prowess. With Steve Tidball he ranks fifth among American tandems. So it wasn't surprising that he won a couple of doubles events with pickup partners in Europe.

One was at Ostend, Belgium, where he had to communicate with Hungary's Zoltan Vargas by signs because of the language barrier. The other was at Montana, in Switzerland, partnered by Barry Phillips-Moore of Australia.

Back in the States, however, he began to make waves on his own. At Southampton he lost to the top-ranking Aussie, Bill Bowrey, but learned a few lessons that served him in good stead. At Merion, Pa., in the Eastern

known Davis Cuppers, Richard Russell of the British Caribbean and Jean Louis Rouyer of France, before losing to Australia's Ray Ruffels.

Then in the United States Nationals at Chestnut Hill, Barth asserted himself, knocked out a couple of seeds, Jim Osborne and Bowrey, and then lost to Bob Lutz, whom he's beaten twice in intercollegiate matches.

Here at the West Side Tennis Club in the United States he eliminated Miguel Olvera of Ecuador (after being down two sets), Ron Holmberg, who was the seventh-ranking American before turning pro, and Sweden's Ole Bengtson.

Roy Emerson eventually stopped Barth's progress in the round of 16 by a score of 6—3, 6—0, 6—3. After all it's pretty difficult to best a player who produces a couple of aces each time he serves.

First serve important

"Getting your first serve in is the difference between winning and losing a match," Barth reckoned. "A computer was keeping statistics on that here, and at the end of the third round I was pretty surprised to find that I was No. 4 in the percentage of first serves going in.

"On grass if you get your first serve in deep there aren't many people who can knock off winners against it—except maybe guys like Emerson or Rod Laver, who's an automaton in any case.

"But John Newcombe is one of the few players who has a really tough second serve," he added. "He really socks it as hard as the first. He hits the corners and goes for an ace."

Barth, though not as short as Cliff Richey, is more slightly built than any other high-ranking American player. He concentrates mainly on holding his own serve, rather than expecting to overpower anyone with it. The most potent weapon in his armory is a wonderfully consistent forehand volley.

"My type game is based on percentages," he admitted, "but you can only play that way to an extent. However, my opponents expect me to play steadily, so when I do come up to the net I can often surprise them.

"This year I feel as if I've been moving a lot better. I've been able to return more serves just by being quicker. I've been concentrating more on winning than ever be-

Roy Barth
starting to make waves

Top Ranked Tennis Pros Here Monday

Daytona Beach Morning Journal - Dec 10, 1970   Browse this newspaper »   Browse all newspa

By TOMMY TUCKER
News-Journal Sports Writer

The number four ranked tennis player in the nation, Clark Graebner, and slightly built Roy R. Barth, ranked no. eight nationally, will be in Daytona Beach for two exhibition matches Monday.

Graebner, with the booming, bullet type serve acclaimed as one of the fastest in the game, and Barth will perform at Oceanside Country Club courts at 3:30 p.m., then later, they'll play under the lights at City Island at 7:30.

Graebner and Barth are touring Florida for the United States Lawn Tennis Assn. to teach shots at clinics and talk on sportsmanship and the game of tennis. Tommy Schroeder and Mike Rubenstein, owners of the Oceanside Tennis Shop and pros at Oceanside CC, are bringing the net tandem here.

Tickets are available at both courts in advance of the matches for $1 children, and $2 adults. Graebner will play Barth in exhibition singles, then the two will pair off with Schroeder and Rubenstein in a doubles match. A clinic and brief lecture will follow.

Graebner, a husky, powerful player, is a Davis Cup Team member but works as a sales

executive for a paper firm and lists his home as New York City. He represents Baymeadows Country Club, Jacksonville.

Notable wins for Graebner include the $6,000 River Oaks singles victory over Cliff Richey, the National Clay Courts doubles championships playing with Arthur Ashe and a near miss at Wimbledon in a highly publicized duel with Roger Taylor of England in a match that carried over two days.

Graebner, 26, has been a Davis team member for seven years. He was the first American in 20 years to win two Davis Cup Challenge Round singles matches (1968). He is former U.S. Clay Court singles champion and was ranked no. two in the nation last year. He's married and the Graebners have two children.

Barth, from San Diego, jumped from 13th to 8th in the USLTA rankings in one year. Among his victims are Tom Okker, Ron Holmberg, Bob Lutz, Charlie Pasarell and Barry MacKay.

Barth, 23, teamed with Steve Tidball to win the nation's no. four ranking in doubles. He's a UCLA graduate and comes from a tennis family.

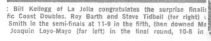

Bill Kellogg of La Jolla congratulates the surprise finalis
fic Coast Doubles. Roy Barth and Steve Tidball (far right)
Smith in the semi-finals at 11-9 in the fifth, then downed Ma
Joaquin Loyo-Mayo (far left) in the final round, 10-8 in

DOMINATING DOUBLES DUOS

Kiawah tennis director Roy Barth stepping down

BY JAMES BECK SPECIAL TO THE POST AND COURIER
JAN 10, 2018

ABOUT THE AUTHOR

Roy Barth grew up in San Diego, California, where he honed his tennis skills on the public courts at Morley Field in Balboa Park. At age 13, he became one of the top junior tennis players in Southern California and went on to win three national junior tennis titles. At UCLA, Barth was a two-time All-American and graduated with a Bachelor of Arts in economics.

From 1969 through 1975, Barth played on the professional tennis tour where he was ranked as high as No. 8 in men's singles and No. 2 in men's doubles in the United States, and Top 40 in the world. He played Wimbledon four times, the US Open eight times, and the French and Australian Open tournaments each once. Barth also competed on the World Championship Tennis (WCT) tour from 1971 to 1973 and played World TeamTennis for the Indiana Loves team in Indianapolis in 1975.

Barth retired from the professional tennis tour in 1975 and settled in Charleston, South Carolina, where he became the resident tennis professional at the Kiawah Island Golf and Tennis Resort. In 42 years under Barth's direction, Kiawah's tennis program was ranked the No. 1

Tennis Resort in the World 12 out of 14 years by TennisResortsOnline. com. In 2006, in recognition of Barth's 30th year at Kiawah, Kiawah's East Beach Tennis Center was renamed the Roy Barth Tennis Center. Barth retired as the Director of Tennis in 2018 and became Director of Tennis, Emeritus.

Barth was inducted into the Hoover High School Sports Hall of Fame, San Diego Tennis Hall of Fame, South Carolina Tennis Hall of Fame, Southern Tennis Hall of Fame, the Intercollegiate Tennis Hall of Fame, and the Professional Tennis Registry Hall of Fame. As a volunteer, Roy served as president of the South Carolina district of the United States Tennis Association (USTA-South Carolina), president of the Professional Tennis Registry (PTR), and chairman of the USTA Davis Cup Committee. Barth has written the *Tips for Better Tennis* instructional manual and produced the *Tips for Better Tennis* DVD.

Made in the USA
Coppell, TX
08 November 2020

40961956R00184